The Spanish Conquest
of the Inca Empire

ALSO BY PETER O. KOCH
AND FROM MCFARLAND

*The Aztecs, the Conquistadors, and the
Making of Mexican Culture* (2006)

*To the Ends of the Earth:
The Age of the European Explorers* (2003)

The Spanish Conquest of the Inca Empire

PETER O. KOCH

McFarland & Company, Inc., Publishers
Jefferson, North Carolina, and London

LIBRARY OF CONGRESS CATALOGUING-IN-PUBLICATION DATA

Koch, Peter O. 1953–
    The Spanish conquest of the Inca empire / Peter O. Koch.
       p.   cm.
    Includes bibliographical references and index.

    ISBN-13: 978-0-7864-3053-6
    softcover : 50# alkaline paper ∞

    1. Peru — History — Conquest, 1522–1548. I. Title.
F3442.K63   2008
985'.02 — dc22   2007034858

British Library cataloguing data are available

©2008 Peter O. Koch. All rights reserved

No part of this book may be reproduced or transmitted in any form or by any means, electronic or mechanical, including photocopying or recording, or by any information storage and retrieval system, without permission in writing from the publisher.

On the cover: Francisco Pizarro, 16th century oil on panel; background map ©2007 PicturesNow.com

Manufactured in the United States of America

McFarland & Company, Inc., Publishers
  Box 611, Jefferson, North Carolina 28640
    www.mcfarlandpub.com

Table of Contents

Preface   1

1. A Fire That Burns Deep   5
2. In Search of Birú   25
3. A Second Chance   36
4. A Test of Will   44
5. Inca Heritage   55
6. The Empire of the Sun   74
7. Return of the Prodigal Son   94
8. The Third Voyage   100
9. Civil War   108
10. Pizarro's March to Cajamarca   122
11. The Capture of the Inca   131
12. The Ransom of an Empire   140
13. Laying Claim to Cuzco   156
14. The Revolt of the Incas   169
15. The Return of Almagro   180
16. The War of the Spaniards   186
17. The End of an Era   194

Chapter Notes   203
Bibliography   207
Index   209

For my dad, Otto, and my sister, Kathy

Preface

The era of Spanish discovery, conquest, and settlement of the Americas is a watershed moment in world history. Initially, the first contact between civilizations that had no prior knowledge of one another ushered in a period of enlightenment that held out the promise of forging a long-lasting and mutually beneficial relationship. Unfortunately, there were many Spanish settlers who, to the great detriment of the inhabitants of the New World succumbed to material temptations and took to claiming, often by force, possessions which rightfully belonged to the natives. Such transgressions coupled with self-righteous Spaniards seeking to impose their religious beliefs upon those with varying views of creation evolved into a manifest destiny that had both papal and sovereign support to expand Spanish interests throughout the Americas. What followed was the systematic subjugation of the numerous tribes that inhabited the islands of the West Indies and the founding of Spanish settlements, which were often built upon the villages of the recently conquered tribe. Once these islands had been exploited for all they were worth the Spaniards sought out other lands to claim for God, country, and themselves, though not necessarily in that order. Many such expeditions to various locations along the coasts of North, South, and Central America met with disastrous results when the Spaniards were met by natives who were more defiant than those they were accustomed to. However, the lure of fortune and fame was sufficient to strengthen the resolve of men willing to risk all that they had, including their lives, for an opportunity to improve their meager status.

Whispers of extraordinary kingdoms that were home to vast stores of gold and silver haunted the imaginations of the intrepid Spaniards who dared to settle along the less hospitable mainland of the Americas. These uncharted lands, once thought to be a gateway to the legendary riches of the Far East, soon revealed themselves to be a New World that had been inhabited by a great many people for a very long time. With each new tribe encountered, the Spanish explorers heard accounts of native realms said to be overflowing with the precious metals that they coveted so dearly. While some of these fanciful stories contained an element of truth many of these tales were simply a clever ruse by natives eager to rid their land of these European interlopers.

By 1520 the stories of Hernan Cortes's campaign in Mexico and the magnificent riches of Tenochtitlan had drifted southward to the struggling Spanish settlement at Panama. The extraordinary wealth of the Aztec empire certainly lent credence to local tales such as that of Dabaibe, a nearby native kingdom said to have a temple sheathed entirely in gold and built to store an unparalleled treasure trove of precious metals and lustrous pearls, or a mysterious land to the south where people ate off plates and drank from vessels made of pure gold. Numerous expeditions set out from Panama to locate other native empires of untold wealth that were ripe for the taking. These campaigns were divided between roving bands of conquistadors who either ventured northward to invade the lands of present day Nicaragua or who sailed southward to search along the shores of Ecuador and Peru in hopes of striking it rich. It was the latter group of Spaniards who, after overcoming a great many obstacles, were destined to meet with greater success. Led by Francisco Pizarro, an elderly soldier of fortune and a veteran of numerous expeditions in the New World, these conquistadors eventually laid claim to the vast domain of the Incas, an empire that had accumulated a wealth of precious metals which eclipsed that known to any civilization of the Old World.

This book, which is a third entry in a series of studies pertaining to the first encounters between the explorers of Europe and the native civilizations of the Americas, focuses on the exploits of Francisco Pizarro and those who followed his obsessive quest to locate the legendary wealth of a region the Spaniards came to call Peru. An examination of the life of this restless soldier of fortune offers insight into the character of those remembered, for better or worse, as conquistadors. In Pizarro, we learn of a man who was driven by an unrelenting ambition to rise above his humble origins and therefore in constant search of any opportunity that might enhance his prestige and enrich his purse. Such resolve enabled Francisco to overcome seemingly insurmountable odds to claim title to one of the largest and wealthiest empires that ever existed, but his less admirable traits led to a brutal end at the hands of men who once swore allegiance to him.

This work devotes three chapters to Inca history, an overview intended to promote a better understanding and appreciation of the greatness and splendor of the vast empire this civilization forged in a relatively brief period of time. From their humble beginnings at Cuzco, a small village nestled high in the Andes, the people who came to be called the Incas forged a vast empire they called Tahuantinsuyu, the land of four quarters. The realm of the Incas, which at its peak stretched for more than 2,500 miles along the western coast of South America, was a varied terrain that encompassed all the known extremes of nature. There were mountains that soared up to the heavens, vast tracts of desert land which rarely saw a drop of rain, jungles so dense with growth that even the sun had a difficult time penetrating its canopy. As many as twelve million people composed of one hundred different cultures speaking twenty different languages all came to live under the rule of the Incas.

An historical account is intended to be a chronological record of important events that are thought to be fact, a recorded rendering which is subject to the interpretation of the historian. A researcher's quest to learn what actually occurred often becomes bogged down with sifting through shards of information filled with suppositions that promote a particular agenda, ideas that happen to support a viewpoint that is currently in vogue, or facts that have been manipulated to suit a specific purpose or misconstrued for whatever reason. There is no denying that the European conquest of the Americas was a brutal ordeal. The conquistadors are clearly guilty of taking lands that did not belong to them, compelling the indigenous population to accept their customs and beliefs without question, forcing the natives to arduously toil for their sole benefit, and introducing a variety of infectious diseases which the aboriginal people had no natural defense against. Such misdeeds, as egregious as they were, tend to blind many to the fact that armed conquest and the tragic consequences related to such forceful acts were known throughout the Americas long before the arrival of the Europeans. It was once believed that the Mayans were a peaceful people who lived in harmony with the earth, only to discover that these city-states waged brutal war with one another to lay claim to precious land and people, the latter of which were either enslaved or sacrificed to their gods. It was commonly taught that the Incas were benevolent overlords who were the purveyors of an idyllic communal society while glossing over the fact that this highland tribe was determined to use whatever means necessary to conquer any tribe that stood in their way and enacted stringent measures which prevented any commoner from rising above their lowly station. There are those who still refuse to believe that the Aztecs took human sacrifice to ritualistically extreme heights despite all the unearthed evidence to the contrary. In every society there can be found customs and accomplishments deserving of admiration as well as practices and feats that are considered objectionable. The same can be said of individuals.

1
A Fire That Burns Deep

I would rather die than surrender and abandon what I have conquered and won by my own endeavor. —Francisco Pizarro

In Search of Fame and Fortune

As Francisco Pizarro stood at the edge of a desolate beach located along the rim of the Gulf of Urabá he stared forlornly at the vacant cerulean tinged waters of the Caribbean Sea, a vast body of water that seemed to taunt him with each wave that gently rolled up along the shore. It had been a full fifty days since his commander, Alonso de Ojeda, had stepped aboard a ship commandeered by an unsavory character named Bernardino de Talavera to sail back to the colony of Santo Domingo in a desperate effort to obtain much needed supplies for his struggling settlement of San Sebastián. Frustrated by the fact that another day was about to pass without any visible sign of relief, Pizarro turned back to look upon the soldiers he had been left in command of, a brave lot who had suffered and endured a slew of horrendous hardships: the blistering and unrelenting rays of a torrid sun, frequent and intensely fierce native attacks, incessant assaults by carnivorous caimans and swarms of bloodsucking mosquitoes, and a debilitating lack of edible food and fresh water. These were men who, just like himself, dreamed of striking it rich in the New World but whose waking thoughts were now consumed with simply summoning enough strength to survive yet another day in this godforsaken land. Fearing that the passage of so much time was an indication that Ojeda had never made it to his intended destination, Francisco Pizarro made a conscious decision to abandon this failed settlement and sail aboard the two vessels that remained in his possession. Unfortunately, these boats were too small to accommodate the present number of men, so he had little choice but

FRANCISCO PISARRO

to wait a bit longer, until the weakest were weeded out by way of natural selection.

Returning to his place among the despondent troops, Pizarro's thoughts turned to the numerous twists and turns of his life that had led him to this very place. He was a long way from Trujillo, Spain, a humble town located in the province of Extremadura. Francisco was the illegitimate progeny of an illicit union between Gonzalo Pizarro, a Spanish infantry officer and a notorious womanizer who fathered many children from his numerous liaisons, and Francisca González, a young servant girl employed at the convent of San Francisco whose reputation suffered terribly from this affair. Gonzalo Pizarro, had served under the renowned Spanish commander Gonzalo Córdoba in the Neapolitan campaigns and fought admirably in the battles for control of Navarre, the latter of which led to his death in the year 1521. According to legend, shortly after his birth, sometime in the year 1471, the unwanted child of this union was left at the doorstep of the church. Other stories state that the young Francisco was raised by relatives. While there is probably an element of truth to each tale, we do know that his education was sorely neglected, for he never did learn to properly read or write. Opportunities for gainful employment were limited at Trujillo and as a lad Francisco had to earn his keep performing the grueling tasks associated with the work of a common swine herder until he was old enough to escape such a dreary existence by enlisting in the army. A tour of duty in which he saw action in the military campaigns of Italy helped foster a lasting sense of adventure in a young and still impressionable Francisco. Though a simple soldier, he was driven by an unrelenting ambition to rise above his humble origins and therefore was always in search of an opportunity that might enhance his prestige and which could potentially line his pockets with fortune. Such an opportunity presented itself in the year 1502.

King Ferdinand and Queen Isabella, the joint rulers of Spain, had recently announced the appointment of Nicolás de Ovando as the colonial governor who was to replace Francisco Bobadilla at the island of Hispaniola. Bobadilla, who had previously been sent by the same king and queen to investigate claims that Christopher Columbus and his brothers were unfit administrators, had grossly exceeded his sanctioned authority when he stripped the famous explorer of his command and sent him and his brothers back to Spain shackled with heavily weighted chains. The promises of untold wealth just waiting to be found in the Spanish West Indies was enticing enough to lure 2,500 adventurous souls aboard the 32 ships destined for the settlement of

Opposite: Portrait of Francisco "Pisarro" [*sic*] (courtesy Library of Congress).

Santo Domingo. Among those who enlisted at the port of Seville was a thirty-one-year-old veteran soldier by the name of Francisco Pizarro.

Ovando's ambitious plans for transforming Santo Domingo into a self-sufficient and prosperous settlement were beset by one unforeseen tragedy after another. The harsh climate and a multitude of disease carrying mosquitoes conspired to claim the lives of hundreds of Spanish settlers in just a very short period of time. Hispaniola failed to reveal enough precious metals to satisfy the pecuniary motives of all who had sailed to the island and this disappointment fueled a growing desire to seek out new lands to exploit. Diego Nicuesa and Alonso de Ojeda were, in the year 1508, granted permission by the widower King Ferdinand to locate and settle a stretch of land that had been explored in 1501 by an expedition led by Rodrigo de Bastidas as well as one commanded the following year by Christopher Columbus during the course of his fourth and final voyage across the Atlantic Ocean. Nicuesa, a wealthy adventurer who had sailed to the New World with Nicholas de Ovando, and Ojeda, a veteran explorer who had sailed with Christopher Columbus and Amerigo Vespucci, bitterly competed with one another for the sole right to settle the lands that rested to the south of Hispaniola, and the official grant to do so was a compromise on the part of the Crown to appease both men. Nicuesa was awarded a claim to a vast tract of land that extended between the Gulf of Darién and Cape Gracias a Dios that was to be called Veragua. Ojeda was granted the right to a neighboring stretch of land to the south that extended into the continent of South America and was to be known as New Andalusia.

By taking advantage of a legal dispute that Diego Nicuesa had become embroiled with involving hereditary claims brought by the heirs of Christopher Columbus, the expedition led by Alonso de Ojeda was able to set sail first. Among the nearly three hundred men who sailed out of the harbor of Santo Domingo on November 12, 1509, there were two of special note: Juan de la Cosa and Francisco Pizarro. La Cosa, an experienced pilot and renowned cartographer of Basque descent, had sailed twice with Columbus, and was an integral member of previous expeditions led by Ojeda and Amerigo Vespucci. He had also sailed with Rodrigo Bastidas on the aborted mission to establish a colony along a stretch of coastline that was later designated as the Spanish Main. He is, however, best remembered as the cartographer who, in the year 1500, drew the Mundi Map, his now famous chart of the then known lands of the Western Hemisphere. Francisco Pizarro, a 38-year-old veteran soldier who was still in search of his share of fame and fortune, had signed on as Alonso de Ojeda's lieutenant. The tall and slender officer exuded an appearance and manner that commanded utmost respect from those who fell under his command. He was a man of unquestionable courage and remarkable fortitude, but who possessed a darker side that was governed by a deceitful and sometimes cruel nature.

Landing at a harbor which was to become the future site of the Spanish port city of Cartagena, Alonso de Ojeda decided to go ashore to officially claim the land for both the Crown and himself. Remembering that the natives of this realm were not a particularly friendly lot, Juan de la Cosa begged his captain to forget about colonizing this region and continue on to a more suitable site, one where the natives were likely to be more receptive to strangers. Ojeda, who had designs on pressing the local natives into service to help in the building of his settlement, had no intention of heeding the unsolicited advice offered by his knowledgeable pilot. The curious natives began to gather along the shore where Ojeda and his men had landed and once they understood that these strangers from the sea were staking claim to their homeland the indigenous population registered its strong objection by taking up arms. The more organized and better armed Spaniards were able to drive their attackers from the beach and they continued to give chase as the natives fled for cover in the nearby jungle. Ojeda and his men soon came upon the now deserted village of Turbaco, the dwelling place of these numerous fleeing warriors. It was here that the Spanish soldiers halted their attack and turned their attention to plundering items from the village which they deemed to be of value, especially those that glittered like gold.

The Turbaco natives, who were silently hiding in the surrounding canopy of the dense jungle, saw that the attention of these intruders had suddenly been diverted and they decided to take advantage of this situation by attacking in full force. The Spaniards responded as best they could to the fury and might of this unexpected assault but their courage began to falter when they saw many of their comrades fall to the ground almost instantly — victims of accurately shot projectiles that were dipped in poison, a toxic concoction from which few wounded soldiers ever survived. The native force, estimated at nearly 1,000 strong, succeeded in dividing the Spanish troops and when Juan de la Cosa saw that Alonso de Ojeda was in danger of being overtaken, the pilot rushed to the aid of his captain. He fought bravely but the renowned pilot and cartographer was soon felled by the poisoned arrows of his enemy. His valiant effort, however, was not in vain, for he provided enough cover for Ojeda to escape into the jungle. Unfortunately, the commander was one of the very few to avoid death that day. Seventy soldiers also suffered the same fate as Juan de la Cosa and many more sustained wounds, many of whom would succumb to their painful and deadly effects shortly thereafter.

After becoming separated from his men, a wounded and disoriented Alonso de Ojeda wandered aimlessly through the dense jungle. The commander was close to death from starvation and exhaustion by the time he happened upon the beach where Francisco Pizarro and the remainder of his troops were still camped. The disparaging news of the natives' victory over the Spaniards was rather disconcerting to the other soldiers, and though they wished to avenge the death of their comrades most feared that the loss of any more men would surely doom their mission. It was during this desperate hour that the expedition led by Diego Nicuesa arrived and, despite their long history of bitter differences, the commander offered his aid to the ailing Ojeda. The combined Spanish force attacked the village, an assault that continued unabated until every man, woman, and child of that village had been unmercifully put to death. It was during this avenging assault that the Spaniards came upon the corpse of Juan de la Cosa hanging from a tree, his swollen body riddled with many an arrow wound.

The victorious Spaniards returned to the beach where they had landed once all of their fallen comrades had been given a proper burial and the native village was thoroughly cleansed of all of its precious items. With a newfound respect for one another the two Spanish commanders decided to join forces to launch raids against other tribes living along the coast. However, it wasn't long before the obstinate captains began to disagree and soon the only thing they could agree upon was that the time had come for them to go their separate ways. Nicuesa and his crew sailed off in search of the riches of Veragua while Ojeda and his men ventured to the Gulf of Urabá where, just to the east, they made landfall to found the colony of San Sebastián. Unfortunately for Ojeda and his men, the spot they selected was an area already claimed by a neighboring tribe and was a vast breeding ground for swarms of bloodthirsty mosquitoes. The natives of this region, just like the tribe at Turbaco, possessed an arsenal of poison arrows and quickly showed that they had no qualms about using them against those who had so brazenly trespassed upon their land. One of the darkest fears of any Spanish explorer was to be struck by an arrow that had been treated with a poisonous substance, for its effects were an excruciatingly painful wound, and death, which was almost certain, was viewed as a welcome relief for the victim.

One day, while foraging for food for his needy soldiers, Captain Ojeda was struck by a poisonous native arrow that pierced his thigh. The swelling of his leg became so severe that the company's surgeon recommended the infected limb should be removed at once before the poison had a chance to spread to the rest of his body. The proud Ojeda threatened to have the doctor hanged from a tree if he dared to cut off his swollen leg. The gaping wound of the commander was closed by the painful means of hot irons pressed against his festering flesh.

The San Sebastián settlement was beset by one disastrous event after another. The food supply dwindled away quickly from both daily consumption and the rapid spoilage caused by the excessively hot and humid conditions inherent to this region. Though there was plenty of food to be found in the surrounding jungle, the men dared not enter this thick forest of tropical vegetation out of fear that they might become the next victim of a poisoned arrow attack. Just when morale seemed to have sunk to a point where all hope was lost, a Spanish vessel pulled into the harbor. Bernardino de Talavera, the captain of the ship, presented himself before Alonso de Ojeda and stated that he and his motley crew of seventy sailors were presently on a trading mission but would be willing, for the right price, to part with some of their staples. In addition to swapping some of their precious gold for the bland, but highly nutritious, cassava bread, Ojeda contracted with Talavera to transport him and the bulk of their collected gold back to Hispaniola so that he could purchase essential supplies and enlist more men to aid in the settling of his ailing San Sebastián colony. Ojeda turned over command of his settlement to Francisco Pizarro and pledged to his trustworthy lieutenant that he would return as soon as possible. Pizarro and the rest of the soldiers watched from the shore until the ship carrying Ojeda and all their gold disappeared beyond the distant blue horizon.

Clinging to the hope that Alonso de Ojeda would remain true to his promise to return, Francisco Pizarro kept the disheartened men busy with a strict regiment of daily chores to ward off their feelings of despair. The natives continued to harass the settlers with periodic attacks and because of their fear of entering the jungle the Spaniards had no choice but to turn to the sea for sustenance, which, unfortunately for them, never seemed to yield enough to satisfy their daily needs. As the weeks began to pass, many began to fear that Ojeda was never going to return. The camp was divided among those who believed that their commander was lost at sea while the others thought that he had left them to die so that he could claim all of their hard earned gold for himself. After nearly two months following the departure of the ship that carried their commander the situation at San Sebastián had become so desperate that Pizarro believed he had no alternative but to abandon this failed settlement. Since the two small boats left to him were not large enough to transport all of the sixty remaining soldiers, Pizarro had to wait until starvation, disease, and mortal wounds had dwindled his crew down to a more fitting number. Once the company of men had lessened to the point where they could all fit aboard the two vessels, Pizarro gave the long awaited command to evacuate the ill-fated colony of San Sebastián. The surviving horses were butchered and the meat was cut into manageable portions and salted to help preserve it as food for their voyage. A short distance from shore one of the boats began taking on water at an alarming rate and the crew was forced to paddle back to the very shore from which they were attempting to escape. In the meantime, Francisco Pizarro and his crew continued on in search of a more hospitable spot to settle.

A Fortuitous Encounter

Francisco Pizarro and his weary crew of thirty soldiers steered in the direction of the harbor of Cartagena where they had the good fortune to meet up with an expedition that had recently sailed from Hispaniola to aid the stranded settlers of San Sebastián. It was from their captain, a wealthy lawyer by the name of Martín Fernández de Enciso, that Pizarro and his men learned of the fate of their former commander.

Once at sea, Alonso de Ojeda discovered that Bernardino de Talavera was not the man he claimed to be. Talavera was no sea trader; both he and his assembled crew of murderers and thieves made their living by taking for themselves whatever items happened to catch their fancy. Even their boat was purloined from an unsuspecting crew they had brutally murdered. Talavera and his cutthroat crew were among the first of the legendary pirates who plied their loathsome trade while scouring the waters of the Caribbean. Ojeda found himself a prisoner aboard their ship while the precious gold which he had brought to purchase supplies for his ill-fated colony was confiscated and divided up among his captors. Talavera continued sailing along the mainland coast in search of other treasures he could take by force before charting a course for the island of Hispaniola. The sudden onset of a powerful hurricane was the cause of a great deal of damage to their already sea worn vessel and it took an extraordinary effort on the part of the beleaguered crew to make for a distant shore they had sighted during this terrifying ordeal. They managed to make landfall at the uninhabited western end of Cuba, an island referred to as Fernandina by its Spanish discoverers. The ship and all of its ill-gotten treasure was lost to the sea, as were the lives of many who were on that fateful journey. Without a ship and with little hope of another Spanish vessel passing along this western side of the island, Talavera, his surviving crew, and the now freed Ojeda made the long and arduous trek through the dense thicket of tropical foliage to the extreme eastern end of the island where they hoped to have a better chance of catching sight of a passing vessel sailing along the waters that connected to the neighboring island of Hispaniola.

A Spanish ship dispatched on an exploratory expedition by Juan de

Esquivel, the governor of Jamaica, and under the command of an ambitious officer by the name of Pánfilo Narváez, happened to spot the stranded Spaniards and immediately came to their rescue. Talavera was quickly recognized for the pirate that he was and once back at Jamaica he was tried, convicted, and hanged, all of which occurred in rapid succession. Alonso de Ojeda eventually found his way back to the settlement of Santo Domingo, but the festering wound he had received at San Sebastián kept him confined to a hospital bed. Before he passed away, Ojeda told Martín Fernández de Enciso, his friend, lawyer and principal financial backer, of the many suffering comrades he was forced to leave behind and that it was his dying wish that Enciso find a way to rescue those pour souls from their desperate plight.

The moneyed Martín Enciso spared no expense when it came to procuring means of transport and essential provisions to provide relief for the many Spanish settlers left at San Sebastián. One hundred and fifty men willingly signed on for this rescue expedition and Enciso set sail shortly after Alonso de Ojeda was laid to rest. They hadn't ventured very far before the entire crew was surprised by the discovery of a charismatic stowaway by the name of Vasco Nuñez de Balboa, an adventurer who was eager to escape the numerous creditors who were harassing him on the island of Hispaniola. Like so many other Spaniards, Balboa had come to the New World to stake his claim to fame and fortune. While these goals seemed to always elude him no one could honestly say it was from a lack of effort on his part.

In 1501 Vasco Nuñez de Balboa sailed to the New World on an expedition led by Rodrigo de Bastidas which explored a vast stretch of coastline that is now part of present day Panama and Colombia. Because of his extensive military training and exceptional skill with a blade — he had earned a living in Spain teaching others how to wield a sword — Balboa was made an officer and had five soldiers who reported directly to him. Juan de la Cosa, the pilot who met his end during the last voyage of Ojeda, was also a member of this expedition. After a year of exploring uncharted territory that yielded little in the way of material profit the expedition disbanded. Many of the disappointed adventurers returned to Spain while others chose to call Hispaniola their new home. Balboa was among those who, after being offered a sizable grant of land by Nicolás de Ovando, the newly appointed governor of the island, and a number of native slaves to call his own, chose to settle down at Hispaniola. During his stay at Hispaniola, Balboa served under Juan Ponce de León on a campaign to subjugate the remaining remote villages of the island. It was during these military operations that Balboa became acquainted with such notable conquistadors as Hernán Cortés and Francisco Pizarro. He also struck up a lasting friendship with Bartolomé de Hurtado.

Balboa tried his hand at farming but it proved to be a position that he was ill-suited for and soon he found himself heavily burdened with numerous outstanding debts. With creditors threatening to have him thrown in jail for his mounting past due obligations, Balboa, with the help of his friend Bartolomé Hurtado, avoided their grasp by hiding inside an empty cask which was placed aboard the ship that was being fitted to sail to the colony of Santo Domingo. Only after they were far from the shores of Hispaniola did Balboa feel comfortable enough to reveal himself to Martín Enciso. Placing himself at the mercy of the commander, Balboa explained his desperate reasons for hiding aboard ship and then offered his services to aid in the cause of the mission. What saved this stowaway from being thrown overboard was his experience as a member of the Bastidas expedition: Balboa told Enciso that he was familiar with the region to which they were headed and he knew where there were natives who were not quite as warlike as those encountered by Alonso de Ojeda and his crew.

Following their chance encounter, Francisco Pizarro and Martín Enciso, along with their respective crews, sailed back to the Gulf of Urabá to rescue those who no longer had the strength or the means to escape on their own. Numerous mishaps along the way convinced a great many of the crew that Enciso was not qualified to lead this expedition. The men soon turned to Balboa as their new leader and he in turn enlisted Francisco Pizarro, a familiar soldier from Hispaniola, as his second-in-command. For refusing to recognize Balboa as his superior, Enciso unexpectedly found himself a prisoner aboard his own ship. He was, however, granted conditional freedom after agreeing to refrain from any efforts to interfere in the affairs of the expedition and pledging to return to Santo Domingo once a suitable location had been located for the new colony. After rescuing the spent survivors of the failed San Sebastián settlement, Balboa charted a westward course in search of a more hospitable region to colonize. Landing along the eastern shores of the isthmus later known as Panama, Balboa staked out a piece of land that was to become the foundation of the colony of Santa Maria de la Antigua del Darién, a settlement more commonly referred to as simply Darién.

Balboa took a unique approach to laying claim to lands that already belonged to the natives, one which served his cause well and that should have served as an example for the numerous conquistadors who were to follow in his wake. Instead of imposing his will solely by means of threats or force, Balboa sought out the chiefs of the neighboring tribes in order to pay homage to them and to ask for permission to settle upon their lands. Such a respectful gesture earned him all that he desired, and then some.

Opposite: Portrait of Vasco Nuñez de Balboa (courtesy Library of Congress).

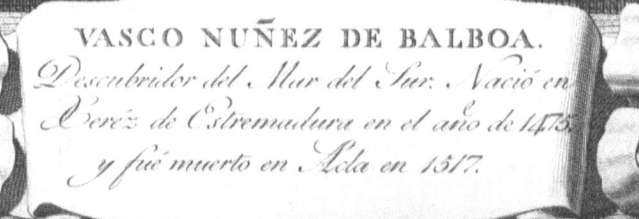

VASCO NUÑEZ DE BALBOA.
Descubridor del Mar del Sur. Nació en
Xeréz de Estremadura en el año de 1475
y fué muerto en Acla en 1517.

Balboa's tactics were admired greatly by Alonso Zuazo, the inspector general of the Indies, who, in 1518, wrote: "Vasco Nuñez had labored with very good skill to make peace with many caciques and principal lords of the Indians, by which he kept in peace about thirty caciques with all their Indians, and did so by not taking from them more than they were willing to give, helping them to resolve their quarrels one with another, and thereby Vasco Nuñez became so well liked that he could go in security through a hundred leagues of Tierra Firme. In all parts the Indians willingly give him much gold and also their sisters and daughters to take with him to be married or used as he wished. By these means peace was spread and the revenue of Your Highnesses greatly increased."[1]

With the help of the natives, Balboa and his comrades were able to quickly clear the land and erect several structures for their new settlement. It was during this time that a ship arrived unexpectedly and which had on board a crew of soldiers so pitiful looking that they all appeared as if at death's door. The commander of the ship was Diego Nicuesa, the wealthy Spanish merchant who had sailed to the New World to found the colony of Nombre de Dios. After parting ways with Alonso de Ojeda, Nicuesa took his five ships and seven hundred and forty men up the coast to a site where the city of Colón now stands. While this location appeared promising at first it soon turned in to a virtual graveyard for the vast majority of the enlisted members of this expedition. Hostile natives claimed the lives of many, disease carrying mosquitoes took many more, and a severe shortage of food claimed its own terrible toll. When their plight became so desperate that the men had to seek sustenance by feasting upon the bodies of the dead, Nicuesa rounded up his survivors, which were barely enough to man one vessel, and set sail in search of a more favorable environment. This search led him to Darién, the settlement recently established by Balboa and Pizarro, and since this location fell within the territory granted to him by King Ferdinand, Nicuesa claimed the colony and all of its precious possessions for himself. Such a request did not sit well with the settlers of Darién, and being by far the stronger group they easily forced the greedy commander and his feeble crew back to their ship.

A greatly angered and disappointed Diego Nicuesa cast off for Hispaniola, where he hoped to seek redress for the transgressions perpetrated by these insolent squatters on his land. Nicuesa's ship, as well as all on board, was claimed by a violent sea, an act of nature that granted both Balboa and Pizarro a temporary reprieve for having the audacity to expel the rightful governor of this region. Shortly thereafter, Martín Enciso and the few men who remained faithful to the deposed commander were permitted to return to Hispaniola and once there he wasted no time laying his numerous complaints before Diego Colón, the son of Christopher Columbus and the newly appointed governor of Hispaniola. Unable to enlist the aid of the governor, the lawyerly Enciso returned to Spain in 1512, where, when he wasn't busy seeking redress from the king for the wrongful acts committed by those who had usurped his authority, he passed the time by writing of his adventures and discoveries in the New World, a compilation of stories which led to the publication of *Suma de Geographia*. Shortly after having chased off Diego Nicuesa and expelling Martín Encisco, Balboa sent emissaries to Hispaniola to explain to Diego Colón the reasons behind his extreme actions.

Meanwhile, Balboa and Pizarro continued with the work that was necessary to ensure the success of their new settlement. More land was cleared for the erection of additional buildings and the planting of essential crops, and new alliances were forged for the explicit purpose of carrying on profitable trade and as a means of protection from potential native uprisings. All of the Spaniards made some form of sacrifice for the betterment of the settlement, though some were certainly less painful than others; Balboa did his part by accepting the hand of Ceretita, the beautiful young daughter of a neighboring cacique named Caret.

Even with all the hard work before them, the Spaniards still kept their eyes peeled for gold, the precious metal which stood as every European's measure of wealth. The natives, who, even though they had difficulty understanding the strange and extremely covetous nature of these strangers, were well aware of the Spaniards' insatiable craving for any item that contained an element of gold. They told them tales of a rich land resting along the banks of a great river approximately forty leagues to the south of Darién that was ruled by a chief so endowed with gold that he had built a magnificent temple entirely out of the substance that shone as bright as the sun.

Having heard of the wealth of Dabaibe, a native city that boasted a golden temple housing vast amounts of precious metals and lustrous pearls, Balboa led a company of 150 men in June of 1512 to search for this magnificent realm. He also brought along the parts required for the assembling of two brigantines that would enable him and his men to explore along the river that was said to be teeming with gold. Balboa's search led them to a large river which they christened El Río de San Juan. It was here that the commander divided his forces, sending Rodrigo de Colmenares and roughly fifty soldiers to explore the main stream, while Balboa and the rest followed a nearby promising tributary. Balboa and his troops came upon a large village that had been vacated the moment the inhabitants learned of the approach of these strange men aboard strange vessels. The Spaniards helped themselves to two of the natives' canoes and approximately 7,000 pesos of crude gold.

Balboa, once he realized that this was not the fabled city the natives had spoken of, gave up his search along this branch of the river and rejoined Colmenares and his soldiers, who also had no luck locating the legendary golden temple. The explorers eventually came upon another branch of the great river which, because of its darkened water, they christened the Río Negro. It was along this river that they came upon a large town composed of approximately five hundred houses. The inhabitants valiantly defended their village but they were soon overwhelmed by the superior weapons of the Spaniards. Though disappointed by the fact that this was not Dabaibe the Spaniards comforted themselves with the thought that this was a more promising region and that perhaps the elusive kingdom might be around the next bend.

Balboa left half of his men at this village while he and the rest of the soldiers continued upriver in search of the elusive realm of Dabaibe. The Spaniards soon came upon a tribe who, because of the frequent flooding of the river, made their home in the trees. The only way the soldiers could get the people to come down from their elevated huts was to begin chopping down one of the large trees where the natives dwelled with the axes they had carried with them. Frustrated by the lack of gold this place had to offer Balboa and his men left this curious village and continued exploring along the river. News of their approach had clearly preceded them, as evidenced by the fact that each village they came upon was found to be entirely abandoned. The frustrated soldiers sought relief by plundering all of the food and valuable items the natives had left behind. A disappointed Balboa made his way back to those stationed at the first village. An advance party of his soldiers arrived just in time to help Colmenares and his besieged troops put down a hastily organized uprising of the natives.

Balboa decided the time had come to cut his losses and return to Darién with the meager amount of gold he had confiscated on this expedition. He still, however, held out hope that Dabaibe was within reach and decided to leave thirty of his soldiers behind under the command of his good friend Bartolomé Hurtado in order to continue with the search. Unfortunately, Hurtado and his men came under heavy attack and, after most of his men were killed, was forced to return to the Spanish settlement empty handed. There would be other expeditions that sought to find this legendary city, one of which included Francisco Pizarro and Hernando de Soto, but no European ever discovered its whereabouts. The tale of the golden temple was among the first of the numerous chimerical El Dorado tales that stirred and captivated the imaginations of an endless string of hopeful European explorers.

In the meantime, Balboa forged a brotherly bond with Prince Panciaco (also spelled as Panquiaco), who was the son of the Cacique Comogre. As an expression of gratitude for the friendly alliance that existed between them, the prince and the chief presented the Spaniards with a gift of nearly four thousand ounces of their finest gold and a bevy of nubile and beautiful women. The elated soldiers could hardly believe their good fortune and they decided right then and there to divide and distribute the powdered gold among themselves. A division over the distribution of shares was the cause of several verbal and physical confrontations between Balboa's men. Having borne witness to this strange affliction of insatiable greed that transformed seemingly reasonable men into covetous creatures who would not hesitate to kill even their own comrades in order to obtain and preserve a substance that was merely used by his own people for decorative purposes, Panciaco slammed his fist upon the table with such force that it created a cloud of gold dust that rained down upon the startled faces of the Spaniards and the very ground that they stood upon. The enraged prince then said to Vasco Nuñez de Balboa, "If this is what you prize so much that you are willing to leave your distant homes, and risk even life itself for it, I can tell you of a land where they eat and drink of golden vessels, and gold is as cheap as iron is with you."[2] The native prince went on to speak of another great sea located to the west which would provide a watery route to a nearby land to the south filled with riches that exceeded their wildest dreams. Prince Panciaco now had the undivided attention of the Spaniards.

Confident that he was on the verge of a monumental discovery, Balboa wrote to King Ferdinand that he had uncovered "great secrets of marvelous riches," and was aware of "many rich mines ... gold and wealth with which a great part of the world can be conquered. I have learned it in various ways, putting some to the torture, treating some with love and giving Spanish things to some."[3] The Spanish commander was convinced that the simultaneous discovery of this mysterious "Other Sea" and the legendary "Kingdom of Gold" would earn him the respect and gratitude of the king of Spain, who, in turn, would surely reward his success with an appointment as governor of the lands that he and his men had settled.

On September 1, 1513, Balboa and Pizarro, his faithful lieutenant marched out of Darién at the head of a company composed of 190 eager Spanish soldiers, 1,000 native porters, and a pack of hunting dogs across the short stretch of land that separates the two great oceans of the world. The remainder of the troops, which was about equal to the number who headed for the opposite coast, remained at Darién. Though the distance to their intended destination was not all that great — a mere fifty miles, their pace was hindered by a dense jungle path that had to be cleared with sharp blades nearly every step of the way. The Spaniards also learned that they had to steer clear of the numerous swamps and streams that were breeding grounds for ferocious man eating crocodiles and to keep a vigilant watch for a variety of venomous snakes and other poisonous creatures that seemed to call everywhere their home.

After a fortnight's journey, the native guides brought Balboa and his men to the base of a hill which they said the summit of would provide them with a glimpse of the nearby other sea. Balboa scaled the mound first and once at the top he was rewarded with a spectacular view of an ocean that was unknown to the Europeans. The commander took a moment to ponder the vast implications of this momentous discovery. While he could lay claim to this sea for his homeland and its sighting seemed to lend credence to the native tales of the existence of a rich empire to the south, his discovery also confirmed what many had long suspected: the famed explorer Christopher Columbus had not discovered a western route to the riches of the Indies but instead had happened upon a New World that was known only to numerous generations of natives who called this land their home. Balboa then beckoned to his men who had waited patiently down below. The company of adventurers, which included Francisco Pizarro, climbed up to join their commander, and once they saw what Balboa had already seen, they knelt down in unison to give thanks to God Almighty for granting them the privilege of such a discovery.

The Spaniards set up camp at the base of this peak, after which Balboa, Pizarro and a select company of twenty-six soldiers headed in the direction of the coast. This short trek to the sea, a route which because it crossed over extremely difficult terrain took the small band of adventurers an additional four days to reach the shoreline. After reaching a bay which they christened San Miguel, Balboa waded out into the water with the flag of Spain in one hand and his sword in the other to symbolically claim the "Other Sea," which he named El Mar del Sur (the Southern Sea), for his homeland. The rest of the men, including Francisco Pizarro, then sloshed their way through waist deep water to stand alongside their revered leader.

The soldiers and natives who had remained back at camp were summoned at once to San Miguel. The Indian porters carried on their backs the various parts of the boats that were to transport all of them to the rich kingdoms that Panciaco had said could be found directly to the south. Once the parts of the boats were assembled the Spaniards set sail in search of these lands which reputedly overflowed with gold. Unfortunately for the intrepid explorers, they encountered contrary winds and currents that kept them from reaching their intended destination. It was all that they could do to reach the Pearl Islands, a group of small islands situated in the Gulf of Panama. Balboa, Pizarro and the rest of the men were met with determined resistance from the natives of these islands but, once again, the superior weaponry of the Spaniards was sufficient enough to overcome the superior numbers of those who dared to oppose them. The end result was that the natives sued for peace by presenting the Spaniards with a basket filled with their finest pearls. Pearl diving was one of the principal occupations of the islanders. These lustrous gems of the sea were treasured as ornaments and also served as a basic form of currency in matters of local trade. Once it became clear to all that the vessels they had brought were not capable of penetrating beyond the waters of these islands the decision was made by Balboa to return to Darién in order to build bigger and sturdier boats that could steer them to the lands that were laced with gold.

The disappointed, but still hopeful, adventurers returned to Darién on January 19, 1514. Balboa wasted little time in preparing for a second expedition across the isthmus but his plans were foiled by the arrival of an armada of twenty vessels that had carried across the breadth of the Atlantic more than two thousand soldiers and settlers as well as entire boatloads of supplies and materials necessary for the establishment of a new colony which was to be known as Castilla del Oro. This crew included a number of future conquistadors, the most notable being Hernando de Soto, Bernal Díaz del Castillo, Pascual de Andagoya, Sebastián de Benalcázar, and Diego de Almagro, who would leave their own indelible mark upon the conquest and settlement of the vast frontiers of the New World. The newly appointed governor of the lands that had been explored and settled by Vasco Nuñez de Balboa and company was an elderly nobleman by the name of Pedro Arias Dávila, but who was more commonly referred to as simply Pedrarias, a name that came to be feared by the natives of this land as well as the many Spaniards who served under him.

The arrival of Pedrarias had been anticipated, but Balboa had hoped to have been well on his way back to the Gulf of Panama by the time the fleet carrying the new governor and his entourage had dropped anchor at Darién. Before embarking on his first journey across the isthmus, Balboa had sent a message to King Ferdinand in which he detailed his plans to discover both the mysterious "Other Sea" and the legendary kingdom of gold that the natives had spoken of on so many occasions. Unfortunately for Balboa, he was to be betrayed by his own words as well as those of another. King Ferdinand was intrigued by the prospect of the discoveries mentioned in Balboa's letter but was deeply concerned by allegations of misconduct that were brought to his attention by Martín Enciso. The aggrieved lawyer bitterly complained to the king that it was Vasco Nuñez de Balboa, along with the willing assistance of Francisco Pizarro, who was guilty of undermining his right to command an expedition he had inherited from Alonso de Ojeda. He also charged that this usurper, who, he reminded the king, had stowed away aboard his ship to avoid his many creditors, was directly responsible for the death of Diego Nicuesa, the rightful governor of the lands where Balboa had settled, and his crew when he chased them away from his settlement, an act that condemned all to an unknown watery grave. It was for these reasons that King Ferdinand decided the time had come to appoint a new governor to this region of his expanding empire.

Balboa handed over command of his settlement to Pedrarias without any hesitation or complaint. The governor was pleased by such a gracious gesture but was displeased to learn that Balboa had already discovered the "Other Sea" that he had referred to in his letter to the king. The uneasy tension between Balboa and Pedrarias continued to escalate, thanks to the determined efforts of Martín Enciso, who had returned to Darién as a member of the governor's entourage, and Balboa soon found himself confined to a stockade to await being tried for the wrongful death of Diego Nicuesa and his crew. The chief judge, a licentiate by the name of Gaspar de Espinosa, who had sailed over with Pedrarias, found there was insufficient evidence to convict the imprisoned Balboa and, much to the chagrin of both Martín Enciso and Governor Pedrarias, ordered his immediate release. However, his freedom did not restore the titles that he had been stripped of, nor did it provide for the return of the many personal possessions, including his home, which became the royal residence of Pedrarias, that had been confiscated by his accusers.

In the meantime, news of Balboa's discovery of the South Sea had reached the court of King Ferdinand, which, of course, suddenly cast the explorer in a more favorable light among the influential members of the inner royal circle. A grateful Crown promptly rewarded Balboa with the title of Adelantado of the South Sea and awarded him a large tract of land to call his own. Pedrarias, who had been ordered by King Ferdinand to treat Balboa with greater respect, offered the hand of his lovely teenage daughter, Maria de Bobadilla, who at the time was still a resident of Spain, to the handsome and dashing soldier. Balboa, who saw this as an opportunity to get back in the good graces of Pedrarias, accepted the governor's generous offer of marriage to his daughter.

Balboa viewed this sudden and fortunate turn of events as an opportunity to resume his long delayed plan to return to El Mar del Sur. Their familiarity with the rugged terrain of the isthmus now made for a much faster crossing to the opposite coast. Once there, the arrival of a group of curious but friendly natives gave Balboa and his men good cause to assemble their vessels as quickly as possible. Besides providing confirmation as to the existence of a rich and powerful nation to the south, where people ate off of plates and drank from cups made of pure gold, the natives drew in the sand a picture of a llama, a creature which to the Spaniards looked very similar to a camel, the beast of burden that carried on its backs the many exotic treasures of Africa, Arabia, and Asia. Unfortunately for the Spaniards, these larger and sturdier vessels were still no match for the powerful winds and contrary currents of these turbulent waters, and once again they could navigate no farther than the Pearl Islands. Forced to admit defeat, Balboa and his men returned to the mainland and from there the dejected Spaniards began their somber trek back to Darién.

Even though Balboa had failed in his quest to reach the legendary rich lands of the uncharted south, Pedrarias still saw his betrothed son-in-law as a threat to his command and therefore schemed to have him arrested on the trumped up charge of conspiring to overthrow the present government, something that he had been thought guilty of in the past. With promises of a prominent role in his administration and a forgiveness of all past transgressions associated with Balboa, Pedrarias was able to enlist Francisco Pizarro, who did not participate in the second expedition to El Mar de Sur, to his cause. An unsuspecting Vasco Nuñez de Balboa was lured to a meeting at the settlement of Acla where he and his comrades, Andrés de Valderrabano, Luis Botello, Hernán Muñoz, Hernando de Argüello, and Andrés de Garabito, were met by the governor and a peculiarly large contingent of well armed soldiers. As Balboa reached out to greet the governor he was abruptly seized by several soldiers and formally placed under arrest by Francisco Pizarro, the officer who had faithfully stood at his side during so many previous adventures.

The fate of Vasco Nuñez de Balboa and four of the unfortunate comrades who had accompanied him to Acla had been foreordained by a deceitful Pedrarias. Andrés de Garabito, who had been arrested with his commander and comrades, saved his own neck by providing false testimony against Balboa and the others. The condemned men were forced to sit through a trial that proved to be a mockery of all sense of Spanish justice. Gaspar de Espinosa, who had recently returned from an expedition of his own, argued that Balboa should be granted a pardon but this time the chief justice, who was overruled by the determined governor, discovered he lacked the authority to save the founder of Darién. Sentenced to death by the tribunal that sat in judgment, Pedrarias ordered that the execution was to occur that night, before the soldiers loyal to Balboa had a chance to disrupt the proceedings. On January 12, 1519, just as the last light of dusk was being pushed back by the encroaching darkness, Balboa and his four companions were led out to the public square and forced to kneel down so that they could rest their heads upon the executioner's block. One by one, their heads were severed from their bodies and then impaled upon poles planted in the ground to serve as a grisly reminder to all of the terrible fate in store for anyone who dared to oppose the will of the governor. Their lifeless torsos were left where they fell and their rotting flesh became fodder for a host of hungry vultures and insects. It is said that Argüello was granted a stay of execution after the others were beheaded but other accounts claim that Pedrarias overruled this last minute show of mercy. This ignominious end to the founder of Darién and the discover of the El Mar del Sur was witnessed by many of the Spaniards who had served under his command, a group that included Francisco Pizarro and another adventurous minded soul by the name of Pascual de Andagoya, a soldier who had served as one of Balboa's shipbuilders.

2
In Search of Birú

Tales of a Wondrous Land

Following the beheading of Vasco Nuñez de Balboa, Francisco Pizarro traveled with Gaspar de Espinosa, one of Governor Pedrarias's most trusted officials, on a return expedition to the Pacific coast. Pedrarias sent them there with a large company of troops to locate and subjugate Urraca, the chief of the Veraguas, all of which they accomplished in a rather expedient but extremely brutal manner. It was during this time that Pizarro struck up a friendship with another soldier of fortune by the name of Diego de Almagro.

Conditions at Darién had, ever since the arrival of Pedrarias and his horde of colonists, deteriorated to the point where soldiers such as Bernal Díaz de Castillo, Bernardino Vazquez de Tapia, and Francisco Montejo left to seek out new opportunities at the island of Cuba, which they found after enlisting in an ambitious expedition led by Hernán Cortés. In the meantime, the tremendous amount of gold confiscated during conquests led by Espinosa and Pizarro was sufficient enough in quantity to entice the covetous Governor Pedrarias to transfer the capital of his Castilla del Oro colony to the opposite side of the isthmus, overlooking the shore of the Pacific coast.

On August 15, 1519, a mere seven months after the execution of Balboa and his comrades, Governor Pedrarias officially transferred the capital from Darién, which was situated along the Atlantic coastline, to the site of a small fishing village that rested near the shores of the Pacific Ocean. This location was known by its native inhabitants as Panama, a name which loosely meant "plenty of fish." Francisco Pizarro was rewarded for his loyal service to Pedrarias with an appointment as lieutenant governor and chief magistrate of the new Panama settlement, posts which he diligently served from 1519 to 1523. He also served on the city council. The veteran soldier supplemented his income at his new residence by becoming a cattle farmer, and even though it provided him with a comfortable living, it was, however, an unsettling reminder of his poverty-stricken days as a swine herder back at Trujillo, Spain.

Even after being designated the new colonial capital by Governor Pedrarias, the town of Panama showed little progress from its days as a humble native fishing village. The huts of the indigenous people stood alongside the few buildings erected to shelter the Spaniards. Only those of the highest rank lived in any kind of comfortable quarters. Most of the soldiers and settlers lived in squalor and yearned for an opportunity to explore other options.

Nearly four years were to pass before there was another serious attempt to seek out the southern lands that the natives claimed were laden with precious gold. In the year 1522, Pascual de Andagoya was commissioned by Governor Pedrarias to sail southward in an effort to learn if there was any truth to the rumors of a rich empire said to exist just to the south of Panama. He was among the group of soldiers who once faithfully served under Vasco Nuñez de Balboa and who, following the execution of their commanding officer, were compelled to join the ranks of those who served Pedrarias. Pascual de Andagoya sailed southward but his best efforts fared only a little better than that of his former commander. The expedition landed at Punta Pinas where the Spanish captain befriended a local chief who told him they were at war with the Birú, a tribe that lived along the river known by the same name. It was Andagoya who christened the land Peru after mispronouncing the native word Birú—the name of the river they navigated for a brief distance.

Sketch of Diego de Almagro (courtesy Library of Congress).

Another version of the naming of Peru claims that the same group of Spanish explorers named it after a chief called Peruquete whose village bore the same title as that of its ruler.

Writing about his adventure in this region many years later, Pascual de Andagoya claimed that he "ascended a great river for twenty leagues, and met with many chiefs and villages, and a very strong fortress at the junction of two rivers with people guarding it."[1] It is believed by some historians that Andagoya learned much on this journey about the Inca empire, but, more likely than not, the adventurer simply heard vague tales of an unseen rich and powerful kingdom that existed somewhat farther to the south. The expedition was cut short when Andagoya injured himself after falling from his horse while attempting to impress the natives with a show of his rather questionable equestrian skills. Pascual de Andagoya returned to the Panama colony with boastfully intriguing tales of native wealth just waiting to be claimed.

Francisco Pizarro had heard similar tales while serving under the command of Vasco Nuñez de Balboa. He was present when an angered native prince knocked over their scale filled with gold and stated that he knew of a land which overflowed with the substance they desired so greatly. He had participated in expeditions to locate the legendary golden kingdom of Dabaibe and had ventured with Balboa on his epic march to El Mar de Sur to search for a native realm that supposedly eclipsed the wealth of all other known lands. He had heard the story of Balboa's second expedition to the other ocean where a friendly native drew a picture in the sand of a beast similar to that of a camel and told the Spaniards of an abundantly rich empire that lay just to the south. The recent discovery and conquest of the wealthy empire of the Aztecs to the north by Hernán Cortés and the recurring tales of a golden kingdom to the south rekindled the old soldier's spirit of adventure.

Francisco Pizarro forged a partnership with his good friend and fellow conquistador Diego de Almagro and the Spanish cleric Hernándo de Luque, both of whom had sailed to the New World with Governor Pedrarias, to seek out the empire rumored to exist to the not too distant south. Almagro and Pizarro were kindred spirits of approximately the same age — both were orphans and both were illiterate — and each had suffered the painful scars of a past that could never be healed. The actual location of Diego's place of birth is uncertain but is generally assumed that the town of Almagro, in the province of New Castile, was where he was raised. He struck up a friendship with Francisco Pizarro during the conquest and settlement of Panama. The Spanish cleric Hernándo de Luque, who was born at Olvera, Andalusia, came to the New World in 1514. He was presently the vicar of the Holy Church of Panama and prior to that he was head schoolmaster at the Cathedral of Darién. He also served as the trusted treasurer of the Spanish settlement. Luque saw this expedition as an excellent opportunity to harvest heathen souls for conversion to Christianity while turning a tidy profit that would enrich the coffers of the church as well as his own pockets. The ambitious priest symbolically sealed the pact between them for the sharing of any and all riches obtained from their upcoming venture by breaking a loaf of bread into three equal pieces and offering one to Pizarro, another to Almagro, and retaining the third portion for himself.

While Pizarro was the more eager of the three to undertake an expedition to explore lands to the south of Panama, he let Almagro and Luque do most of the talking for the group. Diego and Hernándo petitioned Pedrarias, who was a good friend of the priest, for the right to lead such an ambitious venture. The governor granted their request on the condition that they restructure their partnership so that it would entitle him, after expenses, to a share of the profits from this voyage. Pedrarias gave his blessing to the expedition and even provided them with a ship — a ten year old caravel built during Balboa's brief reign as leader of the colony.

Pizarro, Almagro, and Luque were all men of financial means but an expedition of this size and scope required more funds than the three could possibly muster on their own. It was Father Luque who solicited funds from Gaspar de Espinosa, the chief alcalde of Darién and a principal founder of the Panama settlement, who, for personal reasons, wished to remain a silent partner in this expedition. Espinosa, who was descendant from a family of prominent bankers in Spain, had an aptitude for making money off of money. Almagro and Pizarro used their newly acquired capital to purchase another ship, one that had been used by Pascual de Andagoya on his recent expedition. While known officially as the Company of the Levant, many of the wary settlers of Panama thought a better name for the fantastic scheme of Pizarro, Almagro, and Luque was the Company of Lunatics. Francisco had the distinction of being named captain of such a company.

On November 14, 1524, Francisco Pizarro, along with one hundred and twelve other eager soldiers of fortune, many of whom were veterans of the previous Andagoya expedition, and a small number of Indian servants set sail from Panama aboard two ships. Diego de Almagro was to follow the same route once he had rounded up more recruits and additional supplies for the mission. Unfortunately, the explorers chose to leave during the rainy season, a choice which caused their voyage to be severely hindered by opposing winds and turbulent waters brought on by the sudden onset of extremely violent storms. Pizarro sailed to the already familiar Isle of Pearls first and stayed just long enough to take on additional provisions, particularly bundles of grass to feed the few horses they had brought with them.

Leaving the Pearl Islands, the expedition ventured southward across the Gulf of St. Michael to Puerto de Pinas, the farthest point reached by Pascual de Andagoya. It was from there that Pizarro and his crew entered the mouth of the river Birú which they followed upstream for several leagues. Their first landing proved disappointing in the extreme. The captain and his men saw before them only a dismal swampland; a seemingly uninhabitable region that fell far short of the splendid description Andagoya had provided about the land of Birú, or Peru as he called it. Despite their bitter disappointment, Pizarro dropped anchor and led the entire crew, except for the sailors, on foot to explore the surrounding region. For three days they followed the course of the river. All of the adventurers had a difficult time trudging through the muck of the swamps and overcoming the thick jungle growth. The oppressive heat proved unbearable for the heavily armored Spaniards, particularly for a soldier by the name of Morales, who collapsed and died from sheer exhaustion. They all hoped that by venturing inland they would happen upon the wealthy natives that Andagoya and Balboa had heard about on their expeditions. This search took them into a dense jungle filled with the calamitous chatter of howler monkeys and the cacophonous calls of numerous types of exotic birds. A steady rain merely made their passage through the thick foliage, a path that had to be cleared every step of the way with the blade of the sword, an extremely difficult task. Shortly after leading his fatigued men to a clearing where they found nothing of interest except for a view of the distant Cordilleras of the Andes, Pizarro decided that the time had come to return to the ships.

Port Famine

A disappointed Francisco Pizarro and his exhausted soldiers returned to their ships, and from there they made their way back to the ocean where they continued to venture southward. The intrepid explorers hugged the coast in the hope of spotting some sign of civilization. Unfortunately, the route they followed was stalled by constantly opposing winds and currents. It was hoped that by sailing westward, out into the open sea, the ships would be able to break free of nature's tight grasp but, unfortunately, their vessels got caught up in the doldrums, a windless location where they floundered for several long days. A sudden tropical storm finally freed them from the ocean's forceful hold and they immediately headed back toward the coast. Severe storms continued to impede their progress and soon their supply of food and water, which had been strictly rationed up to this point, began to run dangerously low. After ten days of battling storms and bailing water, Pizarro and his crew were forced to make landfall. Their situation, however, failed to improve.

Because of the incessant rains inherent to that particular place and time, the explorers found their present location to be a region thoroughly saturated in water. The shore line where they had landed was punctuated with a dense thicket of mangroves. Traversing through the muck of this swampland and the thick jungle vegetation proved an even more formidable challenge than that which the Spaniards had experienced on their previous landing. Unable to find much in the way of food, the famished soldiers were forced to subsist on the unidentifiable wild berries they happened upon. Many disillusioned men voiced their desire to return to Panama but Pizarro was not ready to give in to the bellyaching complaints of his frustrated troops. To appease his men, Pizarro sent Francisco de Montenegro, one of his most trusted officers, and nearly half of the crew, a group that included those who were known to be the most vocal critics of their present predicament, back to the Isle of Pearls to replenish their now exhausted supply of food and water. Those who sailed had no more to eat and drink than those who were left stranded along the shore.

Once Montenegro set sail, Francisco Pizarro ventured out to locate a nearby village that could help them with their immediate need for food but none could be found in the surrounding jungle. Barter or plunder were the typical means employed by adventurous Spaniards to obtain food whenever they happened upon a native village. Otherwise, they had to forage on their own, and their unfamiliarity with the land and what was edible certainly was to their detriment. The captain tried to ward off an encroaching sense of despair with words of encouragement and a regular regimen of chores. Much of their time was spent building huts upon unstable marshland. All were forced to subsist on the shellfish that the sea deposited along the shore as well as any vegetation they found edible. The soldiers spotted a beach several leagues off that became visible only after the weather had cleared. Pizarro and several men set off to explore this region while the rest remained at camp attending to their various assigned duties. Their efforts were rewarded with the discovery of an abundant supply of delectable and nutritious coconuts. They also found a bushel of maize left behind by natives who scurried away in fear after having sighted the approach of the Spaniards.

Some of the berries that the men ate proved to be poisonous and many a soldier suffered greatly from such ignorance. The survivors grew increasingly thin and pale, their skin taking on a yellowish hue. A Spaniard had only to look at the pitiful sight of his comrades to know how desperate his own plight had now become. Many a poor soul perished from the numerous hardships encountered during this lengthy stay at the spot that Francisco Pizarro would christen Puerto de la Hambre (Port of Famine).

While continuing to reconnoiter the surrounding land, Pizarro and his men came upon a small village that had previously escaped their notice. The fearful natives immediately abandoned their homes when they heard the lumbering approach of the Spanish soldiers. The ravenous troops helped themselves to the generous portions of food that had been left behind but, once their basic needs had been satisfied, the Spaniards were frustrated by the fact that there were few items worth pilfering. Many now wondered if native stories of rich kingdoms supposedly inhabiting this region were simply a fanciful tale told at the expense of the Spaniards. Those lingering doubts dissipated the moment the natives returned wearing ornaments made of crudely wrought gold, a sight which greatly excited Pizarro and his men. It was from the inhabitants of this village that the Spaniards first learned of the rich and powerful kingdom of the Incas, a conquering tribe that dwelled still farther to the south and way up high in a valley amid the soaring peaks of the Andes mountains. The soldiers returned to Puerto de la Hambre with a renewed confidence in the worthiness of their expedition. The men spent the next several weeks staring out to sea awaiting the return of Montenegro, a scenario that seemed all to familiar to Francisco Pizarro.

While Pizarro and his men were making due at Puerto de la Hambre, Francisco de Montenegro and his half-starved crew managed to summon enough strength to make their way back to the Pearl Islands. After quenching their thirst and filling their bellies the men began loading the ship with an abundant amount of corn, fruits — particularly bananas, fresh water, and what little meat they could find to bring back to their famished comrades. Though the distance by sea was relatively short, it still took Montenegro and his men more than six weeks to complete the round trip. The rough waters, strong headwinds, and powerful storms all contributed in part to make for a much longer than anticipated voyage. He returned after this lengthy absence to find a frightfully emaciated Francisco Pizarro and a noticeably diminished crew. The death toll had soared to a count of twenty-seven soldiers by the time of Montenegro's return. He saw that a slim diet of shellfish, seaweed, berries, and a few coconuts certainly had not provided sufficient enough nourishment for his stranded comrades. Even the naturally slender Pizarro appeared deathly frail from a lack of food and showed noticeable signs of the onset of disease. Thankfully, Montenegro had returned with enough food and fresh water to fill the bellies and revive the spirits of all the soldiers. Once this task was complete all were fully prepared to follow Pizarro's lead once more.

Once they had regained their strength, Pizarro and his followers were ready to leave behind Puerto de la Hambre, the dreadful place where they had suffered for far too long, and continue on with the expedition. Diego de Almagro was still unaccounted for during all this time. Though hampered by a steady rain, the revitalized conquistadors continued sailing southward along the coast. Unfortunately, all that they saw before them was a monotonous stretch of marshland and thickets of mangroves. The dense jungle which obscured their field of vision appeared to be one without end. The torrential rains they encountered during this period were accompanied by frighteningly powerful storms that threatened, on more than one occasion, to capsize their ship. The excessive moisture brought on by the steady rains and humid air gave rise to a rot that spread quickly through the clothes of the Spaniards. Mosquitoes were a terrible nuisance, and a few observant men began to see a correlation between the nagging bite of the mosquitoes and the strange and terrible illness that claimed many a Spanish life.

Eventually, Pizarro and his crew arrived at a more promising shore — an area less encumbered by jungle foliage. They dropped anchor and went ashore, where after a brief search they once again happened upon a village, only this one, which was nestled deep within a mangrove swamp, was much larger than the one they had previously encountered. Just like before, the inhabitants of the village fled when they heard the approach of the soldiers. Pizarro and his men found ample amounts of fresh meat and maize as well as a quantity of golden ornaments equal to roughly six hundred pesos, all of which they claimed for themselves. However, the Spaniards immediately decided to return to their vessels when it was discovered, much to their distaste and horror, that the food the natives were presently roasting appeared to be human flesh. The terror of seeing hands and feet boiling in pots was compounded by the discovery that arrows dipped in poison were a part of this tribe's deadly arsenal. The Spaniards were all too familiar with the ominous signs of cannibalism from their previous contact with the ravenous Caribs who regularly launched raids against the more peaceful tribes of the islands to satisfy their craving for human meat. Spanish soldiers had tried their best to stamp out such barbarous behavior by slaughtering every Carib they encountered, while making it a point not to discriminate regarding either gender or age. What the frightened Spaniards probably saw in those pots were merely stewing monkey paws, a delicacy for many natives who lived along the coast.

Seeing that the strain of this arduous voyage on their vessel had prompted a dire need for repair, Pizarro decided to set up temporary camp along the stretch of shore where they had just landed while the ship was to be returned to Panama for a sorely needed overhaul. Before embarking on this return voyage, Pizarro had Montenegro lead a small band of soldiers on a reconnaissance mission of the surrounding area to locate any native villages that could aid them and to find a more suitable site for a permanent place of shelter — one which was less exposed to the extreme elements and more defensible against a possible native incursion. Montenegro and his scouting party succeeded in the first part of this objective in short order, but were forced to pay a heavy toll for such a discovery. Having stumbled upon yet another abandoned village, the Spaniards were to soon learn that the women and children had simply been evacuated to a safer place while the men prepared to wage war against those who had so brazenly invaded their domain. The natives had spied on the Spaniards for some time and when they saw that their forces were divided the warriors decided to launch their attack. As Montenegro and his men were exploring a nearby pass the naked warriors, all of whom were covered in red and yellow paint concocted from the surrounding vegetation, suddenly sprang out from their various places of hiding. The Spaniards were startled by both the stealth and ferocity of these warriors who were armed with bow and arrows and darts. Three Spaniards were killed almost instantly and many more were severely wounded. Montenegro and his remaining troops quickly regained their composure and returned fire with a barrage of bolts unleashed from their crossbows. Then with sword in hand, they launched their own assault, an attack which succeeded in driving off the numerous native warriors. However, the natives immediately regrouped and then attacked with such force that Montenegro had no choice but to issue the call for retreat.

The enlivened warriors followed the withdrawing band of Spaniards all the way back to the camp where they would carry the assault to Francisco Pizarro and his troops who were already under attack from another group of armed natives. Finding himself pinned down by a hailstorm of arrows and darts, Pizarro rallied his soldiers and launched his own offensive against the natives. The captain drew his sword and fought valiantly to defend both himself and his men. The warriors were quick to realize that Francisco was the leader of the group and they set their sights on slaying him. They nearly achieved their objective when the Spanish commander, after sounding his own call for retreat, lost his footing while attempting to lead their escape down the hill. The natives saw what had happened and sought to finish him then and there, but Pizarro, who still had plenty of fight left in him, quickly rose to his feet and ably defended himself by killing two natives with his deft swordplay. Displaying a resolve that would not be denied, the brave captain continued fending off a great many warriors until several of his men, who had noticed the desperate plight of their commander, rushed to his defense. By this time, Montenegro and his band of soldiers had returned and the suddenly strengthened Spanish force was, after much effort, able to repulse the native assault. The men had seen firsthand the skill and valor of their captain and they would, because of his proven bravery in battle, forever after hold him in the highest esteem. Two more Spaniards died during this fierce struggle, raising the total of those killed in action to five, while twenty others were forced to endure the painful effects of their terrible wounds. Pizarro received seven wounds from projectiles that found chinks in his armor, though none were of a life threatening nature.

Captain Pizarro now agreed with the majority of his men that the time had come to depart this hostile region and return to Panama. He had received verbal confirmation of the rumored rich empire that had been told to Balboa and Andagoya, and the sampling of gold he had obtained on this expedition would surely serve as proof to those who still doubted the existence of such an affluent realm. After restocking their vessel with food and fresh water, the Spaniards set sail for Panama.

Upon his return to the port at Panama, Francisco Pizarro learned that his partner Diego de Almagro had already led his own expedition southward and his efforts were rewarded with a rather significant find of gold. Though their paths never crossed, Almagro, who had set sail shortly after his partner's departure, and his crew of between sixty and seventy men aboard a well provisioned caravel, put in at several of the same spots where Pizarro and his men had landed.

Not knowing exactly where Pizarro was located, Almagro hugged the coast and stopped at every spot that seemed suitable to make camp in order to search for his partner. At Pueblo Quemado, the same location where Pizarro lost five of his men before returning to Panama, they saw foreboding signs of an apparent struggle left behind by their comrades. Almagro took fifty soldiers to reconnoiter the surrounding land in an effort to determine exactly what had transpired. They followed a path that led them to a heavily fortified village resting upon the slope of a hill. The Spaniards clearly saw many armed and readied warriors standing between them and the village. The natives were prepared for a possible return of these strangers from the sea, however they had not expected that it would be quite so soon. Almagro and his men continued their advance, believing that such a show of Spanish force would cause these warriors to yield once they had beheld the size and might of their army, but they were soon startled by the shrill war cries of natives intent upon defending their homes. The warriors unleashed a torrential volley of spears, arrows and darts.

Diego de Almagro experienced better success driving off the native warriors than Francisco Pizarro had, but he was fated to suffer more dearly for his efforts. A native spear struck him in the eye socket, and while the wound was not mortal, it did cause the commander to permanently lose sight in that eye. Once the wounded had been tended to, the Spaniards returned to the safety of their ship and resumed their search for Pizarro and his crew. They sailed as far as the San Juan River where they encountered less hostile Indians. Unable to find any further signs of Pizarro and his crew, Almagro feared they all had perished in this inhospitable land. After finding it impossible to pick up the elusive trail of his partner and having already collected a respectable amount of gold, Almagro decided the time had come to return home. Once back at Panama, Almagro was overjoyed to learn that his friend and partner had also returned. Pizarro, meanwhile, was pleased to see that Almagro had returned with even more gold than he had obtained, and both were delighted to learn that each had heard stories of a rich and powerful civilization that lorded over an empire equal in magnificence to that of the Aztecs of Mexico.

3
A Second Chance

A Pact Between the Partners

Shortly before his return to Panama, Francisco Pizarro sent the treasurer Nicolás de Ribera on ahead with a portion of the gold that he and his crew had collected on this expedition. Besides the tribute that was to be paid to the governor, who had made himself a partner in this venture, Ribera was to provide Pedrarias with a full account of the wondrous stories they had heard of far greater treasures just waiting to be claimed. Pizarro hoped this small offering would be more than enough to obtain permission from the governor to embark on another expedition, one which would provide for more men, more supplies, and more ships. In the meantime, Diego de Almagro returned to help their joint cause by adding his larger share of gold to the pot. The explorers were disappointed to learn that Governor Pedrarias was now more concerned with conquering and exploiting known lands situated to the north than he was in exploring for the rumored wealth of unknown lands that lay to the south. Therefore, he had no intention of sanctioning another mission that would surely result in the loss of more Spanish lives for what he considered to be a trivial amount of gold and cheap native trinkets. Such Spanish lives, the governor believed, would be better served in sacrifice toward the conquest of Nicaragua, a land which the governor was convinced contained hidden wealth equal to that of Mexico.

Father Hernándo de Luque, however, was clearly overjoyed by the reports of Diego de Almagro and Francisco Pizarro, both of which seemed to confirm the long-standing rumors of untold wealth said to exist to the south of Panama. This information was also of great interest to Gaspar de Espinosa, the silent partner who had played a prominent role in the founding of the town of Panama. Neither of these partners were about to let such a golden opportunity slip through their fingers because of the doubts of an administrator who lacked their vision. It was Luque who personally interceded on the behalf of his business associates and eventually he managed to persuade Governor Pedrarias to relinquish all claims to the region that Almagro and Pizarro sought to explore for the price of 1,000 gold pesos, a hefty sum that was to be paid in increments. Once this arrangement was agreed upon, Pedrarias granted Hernándo Luque, Diego de Almagro and Francisco Pizarro the rights to all treasure, except, of course, the obligatory royal fifth entitled to the Crown, obtained on their future venture.

On March 10, 1526, shortly after having reached their accord with the governor, Francisco Pizarro, Diego de Almagro, and Hernándo de Luque signed their celebrated contract, a written agreement that entitled each of the partners to a third of all the treasures and lands claimed during their upcoming second expedition. It was an accord that bound the three adventurous souls to the success of their endeavor to discover the untold riches of the lands of Peru, and to this end each swore a sacred oath to uphold their new agreement. On hand were three witnesses, one of whom signed for Diego de Almagro while another attested to the mark of Francisco Pizarro.

Father Luque again managed to round up another twenty thousand pesos, the majority of which, just as before, came from Gaspar de Espinosa, their affluent silent partner, to help finance this second venture. With this money Pizarro and Almagro were able to purchase two larger and much sturdier sailing vessels. In an effort to avoid the terrible pangs of starvation that both he and his men had suffered on the previous voyage, Francisco made sure that the ship's hulls were stocked with an abundant amount of victuals. The partners were able to recruit, though with great difficulty, 160 men for the upcoming voyage. A large number of those soldiers were veterans of the previous expedition. Though the number of enlistments was not quite as many as they had hoped for, it was certainly more than they should have expected considering that the vast majority of soldiers had already been conscripted into service to fight for Pedrarias in his effort to conquer and colonize Nicaragua. Several horses and a relatively large amount of firearms and ammunition were also brought on board, items that the Spaniards sorely lacked on the previous expedition. Bartolomé Ruiz, a capable and experienced pilot, signed on for this second voyage.

First Signs of a Great Civilization

The first landing of the second expedition occurred at the mouth of the Río de San Juan, a jungle coast which was the furthest point reached previously by Diego Almagro. It was here that Francisco Pizarro decided to venture inland with a company of soldiers. This roving band of conquistadors was soon rewarded with the sighting of a small village near the banks of the river which yielded a great many golden items and a fair number of native prisoners. After having relieved the village of a considerable amount of treasure, the Spaniards headed back to the ships, whereupon it was decided that Almagro would return to the Panama settlement with one of the ships and all the gold they had just acquired in the hope that this would be enough evidence of wealth to entice more men to join their cause.

Inspired by their sudden discovery of gold, the Spaniards under the command of Francisco Pizarro continued southward in hopes of discovering even greater quantities of this most precious of all metals. Unfortunately, all they encountered were swarms of mosquitoes breeding along the coastal marshes and a towering forest that seemed to rise all the way up to the clouds. Once a suitable location had been found, the Spaniards went ashore. It was then decided that the pilot, Bartolomé Ruiz, would continue probing southward along the coast with the other ship to search for signs of civilization. Meanwhile, Pizarro and the few who remained by his side would continue with an inland search for more native settlements to sack.

Pizarro and his small band of determined conquistadors soon found themselves lost in the dense and enveloping vegetation of the jungle, which, they quickly found out, concealed a host of deadly creatures both big and small. Man-eating crocodiles lurked cunningly in and around the swamps; anacondas and boa constrictors, enormous snakes that could crush a man to death in a matter of a minutes, were present everywhere. They were also harassed by protective natives who did not take kindly to these strangers trespassing upon their homeland. Several soldiers perished in a desperate effort to return to the more hospitable coast. At the river's edge they set up camp where they were forced to wage a constant battle with pesky mosquitoes and a growing hunger while awaiting the return of either Bartolomé Ruiz or Diego de Almagro. As the food supply dwindled away, Pizarro and his soldiers once again were forced to face the terrible pain and suffering brought on by a prolonged period of starvation. In fact, the only inhabitants who ate well were the caiman, who enjoyed feasting upon the flesh of several unaware soldiers, and the mosquitoes, who dined upon the blood of all the Spaniards.

Such a scarcity of food on land prompted Pizarro to send out small expeditions of soldiers in canoes to search the neighboring swamps for some manner of nourishment. One of those canoes, captained by a man named Varela, unexpectedly ran aground with the sudden onset of low tide. Nearby natives had been furtively tracking their movements from a safe distance and when they saw that this canoe full of Spaniards had become separated from the other boats the natives seized upon the opportunity to punish those who had dared to trespass upon their lands. Warriors in decorative paint let out shrill war cries that sent shivers down the spines of the stranded and unprepared soldiers. They overwhelmed and killed all aboard, after which they stripped the dead bodies of all their earthly belongings. All of this occurred in sight of their comrades who could not reach them until the tide came back in. Francisco Pizarro was deeply saddened by the loss of so many loyal soldiers.

While these tragic events that plagued Pizarro and his men were taking place, Bartolomé Ruiz and his crew came upon the island of Gallo but the pilot wisely decided to forgo a landing once he saw the hostile nature of the armed natives who were steadily massing along the shore. The explorers continued southwestward until they came upon a bay located at the mouth of the Esmeraldas River that Ruiz christened San Mateo (St. Matthew). Here the Spaniards received a more welcome reception from curious natives who came out to catch a glimpse of the strange looking men who floated upon the water in such a mysterious looking vessel. Ruiz and his men stayed just long enough to give their weary sea legs a chance to regain the feel of the ground.

Shortly after resuming their voyage, Ruiz and his crew came upon a large balsa raft complete with a lateen sail and a rudder. Since these were navigational devices that the Spaniards had never before seen employed by natives of the New World, Ruiz and his crew at first believed that they had somehow happened upon another European vessel. As many as twenty natives, both men and women, were on board this large craft. Some of the passengers aboard the balsa were so terrified by the sight of the large Spanish ship that they dove into the ocean in an effort to avoid contact with the Spaniards. These traders, who dressed in more elegant attire and acted in a more civilized manner than any natives encountered up to this point, were carrying assorted wares of gold and silver, items which were more skillfully crafted than any seen before by the conquistadors in this region. Ruiz and his men were also drawn to the finely woven and brilliantly colored garments prominently displayed on board the balsa. Belts, leg armor, bracelets, necklaces, tweezers, mirrors, drinking vessels, and precious stones were also among the many items included in the extensive inventory of these native traders. The Spaniards also found amongst this vast cargo a large quantity of the reddish hue shells of the mollusk, known as spondylus, an item that was greatly prized by many of the people who dwelled along the coast. The natives who did not abandon their balsa were invited aboard the Spanish vessel where a grand feast was held in their honor. Ruiz was able to learn, through the use of sign language, that these traders were from Tumbes (also spelled as Tumbez), a port town to the not too distant south of their present position. When Ruiz inquired about the presence of gold and silver at Tumbes the natives indicated that the sacred palaces not only stored such precious metals but were even sheathed in these substances which shone as brilliantly as the sun. Three of these native traders were retained by Ruiz in the hope that they might be trained as interpreters and to serve as guides for the Spaniards. The rest were set free.

These native reports of nearby temples covered in gold and silver inspired Ruiz to continue on with his southward search. However, shortly after having sailed past the equator without sighting the city that the merchants aboard the balsa called home, Ruiz decided to head back to where he had left his commander in order to issue a full report of all that he had seen and heard, not knowing that he had sailed within two hundred and twenty miles of Tumbes. After an absence of seventy long days, Ruiz and his crew were finally reunited with their comrades and commander. He also brought back with him the natives from the merchant balsa, who to Pizarro and his men appeared to be incontrovertible proof that there were indeed rich civilizations just waiting to be discovered. The news of their amazing discovery helped lift the sunken spirits of those who had suffered and endured the terrible hardships brought on by a severe shortage of food, constant native attacks, an incessant and oppressive heat, torrential rains, and an unrelenting onslaught of many fearsome creatures. Thankfully for all, Diego de Almagro returned shortly thereafter with reinforcements and additional provisions.

Upon his return to Panama, Diego de Almagro was surprised to learn that Don Pedro de los Ríos had succeeded Pedrarias as governor. The newly appointed governor demonstrated that he was much more receptive to such a speculative venture than his predecessor by granting Almagro permission to recruit an additional eighty soldiers, procure another ship, and obtain all the additional supplies and provisions deemed necessary to ensure the success of their mission. However, since so many men had gone off with Pedrarias to conquer and settle the region of Nicaragua, Almagro had a difficult time finding able bodied men who were willing to sail with him. The circulating stories of constant sorrow and tragic deaths associated with their search for the fabled golden kingdom to the south certainly did not help his cause. He did, however, succeed at having himself promoted to the rank of captain, an equal title which would not sit well with Francisco Pizarro.

Almagro finally set sail with a paltry crew of forty soldiers and six horses aboard two fully provisioned ships. After barely weathering a series of intense tropical storms the Spaniards were forced to make landfall at the island of Gallo, where Almagro and his men spent a fortnight making repairs to their severely damaged ships. From there the expedition sailed to St. Matthew's Bay where Almagro and his crew were reunited with Francisco Pizarro, Bartolomé Ruiz, and the rest of their comrades. He was greatly shocked by the sight of the yellow tinged skin and gaunt gait of those he had left behind not all that long ago.

The reinforced and reinvigorated company of adventurers now set off in search of the city of Tumbes. They stopped again at Gallo Island where it was deemed necessary to spend a full fortnight in order to give Pizarro and his weary men an opportunity to further recuperate from their various afflictions. During this time, one of the canoes sent to probe the nearby river capsized and five Spaniards drowned. Shortly afterwards, the expedition continued on to the port of Tacamez, later renamed Atacames, which harbored a town of some two thousand homes inhabited by natives who showed visible signs of being a culture far more civilized than the Spaniards were accustomed to encountering. Unbeknownst to these explorers, they had reached the furthest fringe of the vast Inca empire. Pizarro and Almagro anchored their ships just off shore of this splendid town. They were soon met by an armada of canoes filled with natives who, while brandishing weapons, circled their ships as if trying to block their way. Pizarro made an attempt to bring some aboard for a friendly meeting, but the natives quickly scurried back to shore to join the army of warriors steadily massing along the beach.

Francisco Pizarro, who wished to ingratiate himself before the native nobles in the hope of obtaining additional treasure, went ashore with a landing party which consisted of several armed foot soldiers and an imposing number of horse soldiers. It was a show of strength that the captain-general believed would be significant enough to compel the natives to lay down their weapons. However, more and more natives came out to confront the Spaniards, a sight that quickly forced them to realize that these natives, which they estimated as a unified force of ten thousand armed and ready warriors, were not so easily intimidated and obviously determined to defend their homeland. Finding that his troops were steadily being surrounded, Pizarro realized that he had little chance of defeating such a large force and thus ordered his men to begin an orderly retreat back to the ships. The natives continued to close ranks around the Spaniards and by the time they were near their longboats they found that the way to safety had now been blocked. Pizarro's great adventure might very well have come to an end that day on the beach had it not been for a nervous cavalier who lost his balance and fell off his horse, an embarrassing but comical sight that succeeded in relieving the nervous tension that had engulfed the Spanish troops. Believing that this bizarre creature had split in two, the shocked natives immediately fled from the beach. While the sight of natives dispersing in every which direction was a tempting invitation to sack the town, Pizarro decided not to push his luck and ordered his troops to return to the safety of their ships.

Diego de Almagro and Francisco Pizarro conferred in the captain's quarters where both agreed that Atacames was not worth risking the lives of their men to conquer a town of questionable value. It was at this point that Almagro proposed to take one ship and make another return to Panama to recruit more men and obtain additional supplies to bolster their efforts to conquer and settle these lands while Pizarro would, again, remain behind. Not relishing the idea of once again having to relive the hardships of fending off hostile natives, enduring the pain and suffering caused by a severe lack of food and water, and exposing himself and his men to the constant discomfort of a torrid climate and unrelenting swarms of bloodsucking mosquitoes, Pizarro accused Almagro of always taking the easier path on these expeditions. The captain commented: "It is all very well for you who pass your time pleasantly enough, careering to and fro in your vessel, or snugly sheltered in a land of plenty at Panama; but it is quite another matter for those who stay behind to droop and die of hunger in the wilderness."[1]

A heated exchange ensued, with each partner uttering derogatory remarks that sought to impugn the character of the other, and this war of words escalated to the point where the two commanders reached for the hilt of their respective swords. Fortunately for all concerned, blows were averted by the timely and persuasive intervention of Bartolomé Ruiz, the pilot, and Nicholas de Ribera, the treasurer. While cooler heads managed to prevail at that moment, the bond of friendship that once existed between these two commanders was fated to become a distant memory.

Once the two captains had peacefully settled their differences it was determined that Almagro's plan was, after all, the logical course of action to follow. It was agreed that he would return to Panama with one ship while Pizarro and approximately eighty soldiers sailed the other vessel to a more suitable location, one which would better shield them from the wrath of native discontent. Isla del Gallo (Isle of the Cock), a small island just to the north of their present position was chosen once again. It was here that Pizarro and several men would establish a camp while they awaited the return of Almagro, who was to take his ship and the majority of the men, a group which included those who had expressed an eagerness to abandon this expedition, and sail back to Panama. Dismayed by the prospects of being stranded at such a desolate location, several soldiers wrote to their friends and loved ones back at Panama complaining of their hopeless situation and the utter failure of the mission. Almagro learned of this discontent and confiscated these letters. However, a soldier by the name of Sarabia managed to secretly slip his letter into a bale of cotton earmarked for Catalina de Saavedra, the wife of the governor. The message, which was written in verse, was addressed to the governor of Panama and complained of the harsh manner of Francisco Pizarro and declared that Diego de Almagro was nothing more than a herder of men who were being led to slaughter by his butcher of a partner. The letter of complaint ended with a plea for rescue from their desperate plight

4
A Test of Will

A Line in the Sand

Pedro de los Ríos was shocked by the sight of the emaciated crew that returned to the port of Panama and when he learned of the contents of the letter smuggled among the gifts sent back to his wife the governor flatly refused to grant Diego de Almagro permission to proceed with his plans to enlist additional men to participate in the conquest of Peru. The letter, written by one of the malcontents still stationed with Francisco Pizarro and attested to by several other soldiers, complained of the harsh treatment imposed upon them by both captains. The message cried out for the governor to send a ship to rescue them as quickly as possible. This letter, combined with the reports of hostile natives and the loss of so many Spanish lives, were sufficient enough reasons for Pedro de los Ríos to conclude that this was a venture unworthy of any further consideration.

The governor did everything in his considerable power to keep Diego de Almagro from setting sail again. He did, however, dispatch two rescue ships under the command of an officer by the name of Juan Tafur to the island of Gallo to bring Francisco Pizarro and his forsaken men back to Panama. Captain Almagro and Father Luque managed to smuggle a letter on board the ship commandeered by Tafur which would inform their stranded partner of the reasons for the governor's sudden change of heart. They implored Pizarro to not lose heart, for they were committed to doing everything possible to see to it that the expedition would soon be able to continue as planned.

For the unfortunate souls who had remained behind with Francisco Pizarro at the Isle of Gallo there was no relief from the pain and suffering they were compelled to endure. Their meager provisions were quickly exhausted either from consumption or from the rapid decay brought on by such extremely hot and humid conditions. Since the island had little to offer in the way of food, Pizarro had his men construct a small canoe which was used to carry some of them to the mainland to scour for food. The incessant rains and dark clouds that continually hovered over the region further dampened the spirits of the already disheartened soldiers. The surrounding marshes were breeding grounds for mosquitoes, and there were times when these pesky insects were so great in number that the only way the soldiers could find relief from their unceasing assaults was to immerse their entire bodies in either sand or water. As if this difficulties were not enough to break a man's spirit, the soldiers had to contend with pumas, crocodiles, vampire bats, poisonous snakes, and the eerily haunting sounds of a dark and dense jungle that seemed to come alive the very moment the sun had set. Some soldiers relished death as a release from their mounting troubles. Once again the captain-general found himself standing along an isolated beach staring out at a vast body of water, hoping to catch a glimpse of an approaching ship's mast.

After a month had passed, Pizarro sent the other ship back to Panama ostensibly for repairs, but his true motive was prompted by a growing fear that a mutiny would lead to his death and end with the men sailing themselves back to Panama. Day by day, the starved and disillusioned soldiers stranded at the Isle of Gallo grew more vocal in their complaints. Therefore, the unexpected arrival of Juan Tafur with an offer of safe passage to Panama was one that most were certainly willing to accept. Captain Pizarro, who had no intention of abandoning his own quest, pulled out his sword and drew a line in the sand and, according to one account, said, "Friends and comrades, on that side are toil, hunger, nakedness, the drenching storm, desertion, and death; on this side, ease and pleasure. There lies Peru with its riches; here Panama and its poverty. Choose each man, what best becomes a brave Castilian. For my part, I go to the south."[1]

After his brief speech, a determined Francisco Pizarro crossed over the line he had just drawn. He was soon followed by the pilot Bartolomé Ruiz and then Pedro de Candia, a soldier distinguished by both his large stature and his Greek heritage. The eleven other soldiers who followed suit were Cristóbal de Peralta, Domingo de Soria Luce, Nicolás de Ribera, Francisco de Cuéllar, Alonso de Molina, Pedro de Halcón, García de Jérez, Antón de Carrión, Alonso Briceño, Martín de Paz, Juan de la Torre. The intrepid souls who chose to stand alongside their captain were collectively referred to as the thirteen of glory. The natives from Tumbes also chose to remain in the company of Pizarro and his loyal comrades.

As for the rest of the soldiers, they could not board the ships fast enough for the voyage back to Panama. Tafur adamantly refused Pizarro's request for transport to a neighboring island thought to be more hospitable and was equally reluctant to leave provisions for those who had so recklessly chosen to remain at such a deplorable location. However, in the end the captain found it in his heart to leave Francisco and his companions a meager ration of highly nutritious maize. Moments before Tafur gave the order to set sail, the commander decided that Ruiz should return to Panama colony so that he could inform Luque and Almagro of his determination to complete the expedition to locate the elusive kingdom of gold, a quest that now seemed so nearly within their grasp. In a letter to his partners, Pizarro beseeched them to send a ship laden with additional supplies and men as quickly as possible. He also sent a letter of complaint to Governor Pedro de los Ríos.

Shortly after Tafur sailed away, Pizarro decided that it would be best to seek a new place of shelter, especially now that he had fewer men to fend off a native attack. With the help of some friendly islanders, the Spaniards were able to build their own balsa and sail to the island of Gorgona — some twenty-five leagues to the north and situated about five leagues from the mainland. The tropical isle of Gorgona, which is approximately six miles long, was by far a more hospitable location than the dismal isle of Gallo: here there was a forest to shield them from the blistering rays of a torrid sun, and a small freshwater lake, which swelled from the constant rains, guaranteed that their thirst would always be satisfied. As a means to stave off boredom and to keep their susceptible minds from wallowing in doubt and despair — all of which were potential breeding grounds for rebellion — Pizarro made sure his men were kept busy with a sundry of tasks. Religious services were strictly observed every day, and each man was assigned specific chores that helped to ensure the survival of the group. Huts were constructed for shelter. The island was home to more wild game that was of an edible nature but which, unfortunately, was not nearly enough to satisfy their bellies to the fullest. Pizarro and his men passed much of their time hunting and fishing for food but for the most part they had to subsist on a diet of crawfish, iguana, eggs, and pimento. As he had done so many times before, Pizarro spent a good portion of his free time gazing out to sea, hoping to catch sight of the vessel that his partners had promised to send. It was an act he had performed more times than he cared to remember.

Juan Tafur and his crew managed to make it safely back to Panama while the unsettling events at the Isle of Gorgona were beginning to unfold. Those who had returned with Tafur gave testimony of the many sufferings they had endured on this expedition and spoke of how most of the land they saw was simply a desolate region saturated with water. Such reports merely reinforced the governor's decision to not waste any more men or effort on such a foolhardy cause. While the governor was certainly glad that so many Spaniards had been rescued, he was, nonetheless, annoyed over the sheer stubbornness of Francisco Pizarro and the utter foolishness of those who chose to follow him into certain death. With a clear conscience, the governor felt he could wash his hands of this whole sordid affair, believing that whatever happened from there on out was the result of their own choosing.

The received dictated letter of Francisco Pizarro further strengthened the resolve of Diego de Almagro and Hernándo de Luque to find a way to aid the stouthearted men who had freely chosen to remain true to the cause. Father Luque, who was undeterred by Pedro de los Ríos's lack of faith in their plans, continued to lobby the governor to show compassion toward Pizarro and his followers by allowing Almagro to return with sorely needed supplies and reinforcements. The impassioned pleas and assurances of Luque and his associates eventually wore down the stubborn resistance of the governor, who granted them permission to send one ship to aid their comrades, as well as the right to carry on with their mission. However, there were strict conditions that Almagro and Luque had to agree and adhere to: no more soldiers were permitted to participate in this venture, only sailors — and then just enough to safely man the ship; they were to carry orders that stated the entire crew was to report back to Panama at the end of six months, which also meant that Pizarro must be counted among the band that returned. After several months of negotiations, Bartolomé Ruiz sailed with one vessel manned, as instructed, by only sailors. Almagro and Luque made sure that this vessel, though lacking in reinforcements, was not short on essential supplies and weapons.

The First Sighting of Tumbes

Meanwhile, Francisco Pizarro and his men had to endure a long wait. They passed the time hunting, fishing, and staring out to sea in the faint hope that they would catch sight of a Spanish sail emerging from the distant horizon. Having endured nearly seven months on the island of Gorgona without spotting a relief ship had caused many to abandon all hope. Therefore, when Ruiz and his crew finally discovered their whereabouts, the stranded company of thirteen thought that the approaching vessel was nothing more than a wishful mirage. A great deal of celebration took place once Bartolomé Ruiz docked his boat. Pizarro was greatly pleased with the letter he received from Almagro and Luque, the contents of which made it clear that they were not about to abandon their comrade.

While the bodies of Pizarro and his faithful followers may have been worn down by their many deprivations, their spirits were still willing to continue on with the quest. However, with so few men, it was clear that thoughts of conquest were now out of the question, and their brief time allotted would clearly be better spent gathering evidence of the splendid wealth of this region in an effort to bolster their bid for a third and larger expedition. Their best chance of achieving such an objective was to locate Tumbes, the rich city that Ruiz had learned of from the natives he had encountered on his previous voyage. When the time came to begin their journey to seek out the riches of Tumbes it was determined that two of Pizarro's men, Cristóbal de Peralta and Martín de Paz, both of whom were too ill and frail to cope with the rigors of yet another excursion, were to remain behind in the care of natives who had befriended the Spaniards.

Bartolomé Ruiz steered the ship toward the city of Tumbes, guided by the recollections of his own experience and the advice of the natives who hailed from that location. They ventured southward past the equator and Cape Pasado, the southernmost point that Ruiz had previously explored. The voyage took them past Chimborazo, an active volcanic mountain that soars to a towering 20,561 feet above sea level. On their twentieth day out the adventurers reached the Gulf of Guayaquil. Here they were granted a majestic view of the towering snow capped peaks of both Chimborazo and Cotopaxi.

Pizarro and his men were gladdened by the sight of so many towns along the way, all of which seemed to house natives of a more civilized manner than the warlike natives they had encountered to the north. They eventually dropped anchor at the island of Puná located near the bay of Tumbes, a place which the Spaniards christened Santa Clara. Even though the island appeared uninhabited, which it wasn't, the Spaniards could clearly see that this was a sacred place of pilgrimage for a great many natives. Here the adventurers busied themselves with taking on additional food and water for the next leg of the voyage. While at Santa Clara the Spaniards saw a few finely crafted golden items and were delighted to hear from their native guides, who, now that they had become somewhat familiar with the Spanish tongue, adequately served as their interpreters, that a great deal more of this most precious of metals could be found at the city of Tumbes, which, they declared, was very near. The next day the Spaniards embarked for Tumbes.

After several days of sailing within close sight of the Gulf of Guayaquil's coast the expedition drew near the Río Corrales, a tributary of the Tumbes river. Here they came upon the town of Tumbes, a spot slightly distant from the town that presently bears the same name. As they approached the entrance to the bay a fleet of large balsas came towards them carrying a great many warriors, all of whom were fully armed for battle. Pulling alongside one of the enormous rafts, Pizarro had his interpreters inform the natives that he had come in peace. He was relieved to learn that this war party was headed to do battle with their enemy, the natives who dwelled at the island of Puná. Pizarro persuaded the natives to abandon their current campaign so that they might return to Tumbes to tell their chiefs of his great desire to visit their city. The natives did Pizarro's bidding and returned at once to Tumbes. Shortly thereafter, a number of balsas sailed back to the Spanish ship carrying many of the foods common to their land: bananas, maize, potatoes, coconuts, pineapples. They also sent an offering of fish and several llamas, the latter of which marked the first time a Spaniard had actually seen such a creature.

Several chiefs, or subjugated rulers known by the title of curaca, and an Inca noble, so noted by his elegant attire and the large gold plugs that were inserted into each of his elongated ear lobes, came aboard the vessel to meet with the bearded strangers who had suddenly emerged from the sea. The curacas, as the Spaniards would soon learn, were a subordinate rank of nobility comprising of the rulers of realms that had been conquered by the mighty Incas. Pizarro provided his distinguished visitors with a tour of his ship and made sure they were treated to a sumptuous offering of food and Spanish wine. Through his native interpreters, the captain-general did his best to convince the nobles of the peaceful intentions of his visit and to convey that he was but a vassal of a great and powerful lord who lived well beyond the other sea. He also offered up the standard discourse of how it was the responsibility of the Spaniards to spread the word of their Christian faith. Pizarro told his guests that the sun they worshipped was but an object created by the God of the Christians to give light and warmth for all of mankind. For some natives, Pizarro seemed to be talking of Viracocha, the native god of creation, while others simply thought that he was the one who had been misled. None of the nobles responded to his rather lengthy diatribe. His claim of serving a mighty lord from across the sea also fell on deaf ears: What lord could be more powerful than Huayna Capac, the Inca ruler who was the divine son of the sun? As the Inca noble was preparing to leave, Francisco presented him with an iron hatchet. The delighted emissary reciprocated by extending to Pizarro and his men a formal invitation to visit the city of Tumbes. Since the hour was already late, the captain-general decided to delay a visit to the city until the following morning.

Early the next day, Pizarro sent Alonso de Molina and a Negro servant as his emissaries to Tumbes. They brought with them a hastily assembled array of gifts that included a pig and some poultry as an offering of thanks to the gracious ruler. The citizens of Tumbes came out in full force to see Alonso de Molina and the African who accompanied him. The natives were fascinated by the skin tone of both strangers but more so with that of the man with the skin much darker than their own, whose flesh they annoyingly rubbed and scratched to see if it would peel off like paint. Molina was soon brought before the chief who showed his appreciation for the many gifts they brought by offering both men a delectable drink from elegant vessels made of silver and gold. The two were then given a tour of Tumbes, a splendid city that was once part of the large kingdom of Chimu but which now was part of the vast empire forged by the conquering Incas. Molina and his attendant were especially intrigued by the main temple, a sanctuary that was elaborately decorated with numerous silver and gold ornaments. Both returned that evening to report that the Tumbans were very pleased with their gifts and were particularly excited by the crow of the cock. Molina also told Pizarro of the natives' fascination with his facial hair and the skin color of the black attendant who had accompanied him. Molina spoke of the opulence of the ruler's home, emphasizing the gold and silver dishes he ate from. In telling of his tour of Tumbes, Molina described the temple that had so delighted him as "blazing with gold and silver."

Francisco Pizarro believed that Alonso de Molina had greatly exaggerated his details of the magnificence of Tumbes and decided to send Pedro de Candia, a native of the island of Crete, the next morning to obtain a more reliable account. Pedro cut a fitting figure as he strode ashore dressed in full armor and brandishing his trusty arquebus. Pedro de Candia was a man of such great height — supposedly close to seven feet tall — that he was even more of an oddity to the natives than the African servant who had previously come ashore. The curious natives marveled at the strange outfit the giant Spaniard wore, the gleam of which to the natives had the look of silver, the substance which was thought to be the "tears of the moon." The natives asked for a demonstration of the might of the strange weapon he carried and Candia obliged by setting up a wooden target which he split with a single shot from his arquebus, a predecessor of the musket. The thunderous sound and the flash of light and smoke frightened the throng of onlookers and many dropped to the ground out of fear. A great many natives were now convinced that the gods had returned and cried out the name of Viracocha, the god of creation who long ago had departed their land by way of the sea. Pedro was then led to one of the royal houses where he was served a banquet of their finest food and drank chicha, their royal wine made from fermented maize, out of drinking cups crafted of fine silver and gold. Pedro was accompanied by the expedition's interpreter. He was also given a tour of the city, and at their temple dedicated to the revered sun he saw on display the great store of wealth that the Spaniards had set out to discover.

Pedro de Candia returned to tell his commander that he saw a temple "literally tapestried with plates of gold and silver." He also told of his visit to a temple that housed cloistered maidens who were known as Virgins of the Sun. Inside, he said, was a garden that blossomed with gold and silver facsimiles of the many fruits and vegetables indigenous to this land. He also claimed that ornaments made of gold and silver could be found everywhere in the city. Candia also brought back a canvas that provided the Spaniards with a fairly detailed map of the city. His report, which seemed to validate the fantastic account given by Alonso de Molina, was confirmation to the men aboard ship of the tremendous stores of precious metals their native guides had claimed could be found at Tumbes. The Spaniards rejoiced, for at last there was finally an opportunity to receive a reward large enough to compensate for all the grueling hardships they had suffered and endured up to this point.

After having fully heard and weighed the reports of both Alonso de Molina and Pedro de Candia, the captain-general decided that the time had come to see for himself the great wealth said to be on display at Tumbes. Realizing that he had neither the manpower nor the time to sack the city, he informed his deeply disappointed crew that this was merely a reconnaissance mission and that the time for wealth and glory would have to wait until the next expedition. The captain instructed those who were to go ashore with him to avoid offending or mistreating the natives in any way or manner, and under no circumstances were they to take any items of value. He explained that he planned to earn their trust so that when they returned later to claim the land for both Spain and themselves the natives would be caught off guard, thereby making the conquest a far less risky endeavor.

Following this briefing, Pizarro and several soldiers went ashore and were immediately welcomed by the royal elite of Tumbes. The Spanish commander's first impression of the city was somewhat disappointing — the houses were relatively small, the streets were slightly narrow, and the people were rather plainly dressed, not at all what he expected to see after hearing the glowing reports of his two emissaries. However, his perspective changed dramatically once he caught a glimpse of the temples that shone so brightly from their numerous ornaments crafted out of gold and silver. Pizarro did his best to contain his joy over such a spectacular find. He now knew for sure that those stories he had heard so many times before at Panama of untold riches just waiting to be discovered were indeed true.

After a brief stay at Tumbes, Pizarro bade farewell to the kindly ruler of the city and left him with a pledge that he would soon pay him another visit. With a renewed confidence in the worthiness of this expedition, the Spaniards continued sailing southward, hugging the coast in hopes of spotting signs of another affluent civilization. Approximately ten miles into their voyage they were disappointed to discover that the verdant coast they had become accustomed to was steadily giving way to a parched landscape. They had reached the northern border of the barren Sechura Desert, a region so dry that it can support very little in the way of vegetation. What little precipitation it receives comes from the residue of the thick fog banks that periodically roll in off the ocean. Numerous ravines are formed by the waters of the melting snows of the distant Andes that steadily roll toward the ocean. Such small rivers and streams proved sufficient enough to support a number of large cultures down through the ages.

A sudden surge of heavy winds forced the small group of explorers far out to sea but they were able to maintain their bearings by keeping sight of the majestic peaks of the distant Andes. Pizarro and his men passed Cabo Blanco and soon made landfall at the port of Paita. It was here that they had another encounter with a flotilla of balsas on a trading expedition. After a friendly exchange of words and goods the Spaniards continued southward to Punta de Aguja where they happened upon a great multitude of seals and sea lions basking along the coast. The continual roar of snorts, grunts, and cries emanating from these creatures of the sea were deafening to the ears of the wary but fascinated explorers. At each port of call they were welcomed by natives who amazingly had received advance word of their coming and who rewarded them with bountiful amounts of the local cuisine. Their good behavior at Tumbes had clearly paid off. The Spaniards repeatedly heard reports of an omnipotent ruler who lorded over a vast realm from atop his mountain kingdom. Pizarro and his men went out of their way to show the utmost respect toward the natives of each village they encountered. They carefully avoided all temptations to plunder — the time for such thievery would come soon enough.

The intrepid explorers continued southward but their progress was severely hindered by steadily adverse winds. The dearth of rain in a land with few noticeable rivers caused many men to wonder how they would be able to replenish their rapidly diminishing supply of fresh water. At a place called Collique, just before the Lambayeque Valley, Pizarro and his crew received an exuberant welcome from the proud natives who were once part of the mighty Chimu empire. A soldier by the name of Andrés de Bocanegra was so enamored with the lavish attention showered upon him by these friendly natives that he asked the captain-general for permission to leave the expedition so that he might live as one of them. Pizarro consented to let him stay and the delighted natives welcomed Bocanegra as a member of the tribe by parading him around in an elegant litter.

Pizarro and his crew eventually made their way past Chan-Chan and though they never knew it, the Spaniards had sailed past the sacred burial grounds of the Chimu nobles. These ancient burial chambers beneath the ground were a final resting place for many of the deceased nobles of this land. Each was buried with their own personal treasure trove of gold and ceramic items. Had the Spaniards known of such a place and practice then surely they would have added grave robbing to their long list of transgressions already committed in this land. The opportunity to exhibit such ghoulish behavior would, however, present itself at a later date.

At about the ninth degree south of the equator, a distance of approximately five hundred miles beyond Tumbes, Pizarro decided to yield to the numerous complaints of his crew and began the long voyage back toward Panama. They now had verbal confirmation of a great empire similar in might and wealth to that of the Aztecs of Mexico and seen sufficient evidence to indicate that there was much gold and silver just waiting to be claimed. Pizarro hoped that the small number of gifts they had received at each port of call, a list that included several garments, a few llamas, and fair sample of gold and silver cast into various forms, were collectively enough to convince a skeptical governor to grant him and his partners the authority to embark on a third expedition, one which would be for the express purpose of conquest.

At one of the village stops before their return to the Panama settlement, a simple-minded crew member by the name of Pedro de Halcón asked Pizarro if he might, just like Andrés de Bocanegra before him, remain amongst the people of this land. Pizarro feared that the unstable Halcón might jeopardize the greater cause if he were to stay behind with the natives. The concern of the captain was quickly proved valid when Halcón, shortly after being denied his request, went stark raving mad. The crazed soldier grabbed a broken sword and proclaimed to the natives, "Now, now you rogues, this land is mine and of my brother the king, and you have usurped it from me!"[2] The quick thinking Bartolomé Ruiz knocked Halcón down with an available oar. The mad soldier was chained below deck for the remainder of the voyage.

On the way back home the explorers put in once again at Tumbes, where, as part of a cultural exchange, Alonso de Molina, the soldier who was enamored by the splendid sites of the city, and a sailor named Gines elected, with the permission of their commander, to remain behind while the ruler of the city allowed several of his citizens to return with Pizarro and his crew to Panama. Two of these natives were destined to be trained as interpreters in order to better serve the Spaniards in overcoming the difficult language barrier during the epic quest that was to follow. These young men were Martínillo, a lad of noble lineage who was the nephew of a mighty lord from Poechos, while the other was a mere commoner from Chimor who went by the name of Felipillo. Francisco Pizarro and his men then returned to the island of Gorgona to pick up the two sickly soldiers they had left behind eighteen months earlier. Unfortunately, one of the men had succumbed to his illness shortly after the departure of his comrades. The ship then set sail for the port of Panama.

5
Inca Heritage

Legendary Beginnings

One of the more popular creation legends of the Andean people speaks of a white bearded supreme being named Viracocha who rose up from the murky waters of Lake Titicaca many ages ago to create the world that he had long envisioned in his mind. This vast body of water, which measures nearly seventy miles wide at its farthest point and stretches nearly 138 miles in length, encompassing an area of approximately 3,500 square miles, is a vast oasis amid the parched lands commonly referred to as the Altiplano. At 12,506 feet above sea level, Lake Titicaca is generally regarded as the highest navigable lake on earth. Because of this extreme altitude, the high plateau that surrounds the Titicaca basin is but a bleak and cold tundra nearly devoid of trees. Most of this land is blanketed with stone and that which is not contains but a very thin topsoil lacking in the essential minerals needed for most forms of vegetation to grow.

Viracocha created life in a world that was deprived of light. This new world was populated by giants whom he had shaped out of the clay of the earth. The giant beings he created in his likeness fumbled about in perpetual darkness and Viracocha, who grew weary of their constant bickering, punished them by turning many back to stone, where they can still be seen at a place called Tiahuanaco. The rest of the earthly giants were drowned by a great deluge that lasted for sixty days and sixty nights.

Disappointed by his own efforts to create meaningful life, Viracocha returned to the dark abyss of the lake to ponder over how he could give form to the chaos of the earth above, a stark land punctuated with numerous erupting volcanoes and prone to constant and destructive earthquakes. He eventually emerged from the womb of Lake Titicaca a second time and summoned forth the sun, the moon, and the stars, all of whom arose from islands situated upon the water. These luminous celestial bodies ascended to their rightful place in the firmament that holds the heavens in order that the next race of beings would always have a guiding light from up on high to follow. Viracocha commanded Inti, the sun god, to give light and warmth to the day and ordered Mama Quilla, the moon goddess, as well as the numerous stars to shed light upon the darkened night sky. Each sunrise caused the waters of Lake Titicaca to shimmer as if gilded while every moonlit night cast a silvery shadow upon that same body of water.

This god of creation then gave shape to the earth by "making plains of the hills and of the plains mountains, and bringing forth springs in the living rock." Viracocha was "the Maker of all things, their Beginning, Father of the Sun."[1] He then proceeded to make clay figurines of the various kinds of creatures he wished to inhabit the earth and then gathered the shattered stones that littered the shores of the great lake and forged a new and smaller race of human beings to dwell upon the land. Viracocha breathed life into his many creations, after which he sent them forth to inhabit and populate the far four corners of the earth. Viracocha charged lesser deities with the responsibility of the earth's care: Illapa, the god of thunder, lorded over the weather; Mamakocha was the mother of the sea and all other bodies of water; Pachamama was mother earth; Kolka looked over the stars of the heavens. Once all was in place, Viracocha rested and took time to enjoy the fruits of his labor.

So it came to pass that Viracocha had a son, whom he named Taguapica. Over time, Taguapica grew envious of the adulation accorded to his father and the ensuing malice that took hold of his heart caused him to disrupt all things on earth. He found a multitude of ways to corrupt the hearts and souls of mankind and the means to divert or dry up rivers so that vast tracts of once verdant land soon turned into barren deserts. Viracocha and two faithful men he had retained as disciples set out across the land to correct the many transgressions of his only son and to make sure that all of mankind was guided back along the righteous path.

Viracocha, along with his two followers, ventured northward to survey the terrain and to see if all were living as he had commanded. In an effort to cover more ground the god of creation sent his two disciples off in different directions: one devotee traveled along the coast while the other true believer ventured deep into the jungle forests of what is now part of the Amazon. Viracocha chose to follow the rugged mountain path of the Andes, disguising himself sometimes as an old and beggarly looking man. The ancestors of old remembered that "out of the regions of the south there came and appeared among them a white man, large of stature, whose air and person aroused great respect and veneration."[2] The earthly manifestation of the god Viracocha wore a white garment that touched just below his ankles. His penetrating eyes cast a brilliant emerald glow. The hair upon his head was closely cropped while his kindly face flaunted a long and flowing beard. Viracocha was known by various names at various places: in some regions he was known as Pachayachachic — "Teacher of the World" while another realm came to call him Pachacamac, "Maker of the Earth." Wherever he stopped, Viracocha preached goodness toward one another — imploring mankind to respect the gods, nature, and one another.

Wherever Viracocha stopped he was well received by the people and the benevolent deity promptly rewarded their acts of kindness by healing the sick and enlightening all with his worldly insight as to how best to live an honorable and just life. There was a place, however, that chose not to embrace him. The people of the town of Cacha did not take kindly to the preachings of the old man and threatened to stone him to death. Viracocha knelt before his accusers and lifted his arms up toward the heavens. Suddenly there was a loud eruption and the blue sky above turned red with a tumultuous fire that began to rain down upon the mountains near their town, setting them all ablaze. The disbelievers who moments earlier had mocked him now begged wholeheartedly for his forgiveness, and Viracocha saw it in his heart to put an end to the fires by lifting up his staff and dousing the flames with a mere verbal command. However, by the time the fires were put out they had already charred a quarter of a league of the mountain range. The grateful people of Cacha erected a holy shrine and carved a sacred statue of stone that paid homage to Lord Viracocha.

Viracocha continued on to the Tambo of Urcos where he climbed up the highest peak to urge those who sheltered themselves in the caves to venture out into the sunlit world. The thankful natives showed their gratitude by building a bench made out of their finest gold upon which they set a statue carved in the likeness of the god of creation. Viracocha then wandered on to the verdant Valley of Cuzco, a distance of about six leagues from the Tambo of Urcos. From the Valley of Cuzco, the great lord of heaven and earth ventured to the province of Manta where he met up with his two disciples and once reunited they set out for the coast. Once there, Viracocha removed his cloak and spread it upon the water for him and his followers to use as raft that would straddle the white foam of the waves that were to carry them off to the distant horizon of the western sky.

The Journey of Manco Capac

The legendary history of the Inca, the chosen Children of the Sun, unfolds with the emergence of four brothers and four sisters, from a cave at a hill known as either Pacaritambo ("Inn of Origin" or "Inn of Dawn") or Tambu-tocco (Tavern Hole or Tavern Window), located approximately six leagues southeast of the present city of Cuzco. The center cave from which the Inca clan came forth was called Capac Toco and it was flanked by two openings, known respectively as Maras Toco and Sutic Toco, from which there emerged ten other families who were to follow their lead. The four brothers who left the shelter of the cave to venture out into the unknown world were named Ayar Manco, Ayar Cachi, Ayar Uchu, and Ayar Auca, and they were accompanied on this journey by their four sisters; Mama Occlo, Mama Huaco, Mama Cura, and Mama Raua. They all went forth at the urging of the god of creation, with enough food and water to sustain them until they reached the land they were to call home.

These dwellers of the cave had been beckoned out into a world filled with resplendent light and agreeable warmth by the god Viracocha but it was Apu Inti, the Lord Sun, who spoke to them. Manco, who along with his brother and sisters, had to shield his eyes as as he listened intently to the divine words of the sun god. Apu Inti told his children to go forth and found a city and forge a civilization that would honor him. He said unto them, "When you have reduced people to your service, you shall maintain them in reason and justice with devotion, clemency and tenderness, playing in all things the part of a loving father to his beloved children, modeling yourselves on me. For I look to the well-being of the whole world, since I give men my light by which they see and warm themselves when they are cold and make their pastures and fields to grow, their trees to bear and their flocks to multiply. I bring rain and fair weather in their season and each day I traverse the whole surface of the earth in order that I may see the needs of the world to succor and provide for them as the supporter and protector of men. It is my will that you my children follow this my example, sent to the earth solely to teach and aid these men who live like beasts. And to that end I name and establish you lords and kings of all races whom you thus benefit with your instructions and good government."[3] It was therefore decreed by the gods above that the Incas were destined to hold dominion over the four corners of the world, an earthly realm known as Tahuantinsuyu.

Apu Inti then told Manco and the others, "Take this golden rod with you. It is only two fingers thick and shorter than the arm of a man, yet it will tell you how good the soil is for cultivating crops. As you travel, whenever you stop to eat or to sleep, see if you can bury it in the land. When you come to the place where the rod sinks into the earth with one thrust, establish my sacred city, Cuzco, city of the sun. Soft soil as deep as this golden rod will be fertile soil."[4]

The Sun God then sent his children out into the world so that they might bring a sense of order and civility to the many barbarous tribes that currently inhabited the land, people who had been led astray by the black hearted Taguapica. The Children of the Sun set out over the steep mountains with the golden divining rod that was to guide them to the promised land. Each brother and his sister wife led a tribe of faithful followers who had emerged from the adjoining caves: Ayar Manco and Mama Occlo marched at the head of the Maska tribe; Ayar Auca and Mama Huaco guided the Chillka, Ayar Uchu and Mama Raua directed the Tampu, while Ayar Cachi and Mama Cura marched at the head of the Mara. These tribes brought with them an abundant amount of seed for the planting of a variety of crops, most of which were an assortment of various types of potatoes.

With no other clue to go on to lead them to the sacred land spoken of by Inti, the Inca had to inspect each prospective parcel of ground by plunging the divine golden rod, known to the Inca as a tapac-yauri, into the soil of the earth. At each stop, the Children of the Sun founded a village, but were compelled to move on once they found the soil was not as rich as they had hoped. At their first stop, Manco and Occlo conceived a male child that they would come to call Sinchi Roca, and who was born by the time they reached their second stopover. Pallusta was the third location they stopped at, but after several years they moved on after realizing that the ground was not quite as fertile as first believed.

Ayar Cachi, the oldest and the strongest of the four brothers, went to the top of Mount Huanacauri, and flung four stones as far as he could, each cast to the four cardinal points and then claimed all of the land which fell within those borders for Inti. He hurled these stones with such force that they splintered mountains which, in turn, caused the formation of deep ravines that scarred the landscape.

Their next stop for the wayfaring followers of Inti was Haysquisrro. It was here that Manco, the recognized leader of the clans, decided that the disruptive Ayar Cachi, the brother who could split mountains with stones hurled from his mighty sling, had become a threat to his hold on power and schemed to have him removed from the group. Manco told his slightly older brother that it was necessary for him to return to Tambu-tocco to retrieve a golden cup called a tupac-cusi, a small but sacred llama figurine known as a napa, and some forgotten seeds essential for planting. Ayar Cachi did not wish to follow his brother's orders but changed his mind when he was shamed by the scolding words of Mama Huaco: "How is it that there should be such cowardice in so strong a youth as you are? Get ready for the journey, and do not fail to go to Tambu-tocco, and do what you are ordered."[5]

Not wishing to be branded a coward by his siblings, the proud Cachi decided to do as Manco and the others had requested of him. He was accompanied on this journey by a servant named Tambochacay (window entrance bearer) who was given explicit instructions from Manco to seal the fate of his unruly brother. Once Ayar Cachi was deep inside the sacred cave that once was the home of the Children of the sun, Tambochacay created a landslide of loose stone and boulders that covered up the entire mouth of the cave. Realizing that he had been sealed in the cave, Ayar Cachi shook at the boulders with such force that all of the earth trembled, but try as he might, this son of the Sun could not set himself free. Unable to escape and realizing that he had been deceived and entombed by his own servant, Ayar Cachi uttered a spell that instantly turned an unsuspecting Tambochacay to stone. The site where Ayar Cachi was entombed for all eternity was later known as Mauqallqta, one of the many sacred huacas of the Inca empire. It is said that even to this day Ayar Cachi, in an effort to escape, periodically rattles his cave with such force that he causes all of the neighboring earth to quake.

The wandering Incas and their faithful followers continued on to Quirirmanta, which stood in the shadows of the mountain of Huanacauri. They climbed to the top where all were rewarded with their first glimpse of the luxuriously verdant landscape of the Huatanay River Valley. It was here that Ayar Uchu was transformed into stone and forever after became a much revered huaca site. The respective tribes of Ayar Cachi and Ayar Uchu settled where the brothers who had led them met with their ordained end. Auca, a third brother, became a sacred huaca at the plaza known as Huanaypata, located in the center of the city once called Qosqo and now known as Cuzco.

Manco, as he had done so many times before, planted in the ground the golden rod he carried, except this time the land swallowed it whole, the foretold sign that this was where he and his followers were to settle. At that very moment the heavens above gave their sign of approval with a brilliant rainbow that stretched across the entire valley. Manco turned to his wife and said, "It is in this valley that Our Father the Sun commanded us to make our abode in accordance with his will. Therefore, Queen and sister, it behooves each of us to go this way and draw the people to him in order to instruct them and care for them as Our Father the Sun enjoined."[6] Though but a mere sixteen miles from Tambutocco, the cave where the Incas once dwelled, the numerous stops along the way had delayed their arrival at Cuzco, their new homeland, for a great many years.

The people of this valley were simple folk who were quite content to live off the land. Manco sent a message to tell Alcaviçca, the ruler of the small village of Acamama that was quietly nestled in the valley, that he was the true son of the Sun. There were those who disbelieved and they began to mock the messenger. He told Alcaviçca and his subjects to gaze upon the hill of Huancauri where the truth of his master's words would be proven to all. There at the top of the mountain, the people saw Manco standing alone, with captured rays of the morning sun reflecting brightly off the plates of gold armor that were strapped to his chest and back. Convinced that the radiant image they saw was indeed a child of Inti, Alcaviçca and the bedazzled citizens of Acamama bowed before the mighty Manco and willingly accepted him as their god king, their Inca. Manco was bestowed with the title of Capac, meaning rich and powerful lord.

The name of the village of Acamama, formerly known as Qosqo, was changed to Cuzco (sometimes spelled as Cusco), which in Quechua, the native tongue of the people, means navel — a reference indicating that the city they were about to build stood at the very center of the universe. The sacred plot of land where the golden rod was imbedded in the ground was cordoned off into a square, later called the Coricancha (the golden enclosure), where they erected a simple stone house with a thatched roof that, over time, was transformed into a magnificent temple dedicated to Inti, the sun god. From this first building of the Incas there emerged the splendid city of Cuzco. The city itself was divided into two barrios: Hanan Cuzco, which means Upper Cuzco and inhabited by those who followed the teachings of Manco; and Hurin Cuzco, or Lower Cuzco, where dwelled those who revered the sisters of Manco. It was at Cuzco that myth and history merged to lay the foundations of the legendary Inca empire.

There were neighboring tribes who were wary of the divine claims made by the newly arrived Incas. There was a scarcity of cultivatable earth in the highlands and therefore such fertile lands had to be guarded against invasion by tribes constantly in search of better fields for planting. The Hualla tribe saw that the Inca were rapidly expanding their town and feared that they might begin to encroach upon their designated stretch of land. A war was declared, the tide of which was turned back when Mama Huaco killed one of the leaders of the Hualla with her weapon of choice — an ayuinto — a stone attached to a rope. She then terrified those who had witnessed the death of their leader by cutting open the victim's chest and ripping out both of his lungs. She compounded their horror by inflating the blood soaked lungs with the breath expelled from her own lungs and then held them up high for all to see. The Hualla warriors fled in fear when they saw what Mama Huaca had done.

The Theocratic State of the Inca

The Incas saw themselves as children of the sun god Inti and therefore felt it was their sacred obligation to enlighten the neighboring tribes, all of whom were deemed to be hindered by their barbarous nature. It was, for the most part, a peaceful but somewhat limited expansion of the fertile lands that surrounded the newly established city of Cuzco. The people of the valley willingly submitted to the rule of the benevolent Manco, and consequently the following of the Inca grew steadily larger. Word of the Inca's good will spread throughout the land and soon many people migrated to Cuzco. Manco and his four sisters nurtured the material and cultural development that, over time, evolved into the Inca civilization, an advanced society destined to become a vast and powerful empire. Manco Capac, the first ruler, proved he was a man possessed of considerable compassion and reason, and because of these saintly qualities he was greatly revered by all of his subjects. The prophecy of the sun god was on the verge of being fulfilled.

The Inca ruler was sincerely interested in the welfare of his subjects and strove to make a better way of life for his growing number of constituents. Manco taught the men how to irrigate, plant, and harvest in a manner that would permit the land to yield plentiful amounts of food that would sustain them throughout the entire year. He showed his followers the proper use of the takla, a pointed digging stick used to create furrows for the planting of seeds, and the hoe in order that they could better cultivate their fields. Manco also gave his people various types of tools to help them in the building of Cuzco and showed them how to properly irrigate the land with fresh water. This was an agrarian based economy that thrived on the mass harvesting and consumption of beans, tomatoes, potatoes, peanuts, squash, and maize. The latter staple, which can fully grow and ripen only at altitudes below 2,000 meters, had to be imported to Cuzco, a city which stands at 11,207 feet above sea level. The need for corn was but one of many reasons that compelled the Incas to expand their boundaries beyond the confines of the Valley of Cuzco.

Mama Occlo, in the meantime, taught the women of Cuzco more efficient means of food preparation and how to best care for their beloved children. She also taught them how to weave garments out of cotton and wool that would better protect their bodies from the chill of the mountain air. Ancient Andean weaving techniques were vastly superior to those of their distant and unknown European contemporaries. They created mantles, headbands, hats, and garments of exquisite design and outstanding quality. The skill of these weavers was said to be so great that they could create garments as soft as silk out of tiny hairs plucked from the skin of bats, but the extreme shortness of these hairs has rendered such claims suspect. The subjects of the Inca also learned to excel in the fields of pottery, masonry, and jewelry.

Of the many creatures brought to life by the god Viracocha, none served the Andean people as well as the llama, alpaca, and vicuna, all of whom bear a slight resemblance to their distant relative the camel. The llama's ability to trek across difficult mountainous terrain while hauling a load weighing as much as one hundred pounds made it an excellent beast of burden. Though prone to sulk and take frequent breaks, abrupt halts where the beast would suddenly lie down or just stand still, the llama moved at a slow but steady pace, which, on an average day could travel a distance of some twenty miles. The llama was also an excellent source of meat and its hide was used in the making of sandals and rope. The dung of the llama was utilized as a fuel for sustaining fires and its body fat was employed in the making of candles. Their shorn wool was used for creating garments, but because of its coarseness it was worn primarily by the peasant class. Pieces of this needful animal were sometimes employed for ceremonial sacrifices to the gods and in some instances a whole llama was slaughtered to appease the gods.

The alpaca is somewhat smaller than the llama and therefore unable to shoulder the same burden as its Camelus cousin. However, its softer coat of wool was greatly prized by those of the upper class. The even smaller vicuna produces a coat of wool so luxurious that it could only be worn by members of Inca nobility.

Meat was of limited supply in this part of the world. Llamas, guinea pigs, and small dogs, most of which were domesticated, were the primary sources of meat. The flesh of these animals were cut into small strips and then dried, to create a cured product called charqui, or charki. To replenish their naturally restricted supply of meat the Inca periodically organized royal hunts. Known as a chaco, these public hunts involved thousands of men who formed an enormous ring around the land that slowly closed in on the creatures caught within the circle. Captured vicunas were shorn of their precious wool and released while most of the various other animals captured were killed for their meat. The nourishing meat was divided up among the participants but the wool of the vicuna was reserved for just the Inca nobility. The sheared wool of the llama and alpaca were stored and eventually distributed amongst the people, the portion of which was dictated by the size of the household.

The tribes of the valley were taught about the various gods that lorded over the earth and shown how to respectfully honor each and every one of them. Soon, the different beliefs of the many tribes became the one belief of a newly forged Inca society. The most venerated of their pantheon of gods was clearly Inti, the sun god who was considered the father of the inca. The inca ruled by divine right. He was accorded the respect and adulation that was typically shown to the gods, for he was, by his own decree, the son of Inti. He ate off plates made of either gold, silver, or fine china. The slightest stain to his clothes was enough to prompt an entire wardrobe change. All that he touched became sacred and items such as discarded clothes and uneaten food were stored and ritually burned later so that these articles could not be tainted by the touch of mere mortals. The fallen hairs of the inca were swallowed by servants in order to prevent them from falling into the hands of evil sorcerers who might use them to capture his soul. The inca never expectorated on the ground; instead an attendant would hold out a hand for him to spit upon. All who were presented before the inca humbled themselves by appearing barefoot and bearing a burden on their back or shoulders, usually just a token weight, sufficient enough to force them to bow in a subservient manner.

While the ruling inca was entitled to a harem of hundreds of concubines to satisfy his carnal desires, his queen, or coya, was often a full blooded sister, a seemingly natural choice considering that the same divine blood coursed through their veins. The coya was often referred to as Mamanchic, "our mother," a term of endearment uttered by her loyal subjects. It was only the sons of this blessed union who were considered to be legitimate successors to the royal throne. All other sons were referred to by the title of royal prince.

The House of the Chosen Women, known as the Acllahuasi at the city of Cuzco, was home to several thousand women selected as priestesses to serve the many needs of the gods, which of course included the various needs of the ruling inca as well. Young girls of noble lineage who had not yet reached puberty and judged to be of superior looks or who exhibited an exceptional talent for weaving were honored by being selected as Virgins of the Sun. Fifteen hundred young girls, who were henceforth known as aclas, took a solemn vow of chastity. Once they came of age, the most beautiful of these virgins were selected to become Chosen Women, or acclacunas, and were carefully groomed to serve as concubines of the emperor. When they reached maturity, these women were known as mamaconas and they were cared for by the younger Virgins of the Sun. The cloistered mamaconas were revered almost as greatly as the inca himself. Only the emperor was permitted to lay down beside one of the mamaconas. Any woman who broke her sacred vow of chastity was buried alive, while her adulterous lover was hanged and all of his family members were executed. These Women of the Sun daily prepared food and drink as an offering to Inti. His favorite meal consisted of an offering of golden corn and chicha, the latter a delectable drink made from the fermented substance of the former. They also wove garments of exquisite design and then ritually burned them so they could ascend into the sky to be worn by the god of light and warmth.

The second most powerful figure in Inca society was the high priest, often a close relative of the ruler, such as a brother or uncle, who held the revered title of vilaoma. Besides lording over the other priests, of which there were a great many, the vilaoma, who was the direct line of communication between the gods and mankind, advised the ruling inca on almost all matters of state. He presided over all religious ceremonies that paid homage to the gods and usually was the first to embrace the appearance of Inti in the morning sky with a mocha, a ceremonial kiss thrown to the sun. Nearly every sacred service involved a blood sacrifice to the gods. These sacrifices, in most instances, involved the ritual killing of a llama. Female llamas were never sacrificed to the gods or killed for their meat, only males were selected for such fates. White llamas were set aside for Inti, brown for Viracocha, and multicolored for the god of thunder. The llama that was to be sacrificed was brought forward to face the effigy of the god that was to be honored and then its throat was slit open. The blood of the animal was collected in a bowl and ceremonially cast toward the four cardinal points. The entrails and lungs of the sacrificed animals were used by shamen to divine the future. The lungs were inflated with the breath of the priest so that the veins could be read to foretell of a future event. The placement of the entrails on the ground also provided insight into the various questions and concerns of the inca. After these body parts were examined by shaman and priests for signs that might be omens they were, along with the carcass from which they were taken, burned in a ceremonial fire.

Human sacrifices, though relatively rare, occurred when called for by acts of an angered god. Such events were usually a last resort to appease the gods in a desperate effort to avert a predicted calamitous event or bring an end to one that was ongoing, such as a lack of rain, an illness that struck a village, or famine brought on by a crop failure. Sacrifices were made to Inti Illapa, the feared storm god who caused the sound of thunder with the banging of his club and created bolts of lightning with the crack of his sling, during extended periods of drought. Offerings during such times of need generally involved the sacrifices of a child who was no more than ten years old. Only the most beautiful children were selected for sacrifice to the gods, and these were usually selected from the families of the noble elite. The choice of one's child to offer up his life to ensure the well-being and prosperity of the many was viewed as a great honor. The life of such a small victim was, depending on which god was being appeased at that moment, extinguished either by a blade slashed across the throat, strangulation, or having his head bashed in by a club or ax. In some instances, a person was buried alive, though they were often drugged or made drunk with chicha to help ease the pain of their suffering.

It was believed that the supreme inca, like his father the sun, was immortal and that his soul was simply called home to the heavens so that another child of the sun might temporarily rule over the land. The resurrection of the body was also an integral part of Inca religious belief, and for this reason the bodies of the deceased rulers were preserved and attended to with the utmost care. Their earthly remains were preserved by an arcane method of special herbs, ointments, and wraps that rivaled the results achieved by the Egyptians in preserving the bodies of their deceased rulers. The mummification process involved the removal of the intestines, lungs, heart, and muscle tissues, all of which were preserved in specialized containers. The body was allowed to dry and then carefully treated before being securely wrapped in white linen. Their faces were covered with a mask of gold that was beaten into a shape that resembled their likeness. The period of mourning for a deceased inca went on for nearly a year and he was remembered in song, in which his many great deeds were recited during grand festivals. Those who served the inca ruler on earth were expected to follow their master into the afterlife. A great many of the deceased inca's concubines and servants were strangled while others were made drunk with chicha and then buried alive. All who were sacrificed did so without complaint.

    Each Inca ruler built for himself an elegant palace that was his principal abode on earth and which would later serve as the final resting place for his mummified remains. Much of the wealth acquired by the supreme inca during his reign on earth, which also included his extensive land holdings, was used to care for him in death. The remainder of his royal treasure was distributed among the surviving family members. Since the new ruler inherited only a portion of the estate he therefore had to conquer other lands in order to accumulate his own share of worldly possessions. The estates of the deceased inca were carefully maintained so that when the son of the sun returned to earth he could once again enjoy the comforts he was accustomed to in his previous life. The mummies of the Inca rulers, known as mallquis, were seated upon thrones in their royal palace and positioned to face eastward so that the sun could warmly greet them each and every morning. The responsibility for preserving the body and memory of the deceased ruler was left to the panaca, or royal ayllus, all of whom were descendants of the inca. These royal ayllu groomed the inca mummy and prepared special offerings of food on a daily basis. Bodies of the dead were well protected out of fear that if they somehow fell into the hands of an evildoer then the living members of the royal family would fall under their spell. On special occasions, the most notable being the summer (Capac Raymi) and winter (Inti Yaymu) solstices, the inca mummies were transported by litter and brought before the Temple of Inti for a sacred ceremonial council of all the former rulers. With the aid of their attendants, the deceased incas toasted one another as well as the crowd in attendance, with a drink of chicha contained in a vessel made of silver and gold.

Inca queens were considered the embodiment of Quilla, the moon goddess, and therefore accorded ceremonial burial rites similar to that of their royal husbands. The bodies of the deceased coyas were mummified in the same manner and kept in the Temple of the Moon, a royal hall which was paneled in sheets of pure silver, the precious metal which was considered the sorrowful tears shed by a heavenly moon.

The ruling Inca class imposed rigid societal controls that were specifically designed to instill among their many followers an absolute obedience and an unquestionable sense of duty to the state. Law and order are the trademarks of every great civilization, and Incan society was certainly no exception to this rule. Acts of treason, rebellion, threats against the emperor, or refusals to honor tribute or tax obligations were crimes against the state and therefore punishable by death. Murder, adultery, and blasphemous remarks pertaining to the sun or the crown were crimes against society — and the deterrent for such offenses was, just like crimes against the state, the death penalty. An assault against the nobility or the women selected to the sect of the Virgin of the Sun was the same as an assault against the inca, and therefore warranted a sentence of death. Some crimes, such as theft, were considered a lesser offense and resulted in the guilty party being beaten with a stone. A second offense of the same crime usually resulted in the offender being put to death. A common form of execution called for the guilty party to be hung upside down and to remain in that position until their last breath was expelled. Those who committed heinous or treasonous crimes were often taken to a prison where pumas, jaguars, and venomous snakes were also kept, and the guilty party, following an especially torturous ordeal, was thrown into one of the cages that housed such deadly creatures.

Under Inca rule, one's lot in life was preordained by the state. Men were to marry after the age of twenty-four and women after the age of eighteen. Men of common standing were expected to enter into strictly monogamous relationships. Only the Inca caste were allowed to have more than one wife. They were permitted to marry a first cousin but could not, like the nobles, marry a sibling. A home was provided for each newly wed couple as well as a small plot of land which they could call their own. The commoners were known as the Hatunruna, the "great people." It was the Hatunruna who laid the foundations for the Inca Empire — they tilled the land, paved the great highways, constructed the bridges, and built up the cities and towns. Besides fending for themselves, the common folk were expected to donate a portion of their time toward state projects or to serve in the military forces bent on extending the boundaries of the Inca realm. Children of the common folk were taught only what they needed to know, and that was usually the trade and skill of either their father or mother. A person who attained the age of fifty was considered a senior citizen and therefore entitled to special state sanctioned privileges such as exemption from having to pay taxes in the form of goods or services. They were still expected to contribute to the welfare of society, but with the performance of a greatly diminished workload. The elderly and the handicapped were assigned less strenuous tasks, such as picking coca leaves or making chicha, so they would feel they were still contributing to the betterment of Inca society. The welfare of the people was ensured by the state: food, clothing, and shelter were rights guaranteed to all Inca subjects. Subjugated people were required to wear a ribbon that designated their place of birth, even if they were relocated to a village of the inca's choosing.

Only a full blooded Inca could expect an appointment to any of the esteemed positions that oversaw the official affairs of religion, state, and the military. There were those who, either through marriage to a member of the royal elite or by way of special appointment from the Inca ruler, the latter usually having been doled out for recognition of a meritorious deed to the state or for a political alliance that contributed to the greatness of the empire, managed to rise above their humble origins, but they were usually granted positions of only minor authority. The Incas were the hierarchy of this strictly defined caste society, and the discs inserted in their earlobes served as their easily recognizable mark of distinction. Members of the privileged noble class were immune from having to pay any form of tax.

Since Quechua was only a spoken language, the Incas had to devise their own system of record keeping. The quipu, the Quechua word for knot, was a mnemonic device composed of many strings made of either cotton or wool, died in various colors, that contained knots and strands of various lengths and thickness. Color, length, and the number of knots or frays, all relayed particular and important information to a trained reader known as a Quipu camayoc, a keeper of the quipu. Because there was no written language there was a steady employment of those trained to memorize entire accounts and records relating to every aspect of Inca religion, customs, and history. The renowned Amautas were poet — philosophers of the Incas who retained and recited the epic accounts of the past. They played an important role in extracting and incorporating the various religious beliefs and myths of conquered people into the official history of the Inca conquerors. The Inca people also recorded much of their legendary history on embroidery known as a quellca.

The Beginnings of an Empire

Sinchi Rocco was named the ruler of Cuzco upon the passing of his father, Manco Capac. There are some who say that Manco turned to stone when his earthly reign of nearly forty years came to an end, while others claim that a statue erected in his honor contained the flesh and bones of the revered son of the sun. When the first prince of Cuzco was still very young, the people celebrated the first cutting of his raven colored hair with a ceremony henceforth known as Rutuchico. Each noble took a turn cutting a strand of the prince's soft hair, and each gave the grandchild of the sun elegant gifts. This ten day celebration was filled with much song, dance, food and drink. The twenty year old Sinchi Rocco was married to Mama Cuca, the daughter of Sutic Guaman, the ruler of the town of Sanoc. Marriage to only a sister was not yet the defined tradition for a blessed royal union. Sinchi, like his father, was a benevolent ruler who, also like his father, was greatly revered by his many subjects. Though the fame of the Incas began to spread throughout the lands, Sinchi was merely content to rule over the small realm forged by his father and therefore made no attempts to conquer the other tribes of the region.

The first son of the union between Sinchi and Cuca was named Manco Sapaca but he was passed over as heir to the throne in favor of Lloque Yupanqui. Legend says that Lloque, the third Inca ruler, was visited by a vision of his grandfather, Manco Capac, who told him that he should make himself lord of all the towns located in the Valley of Cuzco as well as those situated just on the outskirts of the valley. The towns of the Valley of Guaro were the first outside the Valley of Cuzco to submit to the rule of the Incas, which they did of their own volition. The leaders of the Ayamarcas and Quilliscachis tribes soon came to Cuzco to swear their fealty to the Inca.

Lloque had many concubines but was without a legitimate wife who could bear him a recognized heir. Mama Cachua, the beautiful daughter of the lord of the town of Oma, was selected to be his rightfully wedded wife. She came to the city of Cuzco with a large entourage along a paved road that was decorated with the most beautiful flowers known to the valley. Because the Inca had ordered that after each half league the royal entourage was to make camp so that his future queen would not grow weary from the journey, the short distance of travel from Oma to Cuzco took four full days to complete. Mama Cachua was royally fed and lavishly entertained at each stop. Lloque Yupanqui and his entourage of nobles came out to meet the soon to be queen once she reached the walls of the city. Within a year of their marriage they were blessed with a son whom they named Mayta Capac. The young auqui, or prince, was supposedly born with all his teeth already in place. He grew at a vigorous rate, so much so that by the celebration of his first year on earth he was as tall and possessed the strength of a typical eight year old lad.

Unfortunately, Lloque Yupanqui died while his son was still very young. Apu Conde Mayta and Tacachuincay, both of whom were sons of Sinchi Roca and therefore the paternal uncles of the prince, were appointed as regents until Mayta was old enough to assume the reins of power. A regent of a young emperor not yet of age was commonly referred to as a Shepherd of the Sun.

The young Mayta frequently quarreled with those who were much older than he. One day while the rambunctious prince was playing with some other noble sons there was one youth who appeared to be annoyed with, and perhaps a bit jealous of, the future Inca ruler and brazenly told him that he must learn to be more respectful of others. The fight that ensued ended the moment that Mayta broke the leg of the older and bigger boy, a prince of the Alcaviçca tribe, who bore a grudge against him. Shortly thereafter a determined group of ten young armed assassins were sent to the House of the Sun to punish the brash young prince. Mayta was busy playing ball with others in the courtyard when he saw them enter. The young Inca armed himself with one of the game balls and stood his ground—showing that he was not about to be intimidated by their bullying tactics. Mayta patiently awaited their approach and the moment they were in striking distance he hurled the ball he held with such force that the thug on the receiving end was killed instantly. The prince picked up another ball and performed the same feat on a second would be assassin. As he reached for another ball the remaining assassins fled from the courtyard and returned to their village.

Once it was learned what had happened at Cuzco, the noble Alcaviçca fathers of the dead children planned their revenge by scheming to assassinate all who had blood ties to the young Inca. The plan was revealed to Mayta by one who had first hand knowledge of their murderous plot. Mayta, his two uncles, and fifty warriors wasted no time in storming the house of the Alcaviçca traitors. Several conspirators were killed immediately and those who managed to escape eventually turned themselves in and swore their undying allegiance to the Incas. The Alcaviçca and the Culunchima tribes were forced to recognize the Incas as their sovereign.

When Mayta came of age, he sat upon the throne that was his father's and proceeded to take for himself a wife. She was called Mama Tancaray Yacchi and was the daughter of a noble chief from Collaguas. As a wedding present, the people of her hometown made a splendid house out of copper for the young royal couple to stay, an elegant setting where they could eat off dishes and drink from vessels made of silver and gold, whenever they came to visit. The warrior ways of this mighty ruler led to the extension of the kingdom with his swift conquests of tribes located near the borders of what were already defined as Inca lands. Mayta frequently toured his kingdom upon a litter sheathed in pure gold and decorated with many precious jewels. Sons of nobles from outlying towns were compelled to serve at the court of Mayta where they were indoctrinated in the refined concepts of Inca customs and philosophy. Mayta had many sons by his many concubines but only those borne by his wife, Mama Tancaray, were considered to be legitimate heirs. The eldest son of the Coya was generally considered the rightful heir to the throne but the accepted line of succession was broken upon the passing of Mayta. In this instance, the eldest son, who was considered far too homely to be a child of Inti, was passed over in favor of the younger and more handsome son.

The newly crowned Capac Yupanqui took for his wife a woman of such stunning beauty that she was known by the name of Cori Ilpaycahua, which loosely translates as "golden jewel." She was the daughter of a prominent and well respected Cuzco noble. Though this ruler had many other wives, there was little doubt about who held his heart, for none of the other women were shown the same loving attention that the coya received from the inca. Yupanqui and Cori had two sons, Inca Roca and Apu Mayta. Shortly after becoming the supreme inca, he learned that several of his illegitimate brothers, all of whom he had personally placed in government posts of great importance, were conspiring to unseat him and place another brother, Tarco Huaman, on the throne. Yupanqui diffused their scheme by calling a meeting of all the nobles whereupon he delivered an eloquent speech that heaped so much praise on those in attendance that the conspirators were moved to forget their treachery and thereafter pledged their eternal support to him. Capac Yupanqui then extended the Inca realm by conquering the Cuyumarca and Ancasmarca tribes.

Inca Roca was to become the sixth king of Cuzco. The new ruler was bestowed with the title of sapa inca, "the unique Inca," as a way of distinguishing him from the noble class which had taken to calling themselves the Incas. It was around this time that another mark of distinction came into use to identify those of noble blood from the common folk. Pacha Kutic, a son of an Inca noble, lost both ears in battle and to cover his unsightly scars, he took to wearing small round gold plates. The other princes honored his bravery by following his example. They took to wearing ear spools, known as huancos, that soon became the recognized insignia for the nobility. The ear lobes of the noble caste were pierced and gradually distended until they were large enough to hold the sizable earplugs made of either gold or precious stones. These ear spools were generally five and a half inches in diameter but, as was often the case, the larger the disc, the greater the rank. It wasn't until the arrival of the Spaniards that the Inca nobles were christened with the name of orejones, the "big-eared ones." The gap between the nobles and the commoners widened when Inca Roca, who understood that knowledge was power, proclaimed, "knowledge must be acquired by the nobility and the nobility alone, otherwise the people will become proud. Their pride would prejudice the state."[7]

One day, while in the performance of his daily rituals at the Temple of the Sun, a pious priest heard the voice of the sun god speak to him. Inti told him that his divine son, Inca Roca, must take a wife at once, for soon he would be consumed with the numerous responsibilities of enlarging the realm of the Incas. Inca Roca heeded the words of the priest and took Mama Michay, a Huayllaca woman of extraordinary beauty, as his queen. They had three sons; the eldest was Titu Cusi Hualpa and the younger two were Vicaquirao and Apo Mayta. Unfortunately, Mama Michay had been previously pledged to Tocay Capac, the chief of the Ayamarca tribe, and war was declared against the Huayllacca because of this broken promise. The badly beaten Huayllaca tribe sued for peace and one of the conditions was that the first born son of Mama Michay, which Tocay believed should have been his, had to be turned over to the Ayamarca. Some tales state that the eight year old Titu Cusi Hualpa was handed over to the aggrieved chief while others speak of the prince being kidnapped from his palace. Whichever was the case, when Tocay explained to Titu why he had been taken from his mother and father, the young prince boldly proclaimed that he was the proud son of Inca Roca and Mama Micay, and therefore would never recognize the claims of the ruler of the Ayamarca. Such a statement greatly offended Tocay Capac and he ordered his warriors to take the boy away and have him put to death. Fearing for his own life, the young prince said to Tocay, "I tell you that as sure as you murder me there will come such a curse on you and your descendants that you will come to an end without any memory being left of your nation."[8] The young prince lent credence to his dreaded prediction by weeping sorrowful tears laced with blood. The chief now feared doing any immediate harm to the prince and ordered him imprisoned, with silent instructions to his guards that he was to be slowly starved to death. Chimpu Orma, a concubine of Tocay Capac, helped Tito safely escape back to the welcome arms of his true parents.

Inca Roca enlarged the empire with several conquests, some occurring by peaceful means but most being the successful result of an armed conflict. When the sons came of age, they served their father well by leading an army that forcefully subdued many of the towns along the road that led to the southern province of Collasuyu. They first vanquished the towns located in the Valley of Moyna. Here they captured the chief named Moina and a noble by the name of Caytomarca. Another chief, known by the name of Guaman Tupa, fled from the field of battle when it became clear that the Incas were the superior army. To avoid capture, he jumped into a nearby lake and was never heard from again.

When Titu Cusi Hualpa succeeded his father as sapa inca he came to be known as Yahuar Huacac, "He Who Weeps Blood." Fearful of becoming a prisoner once again, the seventh sapa inca did not personally participate in any of his planned military campaigns. His failure to accompany military expeditions he had sanctioned did not go unnoticed by his constituents and led to his being labeled a coward, though such words were only quietly uttered behind his back. Yahuar Huacac married Mama Choque Chicllayupay, a woman who is more commonly referred to as Mama Chicya. They had three sons; the oldest was named Pauca (or Paucar Ayllu), the second was Pahuac Hualpa Mayta, and the third, Hatun Tupac Inca, came to be known by the name of Viracocha. Pahuac, the second son, was favored to inherit the throne but never got the chance. The ancient stories claim that the first born son of Yuhuar was openly insolent towards his parents and extremely cruel towards others. When disciplinary efforts failed to correct such unbecoming traits, the Sapa Inca sent his son to Chita, a bleak and bitter cold place, where he was to live a humble life as a shepherd who cared for the livestock of the sun god. Convinced that his first son would never be fit to rule, the sapa inca began to tutor another son as his heir apparent.

Hatun Tupac Inca, the third son of Yahuar Huacac and eighth ruler of Cuzco, chose the name of Viracocha Inca, to honor the creator god who appeared to him in a vision. Viracocha's attendants searched throughout the land for the fairest maiden suitable to become the next coya. Their lengthy search ended at the town of Anta where they met the strikingly beautiful Mama Roncay, the daughter of one of the high-ranking nobles. The future queen was carried to Cuzco on an elegant litter and accompanied by a great number of lords and servants. On their journey, Mama Roncay and her royal entourage passed under many archways that were elaborately decorated with fragrant flowers and fine cloth. Celebrations occurred at every town that the coya and her servants passed through. Viracocha Inca and Mama Roncay had four sons: Pachacuti Inca Yupanqui, Inca Roca, Tupac Yupanqui, and Capac Yupanqui. Some historians have mistakenly credited Viracocha Inca with the numerous deeds and great accomplishments that were performed by his son, Pachacuti Inca Yupanqui.

6
The Empire of the Sun

The Forging of an Empire:

The Inca legends state that while still a prince, Cusi Inca Yupanqui, later known by the name Pachacuti, journeyed to visit his father who was busy presiding over the many affairs of state at Jaquijaguana, a town some five leagues distant from Cuzco. Stopping at the Susurpuquiu spring to refresh himself, Cusi Yupanqui was suddenly attracted to a glimmering light which emanated from the flowing water. What he saw was a crystal tablet and as he moved in for a closer look he saw the ghostly image of a mighty Inca lord, whom he did not recognize, suddenly appear before him. The specter, which had three brilliant rays of light projecting from its body, was dressed in regal attire that included elegant earplugs and a bright red llautu, the latter being the sacred royal headband worn only by the Sapa Inca. The startled prince became frightened and was prepared to run away when suddenly the spirit spoke to him: "Come here, my child, have no fear, for I am your father the Sun; I know that you will subjugate many nations and take great care to honor me and remember me in your sacrifices."[1]

The specter of Inti then produced a series of spectacular images that provided Pachacuti with a glimpse of all the lands and people he was destined to lord over. The vision slowly dissipated, leaving behind the crystal tablet from which it arose. Pachacuti scooped the object from the water and forever after kept it close to him, a talisman which he consulted from time to time. Many years later, Pachacuti would have a golden statue made in the likeness of the apparition that had appeared before him at the Susurpuquiu spring.

Cusi Inca Yupanqui wondered if it was possible for this prophecy to come true, for it was well known that his father favored Urco, also known as Urcon, over all of his many sons, even the eldest legitimate son, Inca Roca. Viracocha Inca was convinced that Cusi Yupanqui was touched in the head because of the vision he claimed that had appeared before him. The opportunity to fulfill his destiny came in the year 1438. This was a time when the Chancas, a mighty nation situated along the coast, decided to expand their empire eastward by invading the Cuzco Valley. Uscovilca, the ruler of the Chanca people, led an army of thirty thousand warriors that easily conquered many towns during their march to the mountainous region lorded over by the Incas. Many of the commanders who marched on Cuzco wore the heads of pumas as helmets of divine protection, a feline creature worshipped by the Chanca people. The number of enemy warriors that advanced on Cuzco was imposing enough to cause the elderly Viracocha Inca to have grave concerns about his ability to successfully defend a city that was without fortifying walls. Rather than confront the Chanca, he decided to abandon the city, as well as many of his loyal subjects, and seek refuge at the mountain fortress called Caquea-Xaquixahuana, situated above the town of Calca and about seven leagues from the city of Cuzco. He brought along his favorite son, Urco, a great number of elite Cuzco citizens, and the bulk of the army to this fortress, where the emperor felt he could better hold out against the Chanca assault.

The leaderless people who stayed behind at Cuzco cowered behind the walls of their homes as the Chanca warriors steadily began to surround the city. Cusi Inca Yupanqui, who chose not to leave Cuzco, urged the fearful citizens to rally behind him in defense of their beloved city. He spoke to the people of the prophecy that had been foretold to him by the god Viracocha in such a convincing manner that all the commoners, nobles, and priests took up arms and solemnly vowed to defend their city to the death. Cusi Yupanqui also was blessed with the counsel of his brother Inca Roca as well as the generals Vicaquirao Inca, Quiliscachi Urco Guaranga, and Apo Mayta. Pata Yupanqui, Muru Uanca, Apo Yupanqui, and Uxula Urco Guaranga were the loyal servants who chose to stand steadfastly beside their brave prince. Many of the neighboring tribes came to Cuzco to offer their aid to the besieged Incas. The prince sent a message to his father asking for help during this, their most desperate hour, but the sapa inca thought his young son was a fool for trusting to his vision and would not consent to sending any troops back to defend Cuzco.

Cusi Yupanqui suddenly began to doubt his chances of victory against such a formidable force and turned to prayer for solace. After much meditation and prayer, the god Viracocha spoke to Cusi Yupanqui: "My son, do not be distressed. The day that you go into battle with your enemies, I will send soldiers to you with whom you will defeat your enemies, and you will enjoy victory."[2] Doing as he was told, the prince and his loyal servants placed weapons and shields on many of the nearby large rocks.

Draped in the tawny hide of a puma, Prince Yupanqui, who was but in his early twenties, led his hastily organized army out on to the field later known as Yahuarpampa ("meadow of blood") to confront a vastly superior number of well-disciplined enemy warriors. The support of the Aymaras and the Quechuas along with the return of those who had previously abandoned the city swelled the ranks of the defending warriors to twenty thousand, which was still ten thousand less than the battle-hardened army that had invaded the valley. The two armies met and immediately engaged in a pitched battle in which great determination and tremendous courage were displayed on both sides. Twice the Incas and their allies repulsed the furious charge of the Chanca warriors but sensing that his army was on the brink of faltering, Yupanqui cried out for the help of Viracocha and the god of creation responded by transforming the nearby armed rocks and stones into an invincible army of bearded warriors, known as Pururaucas, who slew the Chanca with impunity. Victory for the Incas was assured the moment Cusi Yupanqui captured the banner of the Chanca and their sacred mummy, an act which caused the invading army to flee in panic from the field of battle. Uscovilca, the Chanca chief, was taken prisoner and shortly thereafter he was put to death. After the battle was won the warriors made from stone returned to their original form and were forever after revered as sacred huacas. However, the legend of the stone warriors persisted and other tribes would later submit to the Incas out of fear that they would unleash the fury of the Pururaucas against them.

The victorious Yupanqui collected all of Uscovilca's personal belongings: clothes, jewelry, weapons, feathers and set them upon a litter that was to be carried to his father at Caquea-Xaquixahuana. The valiant prince also brought with him several captured Chanca nobles. Viracocha Inca accepted the numerous gifts that his son had brought him but the news of his amazing victory was not as well received. Jealous of his son's great achievement in battle and fearful that the glory of this victory would overshadow his selection of Urco as his successor, the Inca ruler schemed to have his victorious offspring assassinated. These plans, however, were soon foiled by those who were close to the young prince. Many of the people returned to Cuzco and they were warmly received by the benevolent prince. Despite the repeated requests of his dutiful son, Viracocha Inca refused to return to Cuzco and remained at the fortress that stood high above Calca.

After his return to Cuzco, Prince Yupanqui learned that Urco, his envious illegitimate brother, was secretly planning to usurp power for himself. Without letting on that he knew of this treacherous plan, Yupanqui summoned his conspiring sibling to the royal court and told him that he was to lead a military campaign to conquer a town that posed a threat to Inca rule.

During this engagement a captain, who was simply complying with the orders of the prince, slew the untrustworthy Inca Urco. A solemn funeral was held for the dead prince which was attended by Cusi Yupanqui, who feigned much sadness over the loss of his brother.

Even though the citizens of Cuzco looked to Inca Yupanqui as their leader, he repeatedly refused the request of the nobles that he should accept the title of sapa inca. He appreciated their faith in him but explained that as long as his father was alive he could not do as they asked. A great assembly of frustrated nobles went to see Viracocha Inca in hopes of forging a reconciliation between the father whom they once served and the son that they now followed. It was then that Viracocha Inca decided the time had finally come to return to the city he had abandoned. Upon his return, the sapa inca beheld the many improvements that his son had made to Cuzco and saw how much the people revered the savior prince. Viracocha told Inca Yupanqui, "truly you are the son of the Sun and I name you king and lord."[3] He then abdicated his throne in favor of Yupanqui by taking the fringed mascapaycha, known as a borla by the conquistadors, the crown of the Inca ruler which was hewn from the finest threads of vicuna wool and died red, and solemnly placed it on the head of his son.

After being crowned as the ninth ruler of the Incas, Cusi Yupanqui forever after went by the name of Pachacuti ("earth shaker" or "He Who Changes the World"). As sapa inca, Pachacuti was well loved and respected by all whom he lorded over. The prince had valiantly saved the city of Cuzco from being conquered and destroyed. He rebuilt the army, and kept his promise to the god of creation by giving him a place of great honor at Cuzco as well as all the realms that he later subjugated. Pachacuti was greatly feared by the other tribes of the region, for in battle he had proved himself to be a leader and warrior of exceptional skill and valor. Viracocha Inca died ten years after the coronation of his son. The dutiful Inca Pachacuti had the mummified body of his father carried upon a royal litter and accorded a hallowed place of honor within the sacred temple.

The Conquests of Pachacuti

It wasn't until the reign of Pachacuti, the ninth ruler, that the kingdom of the Incas stretched beyond the natural boundaries of the Valley of Cuzco and expanded out into an empire they would call Tahuantinsuyu, the "land of the four united quarters." Each of the four quarters of this vast empire contained numerous provinces and the prominent region of each became the recognized name of that particular realm. To the east of Cuzco, the epicenter of the empire, was Antisuyu, named after Anti; to the west was Cuntisuyu after a region of the same name; to the north lay Chinchaysuyu, in recognition of Chincha; and to the south was Collasuyu, for the realm of Collao (also known as Colla). Each province was appointed an Inca governor to lord over the "Lands of the Sun" and together they formed the Grand Council of the Apocuna.

Pachacuti was eager to personally lead an army on campaigns that would add to his domain but his advisors, who feared that his rashness might be his ultimate undoing, wished for him to first take a wife and father a son, so that the Inca bloodline of succession would not be broken. Pachacuti told them that there were too many deeds he had been ordained to fulfill before he could be tied down to the role of faithful husband and father. The creator god had told him to conquer and unite as much of the known world as he possibly could. As "Children of the Sun," the sapa inca believed it was the manifest destiny of his people to spread the word of the sun. He later relented to the worrisome requests of his advisors by taking as his wife Mama Añahuarque, a young noblewoman who hailed from the town of Choco.

After subduing all the tribes of the Cuzco Valley, Pachacuti then set out to conquer the tribes of the Urubamba Valley. The sapa inca and his army conquered the provinces of Vilcas, Soras and Lucanas without encountering much resistance. Guamanga, which is also known as Ayacucho, proved much more difficult, as the natives refused to relinquish their land without a fight. The inca kept up the siege until the half starved natives surrendered. He then turned his attention to conquering the coastal villages and towns. The province of Vitcos and Vilcabamba were conquered and added to the ever expanding empire of the Incas. After extending the empire to the edge of the rain forests of the Amazon, the inca headed north in the direction of Cajamarca to conquer all of the tribes in between. He then marched south to conquer the Aymara, who inhabited the lands around Lake Titicaca.

Fear of the might of the Incas became so great among the other tribes that soon Pachacuti was able to achieve victory by means of simple diplomacy. When they came upon a town along their march, the inca would send several ambassadors to explain the many advantages of joining the empire and, of course, the disastrous consequences if they should choose otherwise. Such a message, according to one recorded account, invited the ruler and the citizens of the village under siege to submit "in the name of the Sun to acknowledge his authority, upon which they would be treated with honor and loaded with presents."[4] They were promised a certain degree of autonomy and a pledge that none would ever want for food or protection. They would, however, have to accept Quechua as their new language and accept their gods as being supreme. They would also have to pay a specified amount of tribute to Cuzco in the form of either services or goods. The Incas promised that all would either be killed or enslaved if they declined such a magnanimous offer. They were given time, usually just overnight, to discuss the matter while Inca warriors made sure their presence was known by setting up camp and lighting numerous bonfires that were well within view of the town's concerned residents. Such requests often carried enough weight to earn them a victory without blood having to be shed on either side.

It was Pachacuti's intention to conquer the realm lorded over by Colla Capac, a ruler who obstinately refused to submit to the demands of the inca. Near the town of Ayauire the two armies met in a battle that saw a great many fall, but eventually the Inca warriors managed to break the ranks of their resolute adversaries. The Colla Indians then retreated to Pucara. The Incas vented their rage by rounding up the people who had remained behind at Ayauire and summarily beheaded them all. The Incas continued on to the fortress at Pucara, where they engaged and once again defeated the king of Collao and his army. Upon hearing of the Incas' victory over the mighty warriors of Collao, the ruler of the Lupaca nation, whose army was considered the equal of Colla Capac's, decided to submit to the will of Inca Pachacuti without even a struggle.

In 1445 Pachacuti began the conquest of the Lake Titicaca region, the sacred place that was the origin of the heavenly bodies and all of humankind. His armies subdued all of the tribes along the basin, known as the altiplano, that encompasses Lake Titicaca. It is here that large herds of llamas graze and numerous varieties of potatoes grow. It also is the homeland of the Aymara tribe, the ancestors of the Incas, who were quickly subdued. The conquest of the Aymaras provided the Incas with control of the metal mines of the region and the much sought after secrets of combining alloys into the forging of stronger metals.

Pachacuti took time out from his military campaigns to pay homage to the holy Temple of the Sun located on the island of Collao at Lake Titicaca, the very spot where Inti, the sun god, arose and ascended to the heavens. The care of this sacred temple was attended to by six hundred male and a thousand female servants. Pilgrimages to the birthplace of both the heavens and mankind were regular occurrences. Natives came from all four corners of the known world to pay their respects to the omnipotent gods of creation. Pilgrims were transported to the island by way of rafts made from totora reeds and equipped with sails to harness the power of the wind so that they could confess their sins before the presence of Inti. All had to pass through three doorways in order to reach the blessed rock. The first sculpted gateway was Puma-puncu, so called because of the puma figurine that hung from this structure. The next two portals were Quenti-puncu and Pillco-puncu, both decorated with the feathers of the birds that were sacrificed to Inti. After passing through the last door the pilgrims were permitted to gaze upon the sacred stone but could come no closer than two hundred paces. Each departing devotee was given a few grains of maize that had sprouted from the holy island.

At the neighboring smaller isle of Coati stood the Sanctuary of the Moon where inside there could be found a magnificent statue of Mama Quilla, the moon goddess, made entirely of gold from the waist up and solid silver from the waist down. The legends speak of an ancient city that was swallowed by the great flood and remains buried beneath the waters of Lake Titicaca, where it is lorded over by the goddess Copacati, a vengeful deity who seemed to take delight in destroying the works of others.

While on this campaign of conquest, Inca Pachacuti saw the magnificent stone buildings of Tiahuanaco, structures which impressed him so greatly that once he returned to Cuzco he had his engineers and builders emulate that unique style. The waters of Lake Titicaca once washed along the shores of Tiahuanaco but had slowly receded with the passage of each rising sun, until, over time, this once important port city of Tiahuanaco was left entirely high and dry. The city of Tiahuanaco, now located approximately fifteen miles southeast of the great lake, which had been the cradle of civilization for the numerous Andean societies that were to follow, was already abandoned and in ruins by the time of its discovery by the Incas on their march to conquer all of the known world. The Incas found many giant statues at Tiahuanaco that seemed as if they were standing guard over the land. They believed that these towering stone figures were the fabled first men who had failed to honor Viracocha in the proper manner. Hence the name Tiahuanaco, which means "city of the dead" in Quechua. One of the most imposing structures still standing at Tiahuanaco is the Gateway of the Sun. This stone monument, carved from a single slab of stone, is more than seven feet high, and approximately thirteen and a half feet wide, and one and a half feet broad. It is decorated with the carving of a staffed weeping god, identified as probably an image of Viracocha, at its center and forty-eight smaller carvings of strange winged creatures, thirty-two of which appear to have a human face while the other sixteen have the head of a condor, that flank the much venerated Andean god of creation.

Inca Pachacuti now set his sights on conquering the lands situated along the coast, a quest which also included exacting revenge against the mighty Chanca nation, the warrior race that had dared to invade the homeland of the Incas. His march took him as far as Llanos at which point he entrusted the conquest to Capac Yupanqui, one of his half brothers, and provided him with an army of 30,000 warriors. An additional 30,000 warriors were kept in reserve so that the advancing troops could be periodically replenished. The triumphant return of the sapa inca and his conquering army was the cause for much celebration at Cuzco. The Inca ruler had greatly enlarged the empire and the tribute that was to follow made Cuzco the richest city known to this land.

Many coastal towns submitted peacefully to the advancing army of Capac Yupanqui, a growing list that included the Nasco, Pisco, and Ica people. However, the natives of Chincha held out for as long as they could. The Incas encountered similar resistance from the natives of Huarco and Lunaguana, but eventually they too fell before the superior forces that had invaded their homeland. After these brutal conquests, news of the Incas' prowess in battle preceded them when they entered the subsequent valleys of Mala and on through Chilcca, Pachacama, and past Guaura all the way up to the Valley of Chimo where they had to defeat a defiant chief who refused to recognize their claims to his land. Fortresses were built at various locations within these newly conquered frontiers, where Inca warriors were garrisoned to make sure the people remembered which ruler they now served.

Capac Yupanqui took it upon himself to attack Cajamarca, a city allied to the Chimu empire. Minchançaman, the emperor of Chan Chan, sent troops to stop the advance of the Incas, but their efforts were to no avail. Unfortunately for the Inca commander, his victory would prove to be a fatal miscalculation on his part. Pachacuti, who was preoccupied with his plans to rebuild the city of Cuzco was infuriated by the news of the capture of Cajamarca and sent orders that his half-brother was to be executed for having taken it upon himself to advance beyond the area of Yanamayo, the boundary of conquest as decreed by the Inca ruler. A bit of jealousy and a touch of fear that perhaps Capac Yupanqui might be seeking to usurp power were probably the major factors in such a harsh decision. The sapa inca appointed Tupac Yupanqui, his son, to take over command of the army. It was Tupac Yupanqui who, with the approval of his father, led an army to Chan Chan to punish Minchançaman and his subjects for having dared to send an army against the Incas at Cajamarca.

A large stretch of the Peruvian coast is comprised of one of the driest places on earth, a vast tract of desert where rain almost never falls — a stark contrast to the mountain range of the Andes and the forests of the Amazon which receive a rather generous share of precipitation. The coastal towns of this region were dependent upon the abundant schools of fish that congregate along the waters of the Pacific Ocean for their daily sustenance. A recurring change of currents, now referred to as El Niño, has the same devastating ecological impact today as it did during the era of the Pre-Columbian civilizations. The dramatic shift of currents cuts off the nutrients that are a source of food for the fish of this region and as a result they die by the millions. The foul stench of the decomposing bodies is accompanied by a hydrogen sulfide vapor that paints the landscape black. A drastic change in wind direction ushers in torrential rains that wash away essential crops and causes mudslides capable of destroying entire villages.

Chan Chan, the capital of the Chimu empire and a city that spanned nearly nine square miles of coastal desert, was probably the largest of all the Pre-Columbian cities. The Chimu, who were also known as the Chanca, had forged a mighty empire that stretched for more than six hundred miles along the coast. The city, which was built of adobe mud bricks, was founded sometime around A.D. 1,000 and its inhabitants incorporated many of the principles of government and religious practices employed by the Moche, the previous dominant civilization of this region, into their own society. A system of well designed irrigation ditches turned enough of the parched land into a verdant tract that could, in turn, comfortably support a significantly large population. Chan Chan was a virtual oasis of the desert coastal region. Unfortunately, the might of the Chimu had come into question following their crushing defeat at Cuzco and their recent loss of the city of Cajamarca.

Upon entering the Moche Valley, Tupac Yupanqui sent a message to Minchançaman, the ruler of Chan Chan, offering him the opportunity spare the lives of his many subjects by surrendering the city and bowing to the will of the Incas. Minchançaman, who felt secure behind the thirty foot high walls that enclosed the city, refused the request to surrender Chan Chan. Unfortunately for Minchançaman and his subjects, the city had a weakness which the Incas were quick to exploit. Tupac Yupanqui and his men blocked the canals that allowed fresh water to flow to the dry lands of the coast, an act of sabotage that caused the Chimu to surrender without a fight. Without water to satisfy their thirst or to irrigate their fields there was little hope of holding out against an enemy prepared to patiently wait for victory.

The victory over the Chancas marked a turning point in Inca history. It was now the Incas' turn to expand their realm along the coast as neighboring tribes scurried to ally themselves with the mighty conquerors. Minchançaman, the last of the Chimu rulers, was taken to Cuzco along with a vast treasure of precious items confiscated at Chan Chan. Numerous highly skilled Chan Chan artisans were also brought to Cuzco to ply their trade. The Incas melted down the numerous golden objects of the city of Chan Chan and loaded them on to a lengthy caravan of llamas that carefully carted them back to Cuzco where the precious "sweat of the sun" would be used to adorn the walls of their temples and to create magnificent objects of their own design. It was these captured Chimu goldsmiths who were to craft many of the splendid golden ornaments that later captured the attention of the Spanish conquistadors.

The triumphant Inca army returned to a city that was steadily being transformed to conform to the grand vision of Inca Pachacuti. Previously, Cuzco was little more than a series of small buildings designed to house the people who diligently tilled the land and a few holy temples that respectfully honored the gods. The first order of business for the sapa inca was the building of the temple of Quishuarcancha to honor Viracocha, the god who had guided the Incas to victory over the armies from Chan Chan. A gold statue, the height of an average ten year old lad and made entirely of gold, was carved in the image of the vision which had appeared to him at the spring of Susurpuquiu and stored in the temple which honored the revered god of creation.

Much of the gold booty taken from Chan Chan was used in the making of sacred statues and for the forging of the numerous gold plates that were to hang from the walls of the temples that resided inside the sacred plaza known as the Coricancha. Since Cuzco was the capital city of the Inca, the children of the sun, it was therefore decided to put to use as much as possible the material which best reflected the vision of the holy father they worshipped. The inner and outer stone walls of the approximately two hundred foot long Inti Cancha, or Temple of the Sun, were covered with hundreds of plates of gold, made by goldsmiths who beat the precious metal into thin sheets with hammers made of stone. Inside this holiest of temples there hung, directly behind the great altar, a large engraved gold plate embedded with numerous precious jewels. This was the Incas' ceremonial emblem of the sun god. It was in this hall that the mummified bodies of the past Inca rulers were seated. The ground for the reconstructed Temple of the Sun was consecrated with the blood of many slaughtered llamas and the shrine was blessed with several young children entombed alive inside the temple. Five hundred maidens were selected to serve in the Temple of the Sun. Inside the neighboring Temple of the Moon there hung a plate of silver engraved with the features of the moon goddess and seated around it were the mummified bodies of the past Inca queens.

The Spanish historian Pedro de Cieza de León has left us with his own vivid description of the Temple of the Sun that was dedicated to the munificence of the most venerated of all the Inca gods: "Halfway up the wall ran a stripe of gold two hand spans wide and four fingers thick. The gateway and doors were covered with sheets of this metal. There was an image of the sun, of great size, made of gold, beautifully wrought and set with many precious stones. There was a garden in which the earth was lumps of fine gold, and it was cunningly planted with stalks of corn that were of gold — stalks, leaves, and ears."[5]

The golden image of the sun that Cieza de León wrote of was known as Punchau — "the day." This gold disk inside the Temple of the Sun was given a human face and was encircled by a number of emanating golden rays. This mirror image of Inti was positioned so that it would catch the morning light of the sun that shone through the window and reflect them upon the other strategically placed items of gold located inside the temple. The whole temple apartment shimmered with the magnificent radiance cast by the rising sun.

The sacred compound at Cuzco comprised six buildings which collectively were known as the Coricancha, "the golden enclosure." Besides the Temple of the Sun and Temple of the Moon, the Coricancha housed temples that honored Viracocha, the god of creation; Illapa, the god of thunder; Cuichu, the god of the rainbow; and the Pleiades, the cluster of stars that shone from heaven. The total length of the stone wall that enclosed the courtyard of the Coricancha measured thirteen hundred feet. Only those with true Inca bloodlines were permitted to reside in or near the ceremonial center, a district that contained many palaces, schools, religious temples and structures. The imaginary sacred ceque lines, of which there were 41, extended out from every direction of the Coricancha like the rays of the sun to connect the 328 major huacas located throughout the known world. Huacas could be a sacred place, thing, or person believed to be imbued with a divine spirit.

While his son Tupac Yupanqui was off conquering lands that added tremendously to the size and wealth of the Inca empire, Inca Pachacuti concentrated his efforts on making improvements to the various affairs of state. It was during his reign that the governing body became more involved in the general welfare of all its citizens. Advancements in the ways of agriculture were instituted as evidenced by the terraced hillsides that greatly increased the supply of necessary crops. It was Pachacuti who ordered the building of numerous storehouses for surplus maize, dried meat, beans and other essential food items, so that the people would not starve during periods of famine. He made vast improvements to the roads and ordered the building of bridges to connect all the towns and provinces to Cuzco, the center of the empire. Such massive projects required the labor of a great many workers toiling daily over a period of many years. By devising a tribute tax system known as the mita, the divine ruler was able to utilize thousands of conscripted laborers in making improvements to the infrastructure of Inca society. Part of the secret to their success to working long hours at such a high altitude was due to the mild narcotic effect derived from chewing the small leaves of the coca plant. When combined with powdered lime, derived from crushed seashells, the ingested dried leaves of the coca plant provides a boost of energy that staves off hunger, thirst, and fatigue, thereby allowing laborers to work longer and harder. Sensing that many were beginning to take too much delight in its pleasurable effects, the Inca elite later deemed the coca a divine plant and therefore restricted it to their own use, though the common folk were still known to occasionally chew on a wad of its leaves.

Even though it wasn't completed until long after his death, the fortress of Sacsahuaman (the royal eagle) still stands as a monumental achievement of Inca Pachacuti and a testament to Inca ingenuity. The memory of the Chanca invasion was still a vivid memory, so as a safeguard against any future attack it was decided to build a stronghold that would protect the citizens of Cuzco, a city that was not enclosed by fortress walls. Pachacuti ordered the construction of the Sacsahuaman citadel on a hill just to the north of the city. It would take twenty thousand workers nearly fifty years to complete the building of the three staggered and towering sawtooth designed stone walls of the Sacsahuaman bastion. The massive stones used in the building of the fortress, some of which were more than twenty feet high and weighing more than one hundred tons, had to be dragged from the quarries of Guaranga, Oma, and Salu, all of which were several leagues away. One huge stone slated to be used at the fortress never made it to its intended destination. The stone broke away from the five hundred natives who were dragging it to Cuzco and crushed nearly all, a disaster that caused the ground to turn red with blood. The stone, which many believed wept blood, remained at the very spot where it claimed so many lives.

The gigantic stone fortress is divided into three ramparts, the walls of which extend for more than sixteen hundred feet. The first wall has an average height of twenty seven feet, the second wall stands eighteen feet above the first, and the third stands nearly fourteen feet above the second. The walls protected the north, east and west sides, while a deep ravine provided protection against an attack from the south side. If the first wall was breached, the Inca warriors could easily fall back to mount a continued defense from the second rampart. Some of the walls of the Sacsahuaman soar to heights that exceed sixty feet and were meticulously designed to withstand the severe earthquakes that frequently rock the land. The oft told tale of joints fit so tightly that the blade of a knife could not be wedged between the stones is a testament to the skilled mark of Inca masons. Inside the enormous fortress were storehouses and quarters that would enable the Incas to withstand a long siege. The completion of the fortress, which occurred during the reign of Tupac Inca Yupanqui, gave Cuzco a design which resembled the outline of a puma. Sacsahuaman forms the head, the city proper and the great square are the outline of the body, and the twin streams, the Huatanay and Tullumayo, make up the tail.

The Incas forged their far reaching empire in a relatively short span of time. Much like the Aztecs of Mexico, the Incas managed to quickly advance themselves by emulating the great civilizations that had ruled before them. The Incas took the religious practices, social customs, and governing laws which they admired most of the people they subjugated and incorporated them into their own society. While the Aztecs saw the Toltecs and other civilized tribes of the Valley of Mexico as their role models, the Incas extrapolated much from the Chavin, Mohica, Paracas, and Nazca cultures that preceded them, as well as contemporary societies like those of the Chanca. Pachacuti had his historians revise the oral history of the Incas to glorify their own past and to justify their conquest of lands that lay outside the Valley of Cuzco. Pictures of the history of the Incas were hung in the halls of the Temple of the Sun. Over time the myths and legends of the Andean people became accepted as part of their history, and such stories instilled into the mainstream consciousness of all that the Incas were truly divine and benevolent overlords. The Incas readily took credit for many of the accomplishments of the great civilizations that preceded them, and as this became part of the oral history it was soon accepted as fact even by the conquered people who truly deserved the credit.

Towns and villages of the empire were periodically blessed with a visit by the sapa inca and his royal entourage. Pachacuti inspected the lands and people he ruled while being carried on a magnificent gold encrusted litter studded with jewels of exquisite quality. His entourage often numbered several thousand bodyguards and servants. A favorite retreat of Inca Pachacuti was the magnificent mountain city of Machu Picchu, a place that was believed to have been built during his reign. This site was one of the few places within the Inca realm that was never located by the Spanish conquistadors and remained hidden to the rest of the world for several centuries. Lord Pachacuti, whose many deeds and accomplishments contributed greatly to the betterment of Inca society, was, according to some accounts, poisoned to death by one of his concubines.

Inca Expansion under Tupac Yupanqui

Realizing that his time on earth was growing short, an elderly Pachacuti named Inca Tupac Yupanqui as his successor and relinquished the throne to his son while he was still alive. Such a move put to rest any doubts as to who would be the next sapa inca and allowed the father to act as his son's adviser during this period of royal transition. It was Tupac Yupanqui who reinstated the custom that the sapa inca should take as his wife his legitimate sister. He said that it had been told to him in visions of the night that the ruling inca must be pure of blood. With this new precedent in place, Inca Tupac Yupanqui married his sister Mama Ocllo. It was later ordained that his son, and heir to the throne, Huayana Capac would be wed to his sister, Cusi Rimay.

Following in the footsteps of his beloved father, Inca Tupac orchestrated numerous campaigns that succeeded at greatly expanding the size and wealth of the empire of the Incas. Every able bodied man from the age of twenty-five and up could be conscripted into military service at a moment's notice, an enlistment that could last for as long as five years. While the main body of troops was composed of common laborers the positions of officers, known as an auqui, were reserved for those of noble lineage, which of course meant they had strong blood ties to the ruler. As the empire grew larger, the Incas had to rely increasingly on the recruitment of men from the tribes they had recently subjugated, and often these troops were led by one of their own nobles or generals. Those who served the Incas during military campaigns were fed, clothed, and provided with weapons. Their fields were tended to while they were off serving the needs of the state. Conquests by the Incas were made easier by the fact that those they attacked failed to form alliances with neighboring tribes in an effort to oppose them. The Incas, who increased the size of their army with conscripts from towns they had conquered, almost always went into battle with a much larger force.

The Inca army was equipped with a vast arsenal of lethal weapons. They carried slings, bolas, clubs, axes with blades made of stone or copper, a mace with sharp blades and spikes fitted onto a wooden shaft, spears with bronze or copper tips, and bows and arrows when going into battle. Storehouses were maintained along the vast Inca highway system to feed and supply the army during their march. In some instances, especially during large campaigns, wars were put on hold so that warriors could return to their villages to cultivate their fields. The victorious Inca army would return to Cuzco with the heads of defeated chiefs and nobles perched upon the tops of long pikes. Skulls of the vanquished leaders were often used by the sapa inca as vessels for consuming chicha, a fermented maize beverage which was the favorite drink of the royal elite. The flayed skins of some victims were used in the making of drums. Bones of the defeated warriors were sometimes whittled into flutes, and the teeth of a dead enemy were often used in the making of necklaces.

Tupac Yupanqui marched at the head of an imposing army of two hundred thousand warriors along the Antisuyu road that led up and over the rugged slopes of the Andes. Yamque Yupanqui governed the affairs of Cuzco while his brother was off on these military campaigns to expand and enrich the Inca empire. His armies subdued the Chunco and Mojo tribes, as well as the fierce Cañari tribe, the latter of whom would serve the Incas well in future campaigns of conquest. From there the sapa inca marched toward the city of Quito with plans of adding it to his empire. During this campaign, one of his officers, a veteran soldier who hailed from Collao, deserted the Inca cause and returned to his homeland. He spread a malicious rumor throughout the land that the sapa inca had died. This false news was enough to incite a revolt among the members of the highland Collao tribe who were eager for an opportunity to exact revenge against their conquerors. They took up arms and killed all the royal officials that had been appointed by the Inca. The provincial governor dispatched a messenger to Tupac Yupanqui who, upon learning of the uprising, made arrangements for some of his generals to continue with the prosecution of the war while he took a portion of the army with him to put down the growing rebellion. After several skirmishes, the Inca earned another victory over the rebellious Collao people. The two chiefs judged responsible for the uprising were flayed, their skins used for the making of drums and their severed heads were placed on pikes for all to see. Many of the captured warriors were sacrificed to honor the sun.

Shortly thereafter, the Inca ruler and his army resumed the campaign to conquer the kingdom of Quito. The ruler of Quito, who after receiving a favorable forecast regarding the outcome of the war from his trusted oracles, went out to engage those who dared to invade his realm. After a long and bloody battle, the armies of Quito were soundly defeated and their captured king was later put to death. There were several other conquests on the road back to Cuzco, the most notable being the province that was home to the Chachapoya people.

Several years passed before Inca Tupac Yupanqui's next expedition, which ventured out into the province of Collasuyu. He marched at the head of the largest army yet assembled by the Incas in an effort to reach Ticcicocha, the supposed end of the world. The sapa inca and his army were well received at the province of Chucuito, where the people showered him with praise. The nobles of the province told Inca Tupac Yupanqui that he and his men should enjoy the comforts of their homeland and let them take care of the subjugation of the neighboring tribes. Though he appreciated their offer, the inca felt the need to press on toward Lake Titicaca to make a pilgrimage to the sacred Temple of the Sun. His coming had been known to the people of this region for some time, and in anticipation of his arrival a number of rafts had been docked to carry the Inca ruler and his entourage to the island on the lake which honored Inti, the father of all the Incas. The sapa inca and his army continued on to Tiahuanaco where during a brief respite he had an opportunity, just like his father before him, to marvel at the many splendid stone structures of this once magnificent city.

Inca Tupac left Tiahuanaco and proceeded to add many provinces to his empire — a list that included Caranga, Paria, Cochabamba, and Amparaes. Many of the fleeing forces united at a valley in Proncota. Twenty thousand homeless men, women, and children took refuge at a hill that seemed a naturally perfect shelter from any sort of invasion. The inca sent spies up into the hills to make a map of the terrain and the fortress that protected the refugees. Their drawings revealed a gap in the cliffs through which his forces could launch an all out attack. However, further reconnaissance revealed that there were a number of sentries diligently keeping watch over this pass. To overcome this obstacle, the sapa inca had a number of men and women from a subjugated town brought to a spot where they could be easily viewed by the posted sentries. For several nights they performed the "cachua," an erotic dance that climaxed with the impassioned partners engaging in coitus. This went on for several nights under the watchful eyes of the sentries. One night, the women seductively beckoned to the guards, and excited by the prospect of actively participating in the "cachua," they willingly abandoned their posts. While they were being entertained by these seductive women, ten thousand Inca warriors slipped through the pass unnoticed and attacked an unprepared fortress. Those who were not killed by the Incas were imprisoned.

The Assimilation of an Empire

Conquered regions were forced to abandon their old customs and religious beliefs and unconditionally embrace the established practices of the Incas. Quechua became their new official language. Although all subjugated tribes were expected to learn the language of the Incas, obey their laws, and conform to their customs, they were, however, expected to don only the costumes of their native land. Even groups who were transplanted to other regions were expected to dress in their customary attire. It was a rudimentary, but effective, means of census taking and social identification employed by the Inca overlords.

As children of the sun, the Incas felt it was their reverential responsibility to convert all to the faith of the sun, the father of light and warmth. Conquered people could continue to honor their gods so long as they accepted Inti, the sun god, as being the supreme deity. Every city had a Temple of the Sun while the effigies of conquered gods deemed acceptable to the Incas were accorded a home inside the sacred Coricancha at Cuzco.

The noble sons of the rulers from a conquered region were sent to Cuzco where, besides serving as a hostage to ensure that a subjugated ruler thought twice about any plans of sedition, they were thoroughly indoctrinated in the various ways and means of Inca society. Citizens who proved rebellious were removed and placed in towns that had proven their loyalty to the Inca. The rebellious province was, in turn, repopulated with those who were faithful to the emperor. Those who were uprooted, regardless of whether they were recently conquered or those who already owed their fealty to the emperor, were called mitimaes — the people who are sent elsewhere. These moves were often over great distances but much effort was made to place the mitimaes in a terrain and climate that was somewhat similar to their original homeland. Unfortunately, there was no going home for a mitma. Those who tried and were caught were forced to suffer the harshest of consequences. Resettlement proved to be an extremely effective method of social control.

The Incas called their empire Tahuantinsuyu, the land of four quarters. Chinchaysuyu, Cuntinsuyu, Antisuyu, and Collasuyu were the names of these four provinces. The empire of the Incas, which at its peak stretched for nearly 2,500 miles, was a varied terrain that encompassed all the known extremes of nature. There were mountains that soared up to the heavens, vast tracts of desert land which rarely saw a drop of rain, jungles so dense with growth that even the sun had a difficult time penetrating its canopy. As many as twelve million people composed of one hundred different cultures that spoke twenty different languages all came to live under the rule of the Incas. Tupac Yupanqui was the first ruler to order a census taken of all who were the subjects of the Inca.

All who dwelled within the Inca empire had to donate a portion of their time in the performance of duties that were of benefit to the state. Such forced labor could involve tilling land that belonged to the inca, working the roads that connected the empire, or serving as part of the military which enforced or advanced the needs and aims of the state. This forced labor tax that contributed to the welfare of all was known by the term mita. Those who performed services for the state were cared for by the state. All able bodied citizens were expected to work for their keep but those who, for a legitimate reason, could not perform such duties were well provided for. Ensuring sustenance for the helpless was one reason for the state to store food items in great quantity, the other being to feed citizens during times of natural disaster.

A thorough inventory of all products that were deemed of benefit to the empire was conducted at every village. The land was divided into three parts: the first belonged to Inti — the sun god — and was administered by the priests, the second was for the sapa inca, the son of the sun; and the third was for the needs of the people who were watched over by Lord Inti and the sapa inca. The livestock of each village was split into three equal herds and assigned in the same manner as the land. All census and inventory records were carefully maintained on the knotted quipu.

Large storehouses, known as qollaqas, were maintained in each province to house the vast and varied tribute of the numerous communities. There were royal storehouses for goods that were the property of the sapa inca, sacred storehouses which held items set aside for the religious order, and communal storehouses to serve the people during times of need. The latter were used to aid those who were disabled, widowed, or orphaned, as well as the entire population during periods of upheaval, which could be either natural or manmade calamities. Individual storehouses were often filled with food items such as maize, potatoes, beans, and vegetables, dried meats, and even coca, while some stored goods such as tools, cotton, clothing, shoes, and weapons.

The immense empire forged by the Incas was connected by way of a series of well designed roads, all of which led to the city of Cuzco. Wherever the Inca army marched it made improvements to roads that were already in place and then linked them to two main highways that stretched the entire length of the empire. The stone highway, known as the Capac Nan, which crossed the ridge of the Andes to connect the villages and cities of the highlands, stretched for nearly 3,450 miles while the parallel coastal road extended for approximately 2,500 miles. The total distance of the great Inca highway system is estimated to have been as much as 15,000 miles. This intricate road system cut across deserts, spiraled up steep mountains, and extended over vast sierras. Obstacles such as wide rivers or deep gorges were made passable with the building of narrow bridges. The bridge over the Apurímac canyon stretched 220 feet and stood 118 feet above a raging river. The vine cables for these suspension bridges were woven of cabuya fiber (ichu grass) — the thickness of which was strong enough to support the weight of many travelers and sturdy enough to allow the inca to be transported across while seated upon his royal litter.

The royal roads, commonly referred to as the "highways of the sun," were primarily for official use — a path reserved for royal troops, official messengers, and the sapa inca to follow. Commoners, who had little need to venture beyond the borders of their homeland, were only to use these roads on special occasions. This well planned road system allowed the emperor to stay in touch with all of the provinces he lorded over. Relay runners, known as chasqui ("he that receives"), were stationed at small outposts along the roads, with each being just a few miles apart. They were trained to memorize messages verbatim and to carefully handle the quipu, the accounting tool which contained vital statistical information. When called upon to do so, these fleet footed messengers carried fresh fish or game to be served at the table of the sapa inca. The chasqui traveled several miles to the next post where he passed along information to an awaiting runner. Nearby villages were charged with the responsibility of supplying messengers. These runners were selected not only for their ability to run fast and far but also for their talent to remember word for word the message imparted to them. The chasqui announced his arrival at the next relay point by blowing on a conch shell. They needed to be swift of foot and strong enough to endure the steep climbs and descents that the rugged path took. In this manner, information could travel at a rate of 150 miles per day across some of the most difficult terrain found on earth.

Inca armies could move quickly along these stone paved roads to launch a new campaign of conquest or to put down a sudden uprising. Caravans of sure footed llamas frequented the highways to transport tribute to Cuzco or to disperse items of need to storehouses located at other provinces. The royal routes were also used to transfer populations from one province to another. A pile of stones known as an apachita was placed along paths to warn of a treacherous spot. Sometimes these feared spots were the hiding places of evil spirits. The specter of Hapinunu, a woman with elongated and drooping breasts who feasted on travelers she caught, was a terrifying tale that caused any wayfarer to always maintain a watchful eye.

For the convenience of the inca and his army, a shelter known as a tambo was located every four to six leagues between towns. Some of these royal inns, which ranged anywhere from 100 to 300 feet long and 30 to 50 feet wide, were large enough to provide shelter for the inca and his royal entourage, while the army remained encamped outside. The community where the tambo stood was deemed responsible for its care and to make sure it was also well stocked with food and provisions. These tambos were reserved for official business and not permitted to be used by common travelers.

The lay of the land presented numerous obstacles which the Andean civilizations managed to overcome with their persistence and ingenuity. Since there was relatively little flat land available for the planting of essential crops, the people of the Andes tamed the inhospitable mountains by developing stepped terraced fields supported by stone walls that were capable of producing enough food to support the needs of their town. The sloped terraces were built up with topsoil and gravel. The natives of Lake Titicaca employed a concept similar to the chinampas of the Aztecs by dredging up the fertile soil of the lake bed and piling it into rectangular plots — 30 to 300 feet long and 12 to 30 feet wide — that yielded a large quantity of edible crops. The major crops of the Inca civilization included twenty varieties of maize, as well as chilies, beans, squash, avocados, manioc, peanuts, quinoa, coca, cotton, and 240 different types of potatoes. The Incas engineered canals to divert water to irrigate lands naturally deprived of fresh water in order to make it more productive. By tapping into the subterraneous thermal waters and the icy springs of the mountains, the native engineers were able to supply their nobles with running hot and cold water that could be regulated as desired.

7
Return of the Prodigal Son

Seeking a Royal Sanction

Francisco Pizarro's delayed return to the docks of Panama in the spring of 1528 was the talk of the entire Spanish settlement. The veteran conquistador had brought back a varied assortment of treasured items that, when combined, he hoped world be large enough to convince Pedro de los Ríos of the urgent need for a third expedition to the lands of Peru. He presented as tribute to the governor several elegantly attired natives, a few peculiar looking llamas, some splendid samples of gold and silver crafted items, a number of birds exhibiting a dazzling display of brightly colored plumage, and a varied assortment of the finely woven fabrics from the lands he had recently explored. Hernándo de Luque spoke on behalf of the group to seek permission from the governor to proceed with a third expedition, this time to conquer and settle the region. Pedro de los Ríos, who was slightly peeved that Pizarro had failed to return within the allotted time frame, was not impressed with his meager accomplishments and flatly denied their request for a follow up voyage by stating, "He had no desire to build up other states at the expense of his own; nor would he be led to throw away more lives than had already been sacrificed by the cheap display of gold and silver toys and a few Indian sheep!"[1]

Without the blessing of the governor all of the best laid plans of Francisco Pizarro, Diego de Almagro, and Hernándo de Luque were essentially grounded. Such a setback was especially difficult for Pizarro and Almagro to swallow. These seasoned soldiers surely could not help but wonder if fame and fortune, which had eluded the grasp of both for so many years, would ever smile favorably upon them. It was Luque, always the more practical of the three partners, who proposed that they appeal to an even higher authority. The monetarily motivated cleric proposed that they should seek direct approval from Emperor Charles V for the right to conquer and colonize the lands that the partners had just explored. Hernándo, the obvious best choice to appear before the royal court, could not abandon his responsibilities to the church and therefore excused himself from such a mission. The gruff and one-eyed Almagro, whose face was marred with unsightly warts brought on by a steadily advancing stage of syphilis, was hardly a fitting representative for such an ambitious endeavor. The task, therefore, fell to the resolute but uneducated Pizarro. Almagro had no qualms about the choice of his friend Francisco but Luque had his reservations — fearing that this ambitious partner might place his own interests above the interests of the group. The pious partner told Pizarro, "You must negotiate what we have agreed upon, which you are to do without any evil, deceit or cunning."[2]

Both Diego de Almagro and Hernándo de Luque worked diligently to raise enough money for Francisco Pizarro's voyage to Spain in order that he might press their joint cause before the court of the Holy Roman Emperor. Martínillo and Felipillo, the two natives from Tumbes who were to be trained as interpreters, accompanied the captain on this journey as did the ever loyal Pedro de Candia. Pizarro also brought with him the tribute of llamas, the gold and silver, the exotic birds, and the samples of elegant cloth that had been refused by Governor Pedro de los Ríos.

Francisco Pizarro arrived at the port of Seville in the summer of 1528 to plead his case before the Spanish Crown, but as soon as he came ashore he was taken into custody by officers of the local court who hurriedly escorted him to a nearby jail. His ship and all of its contents were impounded by the same court order. Francisco would soon learn that Martín Enciso, his old commander, was in Spain at the time carrying on a protracted legal battle to reclaim the titles, lands, and wealth that he believed had been stolen from him. Enciso still harbored a grudge against Pizarro for having sided with Vasco Núñez de Balboa in the bitter dispute over who was entitled to lead the expedition that he had organized. The lawyerly Martín Enciso claimed unpaid debts were still owed to him by those who had usurped his rightful authority. Fortunately for Francisco, his confinement was a short-lived affair. Emperor Charles V, after learning of Pizarro's incarceration, intervened on his behalf. Besides ordering his immediate release from jail the emperor also rescinded the impound order. It is believed that Hernán Cortés, the conqueror of Mexico, who happened to be in Seville at the same time seeking further recognition for the great service he had rendered unto Spain, used his considerable influence to help gain the release of a fellow adventurer.

After his release, Francisco Pizarro made his way to the city of Toledo, where Emperor Charles V, who had promised him an audience, was presently holding court. Luckily for Pizarro, he had arrived at a most opportune moment, for the emperor was in desperate need of funds to finance the numerous and constantly increasing affairs of his inherited Holy Roman Empire. Francisco's enterprising and tantalizing tale of a rumored wealthy native kingdom had a very familiar ring to it—not that many years had passed since Hernán Cortés had conquered the rich empire of the Aztecs. The possibility of locating another empire as affluent as that of the mighty Aztec kingdom certainly held much appeal to an emperor eager to replenish the rapidly dwindling funds of his royal treasury.

The Capitulation

Emperor Charles V was extremely impressed with the numerous gifts presented by Francisco Pizarro, and expressed a particular fondness for the llamas, and the intricately designed gold drinking goblets that the explorer had received during his stay at the city of Tumbes. The emperor showed his interest in the undertaking of another expedition to the mysterious realm known as Peru by recommending Pizarro's proposal to the Council of the Indies, a committee whose responsibility it was to determine the feasibility of such a plan by carefully weighing all of the factors involved. While such a recommendation clearly meant that Pizarro's proposal was worthy of consideration, the decision process, which more often than not, was hindered and slowed by its own bureaucratic attention to every minute detail and a rigid adherence to its own proper procedure, often took a very long time to reach an agreed upon conclusion.

Francisco was granted a modest stipend which was supposed to afford him enough to live comfortably while he awaited the Council of the Indies' decision. But as those funds began to dwindle away due to the long delay he was compelled to appeal to the queen, who acting on behalf of her absent husband forced a quick resolution that was deemed satisfactory to all parties concerned. After a stay of nearly a year in Spain the capitulation, which authorized the exploration, conquest, and colonization of these newly discovered lands, was finally executed on July 26, 1529. Emperor Charles and the Council of the Indies granted the veteran soldier exclusive rights to explore and settle the lands to the south of Panama, a province henceforth designated as New Castile. Pizarro was appointed governor and captain-general for life of all the lands that he was about to claim for Spain. He was allowed to collect 750,000 maravedies to cover all governmental costs. Francisco was also given a grant of 25 horses from the island of Jamaica and awarded the services of 30 African slaves from Cuba. The Crown appointed García de Salcedo as royal inspector and Francisco Navarro as royal accountant to make sure its interests were respected. Pizarro was also named a knight of the Order of Santiago, a difficult achievement considering that the illegitimate conquistador had to prove his heritage was of good stock.

As for the two other partners, Diego Almagro was commissioned as commander of the city of Tumbes, awarded an annual salary of 300,000 maravedies, and elevated to the status of an hidalgo, the latter being an esteemed rank of minor nobility. Hernándo de Luque was anointed bishop of Tumbes and protector of the Indians of Peru as well as given the promise of an annual salary of a thousand ducats. All salaries and reimbursement of operating costs for the partners, however, were to come from the proceeds that were derived from the conquest itself and not from the coffers of the Crown. As was the case with almost all speculative ventures of that era, Francisco Pizarro and his partners would have to finance their own expedition. The need to recoup their initial investments and a desire to earn the money promised to them always added a sense of urgency to these ambitious expeditions and therefore were major factors that contributed to the eagerness of the conquistadors to plunder any native village or town they happened upon. While each of the three comrades were rewarded for the parts they had played, neither Almagro or Luque received honors and recognition equal to those awarded to Francisco Pizarro.

Several other members of this grand venture were recognized for their past contributions. Bartholome Ruiz, the pilot, was appointed grand pilot of the Southern Ocean and was the recipient of a rather handsome salary. Pedro de Candia was given the important rank of commander of the artillery. As for the eleven other faithful soldiers who crossed the line to stand beside Francisco Pizarro along the sandy shores of the island of Gallo, they were, along with Ruiz and Candia, made knights of the Golden Sword.

Francisco's lengthy stay afforded him the opportunity to visit Trujillo, the town where he was born. Here he was warmly greeted by his four half-brothers, all of whom would willingly join him on his epic adventure. Francisco and Martín de Alcantára shared the same mother while Hernándo, Juan, and Gonzalo Pizarro shared the same father as the bold adventurer. Of the brothers that the elder Francisco met for the very first time, Hernándo, the son of Isabel de Vargas, was the only one not born out of wedlock.

Hernándo Pizarro, who was well schooled and had the opportunity to accompany his father on military campaigns in Italy during the years 1502 and 1503, had the air of an aristocrat about him, but possessed a spiteful side that often alienated others. In 1512 he served the duke of Nájera in campaigns at Navarre. Gonzalo, the youngest brother, lacked a proper education but was skilled in the art of war, experience he is said to have gained while serving with his father in the Italian campaigns. Little is known of the early life of either Juan Pizarro or Martín de Alcantára other than that they also had some military experience. Pedro Pizarro, a fifteen year old relative, joined the expedition as a page. All were proud men eager for a chance to rise above the extreme poverty of their present situation. That opportunity now awaited them all in the New World.

Francisco was able to procure the rights to three capable ships during his stay in Spain: the *Santiago*, the *Trinidad*, and the *San Antonio*. The twenty-eight year old Vincente Valverde was one of six Dominican friars instructed to accompany Pizarro on his conquest of the southern region of the New World. Their mission, besides attending to the spiritual needs of the troops, was to indoctrinate and convert the native heathens to the Christian faith.

One of the many terms and conditions of the capitulation stated that Francisco Pizarro would have but six months to enlist a crew of at least one hundred and fifty able bodied men before returning to Panama, and once there he was instructed to recruit an additional one hundred like soldiers from the colonies. After six months, Francisco was still unable to reach the mandated number of recruits. Fearing that an upcoming scheduled inspection of his progress by the Casa de Contratacion would expose his shortcomings and thus subject the expedition to further review and delay, Francisco decided to set sail in January of 1530. He left his brother Hernándo behind with one ship and its crew, and when the inspectors arrived he assured them that the required number had indeed been enlisted, the difference of which were presently sailing with Francisco. The inspectors accepted the word of Hernándo and gave him permission to depart at once to join his brother.

Hernándo de Luque and Diego de Almagro learned of Francisco Pizarro's return to Nombre de Dios and immediately crossed the narrow isthmus in order to greet their partner as well as to learn if his mission to Spain had met with success. They were delighted to see that their partner had returned with three ships, including the one captained by his brother Hernándo, and 125 new recruits. Their joyful reunion was shattered the moment it was learned that the titles and grants awarded by the Crown weighed heavily in favor of Francisco. Pizarro did his best to convince his partners that he promoted their interests as much as his own but they remained unconvinced. Adding fuel to the flames of discontent was the engaging presence of Hernándo Pizarro, who, from the very beginning, chose not to hide his contempt for Almagro, whom he perceived as having been disrespectful toward his brother and ungrateful for all that he had just been granted by the Spanish Crown. Hernándo frequently referred to Diego as a "circumcised Moor."[3] Pedro Pizarro sided with

Hernándo in his general dislike for Almagro by writing that he was "a profane man, foul mouthed, and who when roused to anger maltreated those around him, even if they were gentlemen; physically strong, he was a brave fighter and popular, a spendthrift though miserly in rewarding his men."[4]

Francisco tried to assuage the concerns of his partners with a promise that there were other lands to conquer and a pledge that the three would share equally in those conquests, but he had forever lost the trust of his partners. Father Luque interceded by extracting a promise from Pizarro that he would petition the Crown for a larger territory for Almagro to govern. It was also agreed that the three partners would share in the profits of the third expedition. Almagro and Luque had little choice but to accept what meager rewards they had been offered.

8
The Third Voyage

The Conquest Begins

Now that he had the backing of the Crown, Francisco Pizarro was prepared to sail back to Peru as a royally sanctioned conquistador. He would now use force to take possession of that which had been granted to him by the Holy Roman Emperor. However, even with the blessing of the emperor, the three partners still could not recruit the number of men they had been mandated to take with them on this epic venture. Seeing as to how nearly everyone was familiar with the tales of hardship and sorrow endured by those who had sailed on the two previous expeditions, most of the colonists at Panama and Nombre de Dios were reluctant to sign up for a similar fate. It wasn't until January of 1531 that the expedition was finally ready to set sail — though they were still far short of the number mandated by the capitulation. Francisco Pizarro set sail with three ships carrying a crew of 180 men and 36 horses. Most of the men recruited were quite young and very few had any combat experience. Those who had been trained as soldiers or had experience fighting natives in the New World were awarded appointments as officers. Diego de Almagro, who stayed behind in an effort to rally more support for their cause, was to join up with his partner as soon as possible.

It was the captain-general's intention to avoid all of those uninhabitable marshlands he had encountered previously and sail straight to the city of Tumbes to launch his campaign to conquer and settle the lands of Peru. Unfortunately, his carefully laid plans were abruptly altered by unfavorable headwinds which slowed their progress significantly. After thirteen days of steady sailing the ships had made it only as far as the recognizable San Mateo Bay, in present day Ecuador, where the crew was forced to drop anchor. They were approximately 359 miles north of Tumbes and just above the line of the equator. It was at this point that Pizarro decided to lead most of the soldiers and all of the horses overland on a southward march while the ships and the remaining crew followed a parallel course along the coast., His objective was to locate native villages that were worth raiding and plundering along the route that led to Tumbes.

The land route proved far more difficult than anticipated. There were numerous streams to cross while the heat, rain and the insects conspired to claim a weary toll upon the bold adventurers. Many soldiers became sick and some soon succumbed to their illness. Guava and plums were among the numerous fruits of this land that helped sustain the Spaniards once they had exhausted their supply of food. A soldier by the name of Diego de Trujillo remembered, "Once when we had nothing more to eat some of our men ate a snake. Two of them died, and another man, who had flavored his portion with garlic, survived but lost all his hair, and was left so ill that it took him a great deal of time to recover his health."[1]

After a long and exhaustive march that yielded little in the way of material rewards the Spaniards finally came upon the town known as Coaque. The natives of Coaque had heard that these strangers who hailed from across the sea had previously shown themselves to be friendly towards the people of Tumbes and because of this they expected to enjoy the same cordial encounter. They quickly saw the true nature of these Spaniards. The conquistadors, without any hesitation or remorse, helped themselves to all the precious stones and metals they saw. The fearful natives quickly fled from their village.

Francisco Pizarro managed to locate the ruler of the village and convincingly told him that it was safe for his people to return. Believing that the Spanish captain spoke the truth the chief instructed his people return at once to their homes. They soon discovered that the cunning Spaniards simply wanted to relieve them of the many valuable possessions still on their person. Realizing they had been duped a second time, the natives fled — not to return until the Spaniards were gone for good. The conquistadors congratulated themselves for the more than satisfactory haul of gold, silver, and precious stones they had plundered with little difficulty. The value of the gold alone weighed in at eighteen thousand pesos. After the obligatory royal fifth was set aside for the Crown, a share of the treasure was divided amongst the troops, with officers and cavalry receiving a significantly larger portion than that of the common foot soldier.

While at Coaque, Francisco Pizarro decided to send two of his ships back to Panama loaded with an estimated 20,000 pesos worth of confiscated treasure from the village, much of which were items crafted out of precious gold. It was the captain-general's belief that such a large display of wealth would help Almagro's efforts to recruit more men, which, of course, it did.

The Spaniards remained in and around Coaque for nearly eight months, and during their stay they had plenty of corn and fruit to sustain them but the lack of meat and fish deprived them of many essential nutritional requirements.

After a period of rest following the departure of the ships, Pizarro and his men continued their march toward Tumbes. Once again the soldiers found themselves forced to deal with the harsh conditions inherent to this region. The unrelenting and oppressive heat weighed heavily on the armored Spaniards. An unknown epidemic broke out among the men — the visible signs being unsightly ulcers. Pedro Pizarro described the strange illness that afflicted the soldiers as being "so bad and tormenting that it caused many men to be wearied and worn by pain just as if they had tumors, and even great sores came out all over the body, and some were big as eggs, and they corrupted the skin, and much pus and blood ran out of them."[2] The treatment of lancing the boils proved fatal for several who bled to death from this prescribed remedy. Several soldiers suddenly became too weak to continue the march to Tumbes.

Luckily for Francisco and his men, a relief ship soon arrived, carrying much needed supplies as well as a number of appointed royal officials: Alonso Riquelme, treasurer; García de Salcedo, inspector; and Francisco Navarro, accountant. Also on board were letters from Diego Almagro and others that provided Pizarro and his men with an update on events unfolding back at Panama. A second ship arrived a few days later at Puerto Viejo with additional reinforcements: thirty eager soldiers of fortune and a dozen horses all under the command of one Captain Sebastián de Benalcázar (sometimes spelled as Belalcazar), a veteran officer who had sailed aboard the third expedition of Christopher Columbus and had served with distinction in Spanish campaigns of conquest at Darién and Nicaragua. The rejuvenated band of conquistadors pressed onward to the Gulf of Guayaquil where along the shores of the Bay of Tumbes they came upon friendly natives from the island of Puná who invited them to visit their homeland. Since the people of Puná were at war with the natives of Tumbes, these natives hoped to form an alliance with the Spaniards to aid their cause, and since this arrangement certainly suited the purpose of Francisco Pizarro, he gladly accepted their offer.

A Disappointing Return to Tumbes

Finding the island of Puná, which was well shaded with trees, to be a rather idyllic location, Francisco decided to make camp here while he awaited the anticipated arrival of even more reinforcements before continuing on to Tumbes. The interpreters, both of whom hailed from the city which Pizarro planned to conquer, warned the captain-general not to trust too much to the flowery words of the Puná natives. The citizens of Tumbes and the people of Puná had been at odds for as long as as anyone from these lands could remember. The captain-general heeded the advice of his trusted interpreters and interrogated one of the local chiefs until he was satisfied that the intentions of his native hosts were truly honorable. The Spanish commander had planned on staying at the Isle of Puná until the rainy season had passed.

News of Francisco Pizarro's return to their land had reached the city of Tumbes and emissaries were immediately dispatched to the Isle of Puná to greet him as well as to warn him of his hosts' ulterior motives. The Puná chiefs did not take kindly to the Spaniard's unconcealed friendly relations with those who were their sworn enemy. When Pizarro heard from his interpreter Felipillo that a number of the Puná chiefs were meeting in secret to plan an all out attack he immediately had the suspected rulers rounded up. Tumbalá, the chief of all the chiefs, was included among the group who were imprisoned by the Spaniards. The captain-general then made the fatal mistake of handing the prisoners over to the emissaries from Tumbes, who, without any hesitation, savagely executed each and every one of them. Once these events were known, the warriors who served Tumbalá took up arms and did the very thing that Pizarro had hoped to avoid: they launched an all out attack. The Spaniards suddenly found themselves embroiled in an ancient blood feud.

The Puná warriors greatly outnumbered their guests but the Spaniards were able to repulse their tenacious assault with the deadly accuracy of their firearms as well as their well-honed skill with the sword and lance. The horse played a pivotal role in this Spanish victory over the natives. Hernándo Pizarro, who received a harsh wound to the leg by a hurled javelin, led a cavalry charge that succeeded in frightening and scattering the attacking natives. Hernándo's horse was badly wounded during this battle and later died. The carcass of his faithful steed was thrown into a cavern so that the natives would not discover that the horse was mortal. For Francisco and his men it was a bittersweet victory that came at the expense of at least three or possibly four Spanish lives and cost them an alliance with those who might have aided in their upcoming plan of conquest.

The Puná warriors soon launched another attack. They managed to kill two soldiers who had strayed from the group to search for gold among the scattered dead natives. Pizarro quickly assembled his men and they proceeded to kill a great many warriors, a slaughter that continued unabated until the natives retreated deep into the woods. Luckily for the besieged Spaniards, two caravels carrying one hundred soldiers, twenty-five horses, and sorely needed provisions arrived on December 1, 1531, under the command of Hernándo de Soto. Included among the crew brought from Nicaragua was a woman by the name of Juána Hernández who, more likely than not, was a prostitute. De Soto, a veteran Spanish officer who was renowned for his exceptional equestrian skill, had recently served in the conquest of Nicaragua under the command of the notorious Pedrarias. Like Benalcázar before him, de Soto was lured into this quest by the wondrous stories of vast amounts of wealth just waiting to be claimed at Peru.

Hernándo de Soto, the progeny of a union between Leonor Aria Tinoco and the hidalgo Francisco Méndez de Soto, was born at Jérez de los Cabalerros, a Spanish town that also boasted Vasco Núñez de Balboa as being another of its favorite sons. Hernándo left home at the age of fourteen to seek fame and fortune and headed to Seville where he is believed to have hitched aboard a vessel that was part of the armada that carried the newly appointed Governor Pedrarias and his numerous hopeful colonists to the New World. It was at Darién that the young conquistador cut his teeth under the command of separate expeditions led by Francisco Pizarro and Vasco Núñez de Balboa. Hernándo served alongside Pizarro on one of the many unsuccessful Spanish expeditions in search of the ever-elusive golden kingdom of Dabaibe. Afterwards, he joined up with Balboa's second campaign across the narrow isthmus of Panama to locate the rumored realm of a great civilization to the south, an effort that met with no more success than that of the first expedition. Following the execution of Balboa, Hernándo de Soto served in campaigns of conquest and plunder orchestrated by Gaspar de Espinosa, the silent partner of the expedition he was to join up with in Peru.

The balance of interest in lands laced with gold tipped from the south and back to the northern regions with the arrival at Panama of Gil González Dávila, an explorer who, along with his crew of one hundred men, had on board his three ships an estimated 112,000 pesos worth of gold cast in various forms. These were the rewards of his explorations of a region known as Nicaragua, which he claimed was as abundant in gold as the oft-told legendary wealth of Mexico. In 1524, de Soto, now a young captain of much renown, signed on for Pedrarias's conquest of Nicaragua, a campaign which was already well underway.

Hernándo de Soto had first learned of Francisco Pizarro's plans of conquest when Nicolás de Ribera and Bartolomé Ruiz, at the behest of Diego de Almagro, came to Nicaragua in the summer of 1529 to recruit more soldiers, procure additional native slaves, and to make final restitution to Pedrarias, a payment that would officially dissolve their old business accord. While at the city of León, Ribera met with Hernándo de Soto and Hernán Ponce de León, both captains who had played pivotal roles in the conquest and settlement of Nicaragua, and both of whom supplemented their income by participating in the illegal but highly lucrative trade in native slaves. Both men were interested in the stories of the vast riches said to exist in Peru. Wishing to keep the elderly Pedrarias, now the governor of Nicaragua and a commander from whose good graces de Soto had fallen, in the dark, Hernándo and Hernán conducted secret meetings with these recruiters from Panama. These talks eventually led to an agreement which called for the captains of Nicaragua to join in the upcoming expedition along with as many soldiers as they could possibly enlist. Both men were assured ranks of distinction, but it was de Soto who was promised the most — command of the army and, should the expedition succeed in its objective, the governorship of a designated province.

Portrait of Hernando de Soto (courtesy Library of Congress).

Hernándo de Soto left Nicaragua shortly after the death of Governor Pedrarias. Those who had sailed from the Nicaraguan port of Posesión with visions of finding vast amounts of precious gold were greatly disappointed by the sorry looking lot of soldiers they had come to join: all were ill and none possessed any gold to call their own. All of the gold that Pizarro and his men had found up to this point had been collected and sent abroad to entice men such as Hernándo de Soto and Sebastián de Benalcázar, two conquistadors who knew each other well, and were friends until differences between Hernándo and Pedrarias forced the soldiers into different camps. Hernándo was probably the most disappointed of all, for he would learn from Francisco Pizarro that he would not be granted command of the army, a promise made to him by Almagro's agents for his agreeing to enlist in the cause. Instead, Francisco retained the rank that he was denied. The thirty year old Hernándo de Soto, however, was given command of the horsemen and his captain was Sebastián de Benalcázar, who was roughly ten years older than his commander. Hernándo Pizarro was put in charge of a company that included younger brothers Juan and Gonzalo.

The Puná natives may have been driven off but they continued to harass their new enemy with small raids shortly after nightfall, the frequency of which were effective enough to encourage the Spaniards to take leave of this island. The well augmented band of conquistadors felt confident that they were now strong enough to impose their will upon the ruler of Tumbes. However, the rainy season forced them to delay their plans for another four months.

Once the weather had cleared, the Spaniards boarded their boats and headed for the nearby port of Tumbes. Some of the soldiers accompanied the Tumban emissaries aboard their balsas and immediately after making landfall they unexpectedly turned on the Spaniards, dragging some into the woods whereupon they gouged out their eyes and then hacked off their limbs. Their horrific screams were silenced only after their bloody torsos were thrown into pots resting over an open fire where they were boiled alive. In the meantime, several other soldiers defended themselves as best they could aboard the balsas and their cries for help were heard by Hernándo Pizarro and several soldiers who quickly rushed to their rescue. The hostile natives fled at the sight of the Spanish horses but not before having claimed the lives of three unfortunate soldiers. Francisco Pizarro was greatly disturbed by the gruesome death of his men at the hands of those he had been led to believe were friends of the Spaniards. The captain ordered Hernándo de Soto to take some troops and punish the people of Tumbes with extreme prejudice. When the natives of Tumbes learned first hand of the extent of the Spaniards' rage they immediately sued for peace.

After recovering from the shock of the unforeseen treachery they had just encountered, the army marched triumphantly into the city of Tumbes only to be surprised by yet another unexpected sight. Instead of finding a bustling metropolis with magnificent homes and temples the would-be conquistadors found a city that lay in near ruin and which was almost entirely abandoned. They also saw that nearly all of the items of wealth, especially those of gold and silver content, had been carted away. This was not the abundantly rich city that Francisco Pizarro and the members of the previous expedition had bragged about to the new recruits, all of whom expected to be amply rewarded once they reached the city of Tumbes.

Pizarro and his troops learned from one of the nobles they had rounded up and interrogated that the entire country was in the throes of a bloody conflict that pitted the armies of two brothers against one another for control of the vast empire ruled by their recently deceased father. He also told them that the Spaniards left behind from the second expedition, including Alonso de Molina, also fell victim to this devastating war. Another account of the demise of the Spaniards who had remained at Tumbes states that they were taken to see Huayna Capac at Quito, but the Inca ruler had died shortly before they arrived. Believing that the Spaniards were the cause of the sapa inca's untimely end, they were all put to death. A different tale claims that Gimes, a soldier who stayed behind with Molina, was executed by the natives of Cinto for having made inappropriate advances toward one of the chief's favored woman.

The neighboring Puná warriors, it seems, were able to assail and sack the Inca town with relative ease because Huascar, the emperor at Cuzco, had failed to come to their aid due to the ongoing civil war with his half-brother Atahualpa, the lord of Cajamarca. The Spaniards also saw signs that revealed death came not only at the hands of Puná warriors but also from another deadly enemy, one which the natives could not fend off with their weapons. The smallpox plague, caused by a virile strain that the Spanish conquerers had unwittingly brought with them to the New World and which the indigenous population had no built up immunity to, had advanced swiftly along the coast and was slowly, but steadily, moving inland. Some estimates claim that possibly as much as two-thirds of the native population had perished from the pernicious effects of both civil conflict and pestilence long before Francisco Pizarro and his conquistadors ever found their way to the town of Cajamarca.

During their stay at Tumbes, the Spaniards happened upon a startling discovery. While searching for treasure a group of soldiers uncovered the bones of a man and woman which appeared to be four times greater than those of a normal person. From the natives they heard the ancient tale of the giants who had come out of the west many ages ago to wreak havoc upon the people of this land.

Though certainly disappointed that the city he had hoped to conquer lay in ruins, Francisco Pizarro was pleased to learn that there was such open dissension within an empire that, from early indications, appeared to eclipse the size and wealth of that of the legendary Aztec empire to the north. He now believed that he could follow a page from the successful tactics of Hernán Cortés and form alliances with the discontented tribes so that he would emerge strong enough to defeat the ruling faction. He soon leaned that the similarities between Peru and Mexico were less than he believed.

9
Civil War

The Reign of Huayna Capac

Titu Cusi Hualpa was recognized by all as his father's successor to the Inca throne but being that the prince was still very young when the soul of Tupac Yupanqui was called home to Inti, the sun god, it was deemed that a council of learned elder nobles would serve as "Shepherds of the Sun" to guide his decisions. After the passage of ten years, the prince was declared mature and wise enough to rule on his own. Tito Cusi Hualpa took the name of Huayna Capac, the "rich and excellent youth," soon after being named sapa inca.

Shortly after becoming lord of the Incas, Huayna Capac learned that his scheming uncle, Gualpaya, had planned to seize power in order that one of his sons could instead sit upon the royal throne. The plot was accidentally discovered when a few opportunistic thieves stole a couple of baskets which they believed contained either prized products of coca or chili peppers, only to discover that they instead contained an assortment of deadly weapons. These were but a few of many such baskets smuggled into Cuzco to arm the would be assassins of the sapa inca. News of this discovery was brought to Apu Achache, the governor of Chinchaysuyu and a faithful uncle of Huayna Capac. He rounded up the remaining baskets, which also contained similar instruments of death, and then arrested the owners, who were tortured until they revealed all the details of this sinister plot. Gualpaya was arrested and executed along with the rest of the conspirators.

Like the Inca rulers before him, Huayna Capac toured the empire from the comforts of his litter, and at many towns and villages along the way he ordered improvements to existing structures and the construction of new buildings, many of which were of his own design. The Spanish historian Cieza de León left us this vivid depiction of the Inca ruler's appearance and demeanor: "Huayna Capac, according to many Indians who saw and knew him, was not large of stature, but strong and well built, of grave, goodly countenance, a man of few words and many deeds; he was stern, and unmerciful in his punishments. He wanted to be so feared that at night the Indians would dream of him...."[1]

Because his father, and his father's father had been so successful in their campaigns to enlarge the Inca empire there were very few worlds left for Huayna Capac to conquer. The opportunity to prove himself a great conqueror presented itself after he had been apprised of sudden uprisings in the distant provinces of present day Ecuador. Huayna left a half brother, Apu Cinchi Roca, in charge of the city of Cuzco while he marched off at the head of a large army along the road to the northern realm of Chinchaysuyu to restore order to his empire.

Along the way the imperial army of the Incas put down an uprising at Chachapoyas. From there they marched to the town of Cajamarca and then to the city of Quito. After many conquests Huayna Capac returned to Cuzco where he was welcomed by his brother who, during his absence, built the magnificent Casana palace to house and honor the triumphant sapa inca. It is said that Huayna's mother loved him so much that she begged him to abstain from anymore military expeditions while she was still alive. The dutiful son remained at Cuzco until her death, which occurred a short time after his pledge. After a proper interment and a brief period of mourning, Huayna Capac set out for the realm of Collasuyu. He stopped briefly at the provinces of Collasuyu and Chucuito to resolve certain affairs and settle several disputes. His army then marched toward the ancient city of Tiahuanaco. His warriors braved the arduous climb over the towering peaks of the Andes to subjugate the barbarous Mojo tribe. Once the anticipated victory had been achieved, Huayna Capac and his army marched to the fertile valleys of Cochabamba where he brought in settlers from the Collao province to inhabit and till the fertile land.

The Inca ruler and his warriors ventured on to Pocona, a town which stood at the extreme border of the empire. After a brief stay, Huayna began the long and arduous march back to Cuzco. He stopped at Lake Titicaca just long enough to make a pilgrimage to the Temple of the Sun, located on the island of Collao, where he ritually sacrificed a small number of prisoners taken on his long and successful campaign. Afterwards, the emperor and his royal entourage returned to Cuzco while the main force of the army was sent on to Cinga where they would make camp and prepare for a future expedition being planned by the sapa inca. The emperor's stay at Cuzco was brief, for the purpose of his return was merely to recruit more men for a campaign to extend the borders of the Inca empire well beyond the city of Quito. Huayna informed the nobles of his plans for expanding the empire northward, a noble quest which many, including several of his brothers, eagerly volunteered to join. The emperor was accompanied on this campaign by the thirteen year old Atahualpa, a son who, though not a child of the coya, was clearly a favored son of the Sapa Inca. Historians seem to disagree over who was the true mother of Atahualpa, but the evidence at hand seems to support the claim of Tocto Coca, a cousin of Huayna Capac.

Huayna Capac and his new recruits soon joined the main army, a combined force which now numbered nearly fifty thousand heavily armed warriors, and together they headed along the royal highway that would take them directly to Tumibamba, the birthplace of the Inca ruler. Once there, Huayna drew up plans for the construction of a royal palace for himself as well as a temple dedicated to the munificence of the heavenly gods. In the latter building he would place a golden statue made in the likeness of his beloved mother. He would entrust the care of the sacred temple to several of his most loyal attendants. It was Huayna's intention to turn Quito and the surrounding region, which included the town of Tumibamba, into a second capital, which was to serve as the epicenter of his planned northern extension of the Inca empire.

The emperor remained at Tumibamba to oversee the building of his palace and of the holy temple while his captains marched out to conquer the neighboring lands. The Inca commanders and their well disciplined army had an easy time subjugating the loosely organized tribes of the surrounding region. Victory was seemingly assured with the capture of a principal chief, but the Incas failed to keep a vigilant watch over their royal prisoner. The chief escaped and rallied his forces to launch a surprise attack that overwhelmed the Inca army and sent it scurrying back to safety at Tumibamba. Fearful of the damage that such a defeat might cause to his reputation, Huayna Capac set out at once on a punitive raid. His army laid waste to every town along the way so that all would once again fear the might and the will of the Incas. Once he had avenged the loss suffered by his captains, the sapa inca then returned to Tumibamba.

While Huayna Capac and his troops sallied forth on several more campaigns that succeeded at enlarging the Inca empire, some of those victories came at a steep price. The Inca invasion of the province of Carangue is a case in point. The Cayambes tribe put up a stoic defense of their beloved homeland that, even though the end result failed to go in their favor, inflicted a numerous amount of losses upon the invading Incas. The Cayambes, whose numbers were not as great as those of the Incas, retreated to a nearby stronghold when they learned of the approach of Huayna Capac's army. The Incas laid siege but were unable to beach the walls of the fortress. At one point during the attack, the Incas were taken by surprise when a number of Cayambes' warriors launched a sortie against them. The ranks of the elite force of the Inca warriors were broken, and because of this the rest of the army began to retreat from the field of battle, leaving Huayna Capac, who had fallen to the ground during the confusion, unprotected. Thankfully, the Inca ruler was saved from harm by two of his loyal captains, Cusi Tupa Yupanqui and Guayna Achache.

After this setback, Huayna Capac ordered his troops to conquer the surrounding villages so that the Cayambes' fortress would be cut off from all outside support. Once again the Inca army laid siege to the fortress and once again they found it impossible to penetrate the defenses of their enemy. The tide quickly turned in favor of the besieged when Auquituma, the Inca commander, was killed during an attack on the stronghold; a disconcerting sight that caused most of the Inca warriors to retreat from the battlefield in a state of panic. The inspired Cayambes warriors gave chase, slaying a great many by slitting the throats of their captured enemy.

The sapa inca, who had stayed behind at Tumibamba during this second unsuccessful engagement, waited until sufficient reinforcements arrived from Cuzco and the neighboring towns before retaliating. Once he felt his army was strong enough, the emperor ordered another assault. The siege of the Cayambes' stronghold continued for several days, with neither side coming close to claiming victory. Knowing their enemy penchant for launching surprise attacks, the Incas gave them a reason to come out from behind the walls of their fortress. The order was given to retreat and when the Cayambes saw their attackers fleeing they once again gave chase. This time, however, they were waylaid by a massed assembly of Inca troops who waited in ambush. At that same moment, soldiers who also had remained hidden entered the now open fortress and began to slaughter all whom they could lay their hands upon. Many frightened citizens tried to hide in some rushes along the lake but all were discovered and brutally slain where they had hid. Because of the vast amount of blood that was spilled that day, this body of water was forever after known by the name Yawar Cocha, the "lake of blood."

After finally overcoming the dogged defense of the Cayambes, Huayna Capac turned his attention to the western coast. He led his conquering army to the Valley of Tumbes. The Incas waged war against Tumula, a chief who lorded over the region of Guayaquil and the nearby Island of Puná. The Incas, by virtue of their superior strength in numbers, eventually prevailed. The sapa inca left a garrison of warriors behind and then returned to Tumbes. The

Puná islanders rallied their forces and promptly slaughtered all of the Incas who had been left behind. After learning of the bloody uprising, Huayna returned to conquer the island once again. After this conquest the emperor returned to Quito but continued to spend most of his time at Tumibamba, a city later known as Cuenca.

It was during Huayna Capac's stay at Tumibamba that messengers from the coast arrived bearing ominous news of light-skinned bearded men who had come from across the sea on enormous floating houses made out of wood. The first of these messages was dispatched by the Inca who met with Francisco Pizarro and his soldiers at the town of Tumbes. The Inca ruler was greatly disturbed by this message and even though it was still daylight, he retired to his quarters to contemplate the meaning behind such strange and unexpected news.

Other messengers soon arrived with even more worrisome information about these strangers who had suddenly come to their land. News of the voyage of Diego de Almagro reached the ears of Huayna Capac shortly after this group of Spaniards arrived at the Río de San Juan. They spoke of how these barbarous men had plundered precious items from the royal buildings and that they showed no fear of the wild beasts that had been caged there by the Inca. When Huayna questioned them about the creatures of his that they had mentioned, one of the messengers replied, "Lord, the only thing to say is that the lion and wild animals that you have in your palaces cower before the strangers and wag their tails at them like tame animals."[2] Huayna, after hearing this, stood up, shook his royal cloak and said, "Signs and auguries, be gone, be gone; refrain from disturbing my domain and power." He then took a different seat and asked the messengers to repeat their stories, hoping that what he had heard was merely a bad dream.

Tales of the depraved manner of the Spaniards sounded much like an ancient legend that was familiar to many of the coastal tribes. It had come to pass a long time ago that giant beings sailing from the west in enormous reed boats came ashore to claim the land and its people for their own. In satisfying their ravenous appetite for food, the giants deprived the natives of the abundant sustenance which the sea and the land had previously provided for them. They forced the women and men to have sex with them, compelled liaisons that, because of their extreme weight, crushed many a poor native partner to death. The giants even had sex with one another, showing no shame over their openly deviant behavior. The people prayed for help and their prayers were answered when out of the sky there appeared a divine being who smote the evil giants. Many natives would come to believe that the Spaniards were a return of these malevolent giants, though a smaller version in stature but not in their ravenous appetite for women, food, and gold.

What followed were a flurry of signs that were interpreted by the Inca ruler's shaman and priests as omens of impending doom. One day the priests of Huayna Capac saw an eagle fall from the sky after being violently attacked by a flock of buzzards. The injured noble bird was cared for but soon died from its massive injuries. Great significance was placed on this event because it occurred during the Feast of the Sun and coincided with reports of hirsute men who came from across the sea.

According to Inca lore, "There followed earthquakes and such unusual violence that great rocks were shattered in pieces and mountains collapsed. The sea became furious, overflowed its shores, invading the land, while numerous comets streaked the heavens, sowing terror in their wake. A curious, mysterious fear had seized upon all of Peru, when one unusually bright night the moon appeared with a halo of three large rings; the first one was the color of blood, the second a greenish black, and the third seemed to be made of smoke."[3] The priests and shaman interpreted the blood colored ring as a coming conflict, while telling the inca, "The black ring threatens our religion, our laws, and the Empire, which will not survive these wars and the death of your people; and all you have done and all your ancestors have done, will vanish in smoke, as is shown in the third ring."[4]

One day there came a mysterious messenger who delivered to Huayna Capac a small black box that contained something of such importance that it only could be opened by the sapa inca. The curious emperor slowly lifted the lid and out flew a great many moths and butterflies: a foreboding sign of death that soon rang true with the arrival of the small pox plague. The Spaniards had brought with them the deadly viral strain of smallpox, and the fleet footed chasquis who carried the messages to the Inca ruler also carried this pandemic disease with them. Mihicnca Mayta, one of Huayna's generals, soon passed away from this terrible pestilence and he was followed to the grave by officers close to him and they, in turn, were followed by the warriors who served under them. It wasn't long before many of Huayna Capac's subjects took ill and then died from the horrifying and debilitating effects of this mysterious illness that quickly ravaged their bodies.

The fearful Huayna Capac, once again retired to his royal chambers to meditate on these ominous signs that were beginning to appear with greater frequency. Three natives of very small stature entered the incas' chamber unannounced and stated, "Inca, we came to call you."[5] The startled inca called out to his guards but when they entered the room the three Indians were no where to be found. It was shortly after this event that Huayna Capac took ill.

As Huayna Capac lay dying, messengers were dispatched to the sacred city of Pachacamac to ascertain from men knowledgeable in the ways of magic as to how the divine inca could be cured. Those closest to the emperor sensed that the hand of death was near and urged him to name a successor. The delirious emperor barely had enough strength to utter the names of Ninan Cuyochi and Huascar before lapsing into a state of unconsciousness without ever mentioning the name of Atahualpa, his favorite son. The first son mentioned by Huayna was a mere infant but because he was the offspring of a union between him and his sister, Mama Cusi Rimay, he was of the purest blood and therefore the favored choice, despite the fact that he was only a month old. Royal emissaries were dispatched at once to inform the sister of the emperor that her son was soon to become sapa inca only to find that both the prince and the coya had been robbed of life by the same mysterious malady that now afflicted Huayna Capac.

The messengers who were dispatched to Pachacamac soon returned to say that the most powerful of the shaman had told them that since the sapa inca was a child of Inti then it was the sun, and only the sun, which possessed the power to cure him. The weak Huayna Capac was carried out from his chambers and laid upon the ground so that he might bask in the warmth of the radiant sun above. Unfortunately, this well-intended advice merely aggravated an already delicate condition and soon the Sun God called the Inca emperor home to the heavens. Such was the condition of Huayna Capac when the other group of emissaries returned to report that the royal prince was dead.

After his death at Quito, the body of Huayna Capac was transported to Tumibamba to undergo the complex and sacred process of mummification. Hundreds of loyal servants were willingly put to death in order that Lord Huayna Capac would be well cared for in the after life. A thousand multicolored llamas were also sacrificed as part of the elaborate funeral ceremony that paid homage to the deceased and beloved sapa inca. The heart and liver of the emperor were to remain at Quito while his mummified body was to be carried by litter over the royal highway to the city of Cuzco, a distance of nearly twelve hundred miles. Once there, the body of Huayna was to be placed alongside the remains of the other rulers, three of which were true mummies while the other five were merely replicas of the lost bodies of the earliest rulers, at the sacred Temple of the Sun. The revered statue of Manco Capac that Huayna Capac had brought with him to Quito was carried on the back of porters so that it could be returned to its proper place at Cuzco. The solemn procession stopped at each town along the way to give the townsfolk an opportunity to pay their last respects and to make additional llama sacrifices to the gods. This event occurred in the Christian year of 1527.

The War of the Brothers

The high priest accompanied the solemn funeral procession to Cuzco in order that he might administer the last rites of Huayna Capac and to crown an awaiting Huascar, the son of Raura Occlo, also a sister of the deceased emperor, as the new sapa inca. In the meantime, Atahualpa, the favored but forgotten son, who was approximately five years older than his half-brother, remained behind to lord over the city of Quito. According to a story later told by Father Bernabé Cobo, Huascar was originally named Topa Cusi Hualpa. On the day of his birth, Huayna Capac had the goldsmiths make a thick golden chain, called a huascar, that was long enough to be held by two hundred native dancers. Following this grand celebration the young prince was henceforth remembered by the name of Huascar.

When the funeral procession finally reached Cuzco, Huascar publicly chastised the Quito emissaries for not having brought Atahualpa to his coronation as sapa inca. Even though the nobles assured the new ruler that there was nothing sinister about his absence, Huascar ordered their torture and when they failed to confirm his suspicions he had them all put to death. The nobles who supported the selection of Huascar were soon disappointed when their new emperor decreed that all the fertile lands set aside for the sun god and the Inca rulers of the past were to revert to his control, a proposal that caused a furor among the various cults that cared for the estates of the gods and the deceased Inca rulers.

Inca Huascar became drunk with both power and drink. There were few days that he was not found to be in an inebriated state. To satisfy his salacious sexual desires he took without asking the wives of nobles who happened to please him and any husband who objected to such a liaison was immediately put to death. Believing it was his divine duty to increase the noble Inca line to fill future governmental posts, Huascar sought to plant his seed with as many concubines as he possibly could manage, a harem which reputedly numbered more than seven hundred women. The time he spent with lips pursed to the cup and his flesh pressed against the flesh of another caused him to neglect his dealings with important matters of state.

Huascar soon learned that Atahualpa was steadily building Quito into a city that was on the verge of rivaling the size and magnificence of Cuzco. Concerned by these reports, Huascar summoned his half-brother to the capital city but Atahualpa, who feared that his rival sibling had a sinister ulterior motive, graciously declined his invitation by saying that the affairs of the province required his continued presence at Quito. Huascar sent a second message that, in much stronger words, requested his presence at Cuzco. Once again, Atahualpa declined this invitation. The inca sent a third message which demanded his appearance at the royal court and if he refused then he would be brought to Cuzco by force.

Atahualpa attempted to allay the concerns of his jealous brother at Cuzco by sending as gifts an assortment of elegantly designed clothes. An outraged Huascar ripped apart the clothing sent to him and threw the shredded items upon the statue of his father and in the face of his mother, who had made the fateful mistake of defending the actions of Prince Atahualpa. He had the emissary who presented the gifts of clothing brutally tortured before being beheaded, after which he ordered that his flayed skin was to be made into a drum that he planned to use to summon an army for waging war against his insolent half-brother. Huascar then sent Atahualpa womanly articles such as clothes, jewelry, and makeup, gifts designed to insult the manhood of the ruler of Quito. The rest of the emissaries were subjected to various forms of torture, after which they were banished from the kingdom.

Atahualpa's advisers warned that if he went to Cuzco the vindictive emperor would either have him imprisoned or, more likely than not, have him put to death. The Inca commanders pledged their loyal support to the ruler of Quito as did the soldiers and citizens of this northern realm of the empire. "Atahualpa was loved by the old captains of his father and the soldiers because he went to the wars with him as a child, and because Huayna Capac had so loved him during his lifetime, allowing him to eat nothing except what he left on his plate. Huascar was clement and pious; Atahualpa, ruthless and vengeful; both were generous, but Atahualpa was a man of greater determination and endeavor."[6] This flawed character study of Huascar was provided to the Spanish historian Cieza de León by Cuzco loyalists who saw Atahualpa as a usurper. The Inca generals at Quito, all of whom had known the prince for his entire life, pressed for the rights of Atahualpa both out of a fondness for him and with the realization that they would not enjoy the same privileges under Huascar, who had already appointed his own military commanders at Cuzco. Atahualpa accepted their overtures to proclaim himself king of both Quito and Tumibamba.

The relatives of Atahualpa still at Cuzco were summoned to the royal palace where Huascar said to them: "I have news that your kinsman Atahualpa is rising in rebellion and wants to make himself king. I wish to send all of you, his kinsmen, to kill him. Bring me his head because I wish to drink from the skull. If you do this, I will hold you as friends and grant you favors. If you do not bring it to me, none of you should return, for if you do I will tear you all to pieces."[7] The relatives of Atahualpa had no choice but to obey the commands of Huascar. Cuxi Yupanqui, a close kin of the prince at Quito, was placed in charge of this reluctant group of conscripted relatives.

Five years after the death of their father the royal sons went to war with one another to determine once and for all who would reign supreme over the whole of the Inca empire. The first battle of the Inca civil war occurred at the town of Tumibamba, where Atahualpa met with defeat and capture at the hands of Cañari forces loyal to Huascar. While the triumphant warriors celebrated their good fortune, Atahualpa managed to engineer his escape by means of a silver utensil smuggled in by a friendly female visitor. His miraculous return to his army at Quito was taken as a sign that this son of Huayna Capac was indeed destined to wear the crown of the sapa inca. However, he suffered an injury during this disastrous engagement that left one ear lobe badly mangled, and since this was considered to be an extremely ominous sign, he had to wear a specially designed cloak that hid his unsightly disfigurement.

Sketch of Atahualpa (courtesy Library of Congress).

The reinvigorated army under the command of Atahualpa returned to Tumibamba and defeated the royal army of Cuzco in rather convincing fashion. The Quito warriors sacked the city and slaughtered a great many Cañari inhabitants. Atoc, the commanding general of Huascar's royal army, was among the many who were taken prisoner during this engagement. He was to suffer a fate similar to that of the unfortunate emissary Atahualpa had previously sent to Huascar — he was flayed, probably while still alive, and his peeled skin was forged into a drum. His severed head was made into a specially designed drinking vessel for Atahualpa. Cuxi Yupanqui, the cousin of

Atahualpa, was captured during this battle and brought before the victorious lord. Atahualpa showed great respect toward Cuxi Yupanqui and after learning that he had been forced to take the side of Huascar because of threats of harm against him and his family, the prince welcomed him back into the fold by appointing him a captain within his royal army.

After this stunning victory, Atahualpa and his generals turned the table on Huascar by launching an invasion into his kingdom. While Huascar had a much larger army, Atahualpa enjoyed the benefits of having superior commanders and battle-tested warriors on his side. Chalcuchima (also spelled as Challcochima or Chalcochima) and Quizquiz were two generals whose brilliant military strategies and fearless leadership had been proven numerous times on the battlefield. Because he had such confidence in their abilities, Atahualpa decided to remain behind at the town of Cajamarca while his generals continued on ahead to prosecute the war for control of the empire. The natural hot springs of this region made for an idyllic spot for Atahualpa and his troops to recuperate from the rigors of a long and hard fought campaign. By tapping into the icy waters of a mountain lake and the thermal underground springs, the Inca ruler and his entourage were treated to the pleasure of running hot and cold water at the installed public baths. The risk of being captured once again surely played a factor in Atahualpa's decision to remain at Cajamarca.

Atahualpa's army had prevailed in convincing manner during battles at Bombón, Jauja, and Vilcas and their stunning string of victories continued at Pincos, Andahuaylas, and Limatambo. Huascar, who had remained at Cuzco during this ongoing civil war, decided the time had now come for him to lead his Inca warriors to victory over the swiftly advancing armies led by Chalcuchima and Quizquiz. The Sapa Inca managed to muster an imposing force of nearly 60,000 warriors for this campaign. The royal army that Huascar had assembled consisted of troops already defeated in battle and commoners with little military training who had been pressed into service, while the army which fought on the side of Atahualpa was comprised of battle hardened veterans whose confidence grew greater with each victory.

Huascar decided he would lead the advance with only five thousand hand picked troops, the majority of which were Inca nobles with little if any battle experience, while the rest of the warriors were divided into several battalions that were to remain at a concealed distance. His plan was to make the enemy think that his army was extremely small and with that in mind he believed that Atahualpa's generals would abandon their well disciplined battle plan and attack in full force. It was then that Huascar would signal from his litter for the rear guard to charge onto the battlefield, an overwhelming force that would throw the enemy into a state of confusion.

Huascar and his small body of troops happened upon a captain and his squadron of warriors who served Chalcuchima and Quizquiz and, because of their superior numbers, they were able to easily overtake them. The captain from Quito was tortured into revealing the whereabouts of the main force, after which he, along with the rest of the warriors who served under him, was put to death. Huascar's easy triumph convinced him that victory was clearly ordained from high above and therefore decided to abandon his own plan and advance upon the camp of Chalcuchima and Quizquiz without bothering to wait for the rest of the troops. In the meantime, the generals of Atahualpa had learned of Huascar's approach from their sentries and prepared for his arrival by strategically hiding a number of armed warriors in a nearby ravine. Huascar's small force was easily annihilated by this hidden army and the badly wounded sapa inca was taken prisoner.

After having learned of the brutal massacre of their comrades and the subsequent capture of Huascar, the leaderless army of Cuzco quickly fled back to the city to contemplate their next course of action. They were closely tracked by the victorious army which served Atahualpa. The citizens of Cuzco became gravely concerned when the defeated imperial army returned with news of the emperor's defeat and capture. Fear and panic took hold once they beheld the size and might of the army of Quito that was steadily advancing toward their city.

Atahualpa's generals sent overtures of peace that proved successful in luring many Cuzco nobles to their camp. The unarmed Inca nobles were greeted by Quito warriors who beat them mercilessly with their clubs. The nobles who survived such a brutal beating were forced to suffer through an excruciating round of gruesome tortures. Those allowed to live were returned to Cuzco in the company of an army of warriors loyal to Atahualpa. Once inside, the Quito warriors encountered little resistance from shocked citizens who were unprepared for such a sudden turn of events; the warriors therefore were able to easily take control of the city. While much of the city was sacked, the conquerors remained respectful of the sacred Coricancha by leaving it untouched.

The generals of Quito demonstrated their capacity for being benevolent conquerors by decreeing that a pardon would be granted to anyone who willingly came forward to swear their allegiance to Atahualpa, the new sapa inca. Those who did not would be considered an enemy of the state and suffer the consequences of extreme prejudice. Unfortunately, such a magnanimous offer did not extend to any of the immediate members of the royal family, for they were fated to suffer terribly at the hands of their captors. Many of Huascar's relatives, as well as members of his inner circle, sought to elude capture by sneaking out of the city dressed as commoners.

The victorious commanders were quick to send news of their glorious victory to Cajamarca, where Atahualpa was presently encamped with the remainder of the army. The demeanor of Atahualpa changed the moment he learned that his army had defeated and captured his half-brother Huascar. He was now the true sapa inca, a godly manifestation who stood above the plane of ordinary men. His expression took on an authoritative look, always masking his emotions with an austere expression. Atahualpa immediately dispatched his cousin Cuxi Yupanqui to Cuzco with directions for the orderly transfer of power and instructions of how he wished to mete out punishment against members of the Huascar household. Once Cuxi Yupanqui arrived at Cuzco he assembled all of the nobles to tell them that Atahualpa harbored no ill will toward the people of Cuzco but wished only to punish the immediate family of the corrupt Huascar. He urged the nobles to prove their loyalty to the new emperor by going out to the four provinces to locate those who were in hiding and have them returned to the city unharmed.

The nobles did as Cuxi Yupanqui asked and searched near and far in every direction for those who were members of Huascar's inner circle. Many were captured and returned to Cuzco but there were many who feared the judgment that awaited them and chose to take their own lives before being taken prisoner. Cuxi ordered a great number of tall stakes placed in the ground on both sides of the main road that led to the city. Many of the concubines of Huascar were hung upside down from those poles and any woman who carried the planted seed of Huascar had her belly slit open to expose the unborn child. Several of the living sons of Huascar were left to hang upon these stakes until there was no more life in their body. Many of the daughters of Huayna Capac, Atahualpa's half sister's, were condemned to die in this same manner. Other lords and family members who were loyal to Huascar were tortured and then had their skulls split open with battle axes. The bodies of the dead were left as fodder for the various scavenging creatures that inhabit the earth. Executions were not restricted to just those methods. Some were burned alive, a few were weighted down with stones and thrown into nearby bodies of water, and others were thrown off steep cliffs. A great many were reportedly hacked to death with hatchets. It was Atahualpa's express wish that the entire bloodline of Huascar was to be extinguished before he entered the city of Cuzco. A harsh punishment was also exacted against tribes that had sided with Huascar in the long and bloody civil war, especially the Canari tribe, whose warriors had maltreated Atahualpa during his brief captivity. Atahualpa instructed his warriors to lay waste to their villages and kill all who dwelled there.

Huascar, his mother and his wife, along with a number of other lords were placed in cages to await their inevitable fate. The once mighty sapa inca was forced to wear feminine clothing, similar in style to that which he had sent to Atahualpa, and his captors humiliated Huascar further by forcing him to eat the foul excrement that littered the streets of Cuzco. Huascar was pulled from his cell so that he could witness the grisly execution of his brothers and sisters, children, and other close relatives who had been captured. Coya Miro and the son she bore Huascar as well as the child of his that she still carried in her womb were all slain before the tearful eyes of the deposed Inca ruler. Another favorite sister by the name of Chimbo Cisa was also killed in his presence. Huascar had been allowed to live so that he might suffer the pain of knowing that all whom he knew and loved suffered because of him. Once these gruesome executions had been concluded, Huascar was transported to the town of Jauja, where he was imprisoned.

As Atahualpa was hurriedly making preparations for his triumphant entrance at Cuzco there came to Cajamarca four messengers from the village of Tallane who said to him: "Unique lord, you should be aware that some white and bearded men have arrived in our town of Tangarala. They bring a kind of sheep (llama) on which they ride and travel. The sheep are very big, much larger than ours. These men come so well clothed that no skin appears but the hand and face. And half of it only because the other half is covered with a beard that grows on it."[8]

The new sapa inca believed that these strangers who came from across the sea just might be the long predicted return of the god Viracocha and his disciples. Since there was a growing fear that these supposed deities had returned to render aid to Huascar, Atahualpa decided to remain at Cajamarca to await their arrival in order to determine for himself if these strangers from the sea were gods or mere mortals.

10
Pizarro's March to Cajamarca

The Founding of San Miguel

Francisco Pizarro remained at Tumbes until the early part of May 1532 at which point he marched at the head of the main force of his army to seek out other towns and villages to claim for both Spain and himself. There were a handful of new recruits who were not pleased by what they had seen so far and asked for permission to return to Nicaragua. Their request was granted on the condition that they leave behind all of their weapons. Francisco Martín de Alcantára and more than twenty-five soldiers — mostly royal officials and those who lacked the will or the strength to march ahead — remained at Tumbes. Antonio Navarro, the accountant, was named captain over those who were to stay behind to enforce Spanish claims to what little remained of the city.

Soldiers were not the only members of the expedition who demonstrated a lack of faith in the quest of their commander. All of the Dominican friars, except for Father Vincente de Valverde, who were appointed by the Crown to accompany Francsico Pizarro to Peru abandoned the mission. According to the conquistador Diego de Trujillo, Father Reginaldo de Pedraza left "taking with him some hundred emeralds he had sewn into his garments."[1]

Francisco Pizarro hoped to take advantage of the fratricidal feud that had left the mighty Inca nation divided and weakened. He now knew that Atahualpa had prevailed over his brother and had proclaimed himself the supreme ruler of the Inca empire, but Pizarro could also see that all not all of the towns were willing to accept him as their new lord and master. The captain-general hoped to exploit such discord to his advantage. What he did not know was that while he was at Tumbes there were spies in his midst, scouts who were the eyes and the ears of Atahualpa.

The very roads that allowed the Incas to govern and control their vast empire provided Francisco Pizarro and his small band of conquistadors with a direct path to the numerous towns and villages within their realm. Since it was his earnest desire to win the people over to his side, Pizarro ordered his men to refrain from any overt pillaging of native valuables. Of course any people who dared to oppose the Spaniards were to be dealt with in the harshest manner. By following the example of Hernán Cortés in his successful conquest of the Aztecs, the captain-general hoped to win over the disgruntled tribes with diplomacy until he had assembled a force of allies large enough to conquer the ruling Incas. However, Peru, as he would soon discover, was structured very differently from Mexico.

After nearly a month of marching along the coastal road, the Spanish expedition reached the banks of the river Piura located in the scenic Tangarala Valley, a distance of roughly ninety miles to the south of Tumbes. Pizarro and his soldiers soon came upon the native town of Paita which the captain-general found to be an idyllic site for establishing a permanent Spanish settlement. The Spaniards, with the aid of the natives who accompanied them and those who called Paita their home, erected a fort, a church, and several buildings to form the basic foundations for the colony that was christened as San Miguel. Before continuing on with his quest, the captain-general collected all of the gold and silver confiscated up to this point and had it melted down and cast into ingots of equal value. After the obligatory royal fifth was set aside, he urged his men to turn over their share, with the promise that it would be paid back at a later date. All agreed to Pizarro's request. The entire treasure was shipped back to Panama to purchase additional provisions and weapons, and, most importantly, to persuade more men to join their bold quest to conquer all of Peru.

Three weeks after the two ships set sail for Panama, Francisco Pizarro decided the time had come to resume his march. His decision to leave San Miguel was prompted by the news that the victorious Atahualpa was camped at Cajamarca, a town that was approximately 350 miles away. The Spaniards were made aware of this fact by a native dressed in peasant garb who claimed to know a great deal regarding the whereabouts and the intentions of the newly crowned Inca ruler. The native who Pizarro and his officers carried on discussions with was actually an Inca warrior named Ciquinchara, who had been sent in disguise by Atahualpa to learn more about these strangers who so brazenly trespassed upon his land. Ciquinchara made sure to obtain an accurate count of the number of soldiers under the command of Pizarro and also made a mental note of their peculiar weapons and the strange beasts that easily bore the weight of even the largest man. He told the captain-general that Cajamarca was but a mere twelve day hike from where they were now, but failed to mention the difficult climb that lay ahead.

Approximately fifty soldiers were left behind to guard the Spanish settlement while Francisco Pizarro set out on September 25, 1532, with the major portion of his troops, a few Indian guides, and his two native translators in search of Lord Atahualpa. While he was unable to enlist the support of the local natives to his side, such as Cortes had done in Mexico, he was grateful that no one along the way sought to oppose his advance. The Spaniards came upon fortresses that were recently abandoned and bridges that were left unguarded. Ciquinchara accompanied Pizarro and his troops for a brief distance before the Spanish captain asked him to go on ahead to inform Atahualpa that he and his men were on their way to meet with the Inca emperor.

The determined captain-general and his band of soldiers crossed the river that flowed before them and soon settled for the night at the town of Poechos. From there they followed the advice of their guides and headed eastward along the route of the Piura river, taking care to avoid the desolate region known as the Sechura desert. After the fifth day out the first stirrings of discontent emerged when a small group of soldiers registered their mounting concerns and fears about marching to Cajamarca, where it was known that Atahualpa awaited with tens of thousands of his fully armed and readied warriors. Pizarro listened to their complaints and then decided to weed out the malcontents by stating that any man who wished to return to San Miguel was free to do so but his share of the rewards that awaited would obviously be far less than those who bravely followed him to Cajamarca. Four foot soldiers and five cavalrymen elected to abandon the mission and were granted leave to return to the Spanish garrison. Those who continued on no longer had any cause to complain for they had freely chosen to follow Francisco Pizarro into the great unknown.

The March to Cajamarca

As they continued their march toward Cajamarca the Spaniards saw further evidence of the devastating effects of the recent civil war. Death and destruction had clearly preceded the arrival of the conquistadors. Pizarro and his men came upon villages that were entirely destroyed and saw piles of corpses that had simply been left to rot upon the ground. Such ghastly sights stirred up a considerable amount of fear and doubt among the troops but their commander was encouraged, believing he could use this internal strife to his advantage. The Spaniards continued on along the tributary Inca road that connected the empire and eventually they reached the village of Zarán where they were warmly received by the curaca, the recognized chief, who housed them all at one of the local large royal tambos. Inquiring as to why there were so few men at Zarán, Pizarro learned that most of them were conscripts in the Inca civil war. It was here that the Spaniards remained to await the return of Hernándo de Soto.

Francisco Pizarro had previously dispatched Hernándo de Soto and several cavaliers to scout ahead for a better route to Cajamarca and to gather intelligence about the Inca garrison at Cajas (also spelled as Caxas). The Spaniards were accompanied by native guides who were quite familiar with this particular part of the region. Soto and his men marveled at the paved royal road that they followed and were delighted by stories from the local inhabitants of large Inca cities that were sheathed in gold. The Spaniards also learned more about the cause and effect of the devastating civil war of the Incas, a conflict that had left thousands of warriors dead and an untold number of citizens homeless in its wake. The Spaniards believed they were now within reach of the great riches they had heard about for such a long time. Along the way, Hernándo de Soto encountered a tribute collector for the emperor and from him he learned much about the capital city of Cuzco as well as Atahualpa, the new sapa inca.

Two days after being sent on ahead to reconnoiter the land, Hernándo de Soto and his company of horsemen came to the village of Cajas. They found that the native town, like so many others along this path, had recently been sacked by Atahualpa's conquering army. Hernándo and his soldiers were disturbed by the sight of many rotting native corpses hanging from trees — a clear sign of just how ruthless the Incas could be. Hernándo and his men listened to complaints from the people of the cruel treatment they suffered at the hands of warriors from Quito and the burdensome tribute they were forced to pay the nobles at Cuzco, tribute that included children who were fated to be sacrificial victims. The Spaniards, however, added to the numerous atrocities already suffered by the people of Cajas by having their way with the sacred virgins who served in the local sun temple dedicated to the sun. The molesting of the five hundred cloistered women was sufficient cause for the citizens to take up arms and challenge the sacrilegious Spaniards. Many natives died in a gallant effort to defend the honor of these revered women but in the end it was to no avail.

During their brief stay at Cajas the Spaniards were met by one of Atahualpa's lords who presented Hernándo de Soto with two stuffed ducks and clay models of two guarded fortresses, the implied threats of which did not go unnoticed by the suspicious Spaniards. Captain de Soto and his men continued on to Huancabamba, which was described as a "fortress built entirely of cut stones, the larger stones being five or six palms wide, and so closely joined that there appeared to be no mortar between them."[2]

Lord Atahualpa already had knowledge of Francisco Pizarro's return to Tumbes and numerous spies kept him informed of their every movement. Hernándo de Soto learned from the emissary sent by Atahualpa that the royal army was still camped at Cajamarca and that the ruler extended an invitation for all of the Spaniards to come meet with him there. Though it was encouraging to learn that the sapa inca wished to meet with them it was somewhat disconcerting to realize that the Inca ruler was already aware of their presence. The emissary who met with Hernándo was, unbeknownst to the Spanish captain, also a spy charged with learning more about the strength of this army of invaders and determining whether they were returning deities or mere mortals.

Captain de Soto returned after an absence of eight days with the emissary dispatched by Atahualpa who, on behalf of the Inca emperor, welcomed Francisco Pizarro and his troops to his lands and urged them to journey on to his camp nestled in a valley beyond the mountains. The Inca ruler had instructed the emissary to present the leader of these strangers with many gifts of considerable value, a list that included two elegant ceramic drinking vessels, some gold and silver embroidered cloth woven from llama wool, and some fragrant perfume. The captain-general showed his appreciation by reciprocating with a hasty offering of two rather plain glass cups, a red cap, and a lace shirt, mere trinkets that paled in value to those offered by the sapa inca. Pizarro also gave the Inca ambassador a message to carry back to Atahualpa which stated that the Spaniards were emissaries of a mighty emperor from across the ocean who wished to form a lasting alliance with the great people of this land. Atahualpa would also learn of the Spaniards' rape of the five hundred mamacunas at Cajas from this returning emissary.

Before setting out for Cajamarca, Francisco Pizarro sent a messenger back to San Miguel to update the troops stationed there as to their present situation and to inform them of his upcoming plans. He also sent back the splendid gifts presented to him by the native envoy. As they marched toward their imminent rendezvous with the reigning sapa inca the Spaniards heard whisperings from the residents of the towns they passed through that the cunning Lord Atahualpa was laying a trap for them. These murmurings of treachery on the part of Atahualpa were disconcerting enough to motivate the captain-general to send four native messengers on ahead to Cajamarca to remind the Inca emperor that the Spaniards came in peace. He also instructed these emissaries to gather as much intelligence as possible, without making themselves too conspicuous, concerning the mood of the Inca and the strength of his army. Pizarro also wanted them to find out if there were any Inca warriors lying in wait alongside the road.

Fearing that the Incas were already too familiar with the route he was taking, Francisco Pizarro chose not to proceed by the path recently probed by Hernándo de Soto. Instead, he marched his troops southward in hopes of finding natives who desired to join up with him and his men. Pizarro found that most of the towns were willing to recognize the Spaniards as their ally but, because of the long and bloody civil war and the sudden appearance of a mysterious plague, both of which had claimed a great number of lives, they were unable to provide any warriors to aid the cause of the conquistadors. In fact, many towns were having a difficult time rounding up enough able bodied men to tend to their fields.

The Spaniards, along with the several hundred native porters who helped lighten their load, marched for three days across an arid stretch of land that had little to offer in the way of either food or water. They were now skirting along the barren stretch of land known as the Sechura Desert. Pizarro and his men eventually reached a more verdant and consequentially more populous region. Hernándo Pizarro went on ahead with a small company of cavaliers to reconnoiter the land. Even though he was well received by the nobles of the towns he came upon, Hernándo decided he could learn much more about Atahualpa's true intention toward the Spaniards by forcibly loosening the tongue of one of the native chiefs. The Spanish commander ordered his soldiers to pluck the nails from the ruler's fingertips and when this method of torment failed to elicit the information he wished to hear, Pizarro then had his eyelids seared with heated blades. It was then that the tortured chief told him Atahualpa was luring them into a trap. The information extracted by this means seemed to satisfy Hernándo but what he heard, more likely than not, were simply the words which the native chief knew would put an end to the torturous ordeal that had been forced upon him.

Included among the reasons that compelled Lord Atahualpa to remain so long at Cajamarca was the hope that the nearby sulfur springs would help cure the unsightly wound to his ear that he had received from the armies of his half-brother during the struggle for control of the Inca empire. Ciquinchara, one of the many spies sent by the emperor, returned to tell Atahualpa, "Unique lord, you ask me and command that I speak. I have so greatly desired to do so, since I found out from the Tallanes who left from here and misinformed you. I don't blame them because when the lord of those viracochas arrived, the one they call capito (captain), I did not understand wither who they were. I was also as ignorant as they." Ciquinchara went on to say, "They are very few. I have counted between one hundred and seventy and one hundred and eighty. Their number does not surpass two hundred. To me they seem to be leaderless people wandering about and thieving."[3]

Ciquinchara also told the emperor of the hollow metal tubes wielded by many of the Spaniards which, on their command, spewed forth a thunderous blast that was immediately accompanied by flashes of lightning and bursts of smoke that inflicted great damage upon its intended target. He also went into great detail about the mighty beasts that bore on their backs the weight of these strangers, a sight that made them appear as if both were one creature. The faithful messenger went on to say that based upon his observations he believed that the Spaniards were not gods or even godlike, as had been reported by previous messengers from the coast, but instead were mortal men with numerous faults. But they were, he conceded, unlike any men he had ever before encountered.

Atahualpa was greatly disturbed by Ciquinchara's ominous observations but was relieved to learn that these men performed no feats or miracles that would lead one to believe they were true gods. This information coincided with reports submitted by other spies. The emissary who had returned with gifts from Francisco Pizarro boasted that it would take no more than two hundred warriors to subdue the Spaniards if their claims of coming in peace proved to be a lie.

After a brief period of contemplation, Atahualpa said to Ciquinchara, "I really want you to return to these men and take them these two tumblers of gold from me. You should give them to the capito, their lord, and you should tell him that I like him very much and that I want to see him. I wish we could figure out this matter and find out whether they are gods or another kind of people who could be gods and arrive angry and do the things you have witnessed."[4]

In the meantime, the captain-general and his exhausted troops had reached the base of the towering Andes, the longest mountain range on earth. Many of the peaks of this cordillera soar to heights so great that even in the torrid zone they remain eternally blanketed in snow. No Spaniard had ever gazed upon such majestic mountains and many feared that the steep snow capped peaks were simply too treacherous to scale. Many of the men urged their commander to take an alternate course, suggesting that they follow instead the royal road which led directly to Cuzco, the recently conquered capital of the Inca empire. But to Francisco Pizarro, the quickest way to lay claim to the entire empire rested along the road that led to Cajamarca. The captain-general saw the path through the mountains as an opportunity to impress upon the people of this land that the Spaniards were indeed men possessed of godlike strength and endurance. To the dismay of many a weary soldier, their commander chose to follow the mountain path that led to Cajamarca.

Before proceeding on this difficult climb, Pizarro attempted to raise the spirits of his men by saying, "Let every one of you take heart and go forward like a good soldier, nothing daunted by the smallness of your numbers. For in the greatest extremity God ever fights for his own, and doubt not he will humble the pride of the heathen, and bring him to the knowledge of the true faith, the great end and object of the Conquest."[5]

The brave band of Spaniards then began their assault of the vast and steep mountain range. They followed along a well defined but dangerously narrow path where the slightest misstep could cause a hapless climber to plummet to an imminent death that awaited below. The ascent forced them to contend with frigid temperatures for which they were unsuitably attired as well an accompanying sense of dizziness and labored breathing brought on by oxygen levels less than half of what they were normally accustomed to. The horses suffered equally alongside their masters and had to be dismounted and led by the bit up the treacherous path that cut through the peaks of the Andes. They would have to navigate hairpin turns made more difficult by the mist that shrouded their range of visibility and had to summon their courage to cross frighteningly long and narrow suspension bridges that wavered above raging waters and deep ravines.

Shortly after passing a recently abandoned Inca fortress near the top of the mountain they were ascending, Francisco Pizarro instructed his exhausted soldiers to make camp. While the famished and frostbitten men were busy tending to their immediate needs there arrived one of the native messengers that had been sent by Pizarro to the Inca camp. He told the captain-general that the path to Cajamarca was free of any danger and that the sapa inca was sending another embassy to greet the Spaniards. The embassy which he spoke of arrived shortly thereafter. An elegantly dressed Inca noble and several attendants sent by Atahualpa presented Pizarro with a gift of ten llamas. They told the captain-general that their ruler wished to know when he could expect to finally meet with the Spaniards. The proud Francisco told them to tell their emperor that the hour grew near that the two leaders would greet one another at Cajamarca. The emissaries carried this message back to Lord Atahualpa.

The refreshed Spaniards resumed their march to Cajamarca the following day. It took two more days of steady climbing before they completed their assault of this stretch of the cordilleras and were ready to begin their descent toward the valley where Atahualpa and his warriors were encamped. As they were coming down from the mountains another embassy came bearing more gifts and another message from the Inca ruler. They brought more llamas and some golden drinking cups filled with the fermented corn juice known as chicha. The Spaniards showed the emissaries every courtesy, though one of them unwittingly committed a slight breach of proper protocol by reaching out to touch the radiant disk that hung from the distended earlobes of one of the Inca nobles.

While the Spaniards were making camp and entertaining the company of men sent by the Inca emperor, another of the native messengers previously dispatched by Pizarro to meet with Atahualpa returned and when he saw the embassy of the Inca he went into an uncontrollable rage and immediately grabbed the ambassador by the ears. After being restrained by the Spaniards the messenger said that Atahualpa refused to meet with him and that he was denied both food and drink. He went on to say that Atahualpa was "in warlike array outside Cajamarca on the plain. He has a large army, and I found the town empty."[6]

The Inca ambassador countered that the army at Cajamarca was not nearly as large as those that were typically brought to do battle. He also said that Atahualpa had refused to meet with the native messenger because he bore no credentials attesting to his claim as an emissary. The ambassador then claimed that the city of Cajamarca had been abandoned in order to provide adequate lodging for the weary Spaniards. Francisco Pizarro, who now feared that the native rumors of his marching into a trap just may have been the truth, was careful to mask his concerns. The Inca noble was dismissed after being given a message that the Spaniards would now make even greater haste toward the town of Cajamarca.

11
The Capture of the Inca

Pizarro Fortifies His Position

After seven grueling days of steady climbing up and down mountainous terrain the weary Spanish troops finally came to a clearing that offered them a splendid view of the lush valley of Cajamarca. From this vantage point, Pizarro and his men could clearly see the town they had heard so much about, while off in the distance they could faintly make out the large camp where Atahualpa and his army patiently awaited their arrival. Cognizant of the fact that their every move was being carefully watched, the proud Spaniards made sure they put on a show of strength by descending the mountain pass in an orderly procession and with an arrogant swagger that clearly signified they knew no fear.

A steady rain fell as the conquistadors entered the town of Cajamarca on November 15, 1532, nearly eight years to the day when Francisco Pizarro had embarked on his first expedition to the unknown lands of Peru. Cajamarca was a city that was home to some ten thousand people on any typical day, but on this day the town had, by order of Atahualpa, been vacated for the much anticipated arrival of the Spanish soldiers. A few hundred townsfolk were instructed to remain behind to tend to the basic needs of the Spaniards.

Francisco Pizarro assembled his troops, which numbered 62 horse and 106 foot soldiers, at the main courtyard where he fully expected to be met by ambassadors of Lord Atahualpa. From this spot the captain-general and his troops had a much better view of the Inca camp. They reckoned there were as many as fifty thousand warriors encamped at the natural hot springs which often served as a resort for Inca nobility. One anxious soldier wrote, "So many tents were visible that we were truly filled with great apprehension."[1]

After having beheld the host of Inca warriors that stood before them and realizing that the much expected emissaries of Atahualpa were not forthcoming, Pizarro feared that the ominous native warnings of his being led into a trap had indeed come to pass. Anticipating a possible attack, the soldiers were strategically positioned along the main square of Cajamarca. Seeing as how Atahualpa would not come to see him, the captain-general decided to send his own emissaries to the Inca camp. Hernándo de Soto was dispatched with fifteen cavaliers and Felipillo, the native interpreter, to officially announce their arrival. Fearing that perhaps he had not sent an impressive enough show of force to earn the respect of the omnipotent inca, Pizarro shortly thereafter sent his brother, Hernándo, with another twenty horse soldiers to bolster Hernándo de Soto's embassy.

Hernándo de Soto and his troops galloped at a swift pace along a paved road lined with a great many Inca warriors who looked on in wary silence. Despite how they really felt, the soldiers were careful not to show even the slightest sign of fear. Proceeding unmolested through the heavily armed camp, the Spaniards had to cross two streams before reaching the court of the Inca emperor. The natives were amazed at the sight of armored Spaniards on horses crossing a wide but shallow stream at full gallop. Many of the cavaliers remained at the second stream while the captain and a few others strode into Atahualpa's courtyard. Here they found the ruler seated upon a low stool, reputedly made of gold, that was reserved for royalty and surrounded by an estimated four hundred noble bodyguards all dressed in elegant attire. Included in this royal entourage were a number of beautiful woman who were concubines of the sapa inca. The forehead of Atahualpa was partially covered with the royal maskapaicha, a fringed and crimson colored cloth laced with gold that is often referred to as a borla, the sacred Inca crown which had only recently been placed upon his head following his stunning victory over Huascar.

Francisco Xeres, Francisco Pizarro's personal secretary, noted that the ruler "Atahualpa was a man of thirty years of age, good-looking, somewhat stout, with a fine face, handsome and fierce, the eyes bloodshot. He spoke with much dignity, like a great lord."[2]

Hernándo de Soto plucked a ring from his finger and presented it as an offering to Atahualpa, a gift which the Inca ruler accepted without any visible display of emotion. His speech to the emperor about the Spaniards being emissaries of a great and powerful king from across the ocean was translated by Felipillo, the native interpreter who had accompanied them. Atahualpa never looked at Hernándo de Soto, his eyes remained cast toward the ground while the Spanish captain delivered the message of his commanding officer. Hernándo Pizarro and his company of soldiers arrived while the request of his brother to meet personally with Lord Atahualpa at Cajamarca was still being translated. One of the nobles spoke for the emperor, saying that he was presently fasting and therefore could not meet with the Spaniards until the following day.

It was only after learning that this second captain was the brother of the Spanish commander that Lord Atahualpa decided to speak for himself. The Inca ruler complained that the Spaniards had mistreated his people along the Chira river, a charge which Hernándo Pizarro denied. Atahualpa went on to say that one of his chiefs had killed three Spanish soldiers and a beast like the one that Hernándo sat upon. A noticeably angered Pizarro boastfully replied that "neither he, nor all the Indians of that river together, could kill a single Christian."[3]

This war of words promptly ended when female attendants of the Inca ruler brought out two elegantly designed golden goblets filled with the intoxicating chicha beverage, one of which was served to Hernándo Pizarro while the emperor drank from the other. Atahualpa then had two silver goblets brought out and filled with the same fermented beverage, which he shared with Hernándo de Soto. According to an Inca account, de Soto and Pizarro feared that their drinks were poisoned and poured the beverage onto the ground. However, considering that both officers had been instructed to do everything in their power to convince the Inca to come to Cajamarca, it seems unlikely that they would have performed a gesture that might have easily been perceived as an insult. Hernándo Pizarro asked the emperor to speak his mind and he responded by saying, "Tell your captain that I am keeping a fast, which will end tomorrow morning. I will then visit him, with my chieftains. In the meantime, let him occupy the public buildings on the square, and no other, till I come, when I will order what shall be done."[4]

Hernándo de Soto could not help but notice that the Inca ruler and most of his entourage kept eyeing the horses. He decided, for their benefit, to put on a dazzling display of his exemplary equestrian skills. After guiding his horse through several intricate maneuvers, the officer charged directly at Atahualpa and then abruptly halted just close enough so that the breath of the mighty beast could be felt upon the face of the emperor. While Atahualpa never so much as flinched many of those around the sapa inca fled or covered their faces in terror. It is said that the emperor had all of the nobles who recoiled out of fear of the horse, a number estimated to be at least forty, put to death shortly after the departure of the Spaniards. Another Spanish account claims that Atahualpa had three hundred put to death for failing to overcome their fear. The Spanish emissaries left the Inca camp with the understanding that the sapa inca would visit Cajamarca the following day.

The two captains returned to Cajamarca to report on all that had occurred during their brief meeting with the Inca ruler. While the captain-general was delighted that his officers had succeeded at convincing Atahualpa to meet with them he was somewhat disturbed by the report that the sapa inca showed absolutely no fear of either the soldiers or the horses. That night, Francisco Pizarro summoned his officers to a private meeting where he let them know of his daring plan to take the emperor hostage. He emphasized that previously gathered intelligence taken in conjunction with the sight of so many armed warriors at this location seemed to confirm that Atahualpa intended to do bodily harm to the Spaniards. To retreat now, he declared, would be an admission of defeat and a sign of weakness that would most likely prompt the Incas to launch an attack against them along mountain passes that were more familiar to the natives. The plan that the commander proposed was similar to the bloody but rather successful tactics employed by Hernán Cortés at Cholula and Pedro de Alvarado at Tenochtitlan during their conquest of the Aztec empire. Once inside the courtyard, the natives were to be overwhelmed by the element of surprise and the overpowering might of their superior weapons. The officers saw that there was no other choice but to follow the lead of their commander.

Francisco Pizarro had good reason to be concerned. During the middle of the night the emperor had sent his general Rumiñavi (eyes of stone), a warrior noted for showing no mercy toward his enemy, and five thousand elite warriors into the mountains to block a potential escape route along the north road to Cajamarca. It was, by some accounts, Atahualpa's plan to capture the insolent Spaniards and sacrifice them later to Inti, the sun god. As for the horses, it was said that he planned to sacrifice a few to the gods and with the rest he hoped to create his own stable of horses. Those soldiers whom the emperor mercifully decided not to put to death were to be castrated and sentenced to serve as attendants to his many concubines.

To keep the soldiers from worrying excessively, the details of the daring plan to capture Atahualpa were not conveyed to them until the breaking light of dawn on the 16th of November. The night before the upcoming encounter the Spanish soldiers were awestruck by the sight of the numerous native campfires that lit up the valley. The nervous soldiers, many of whom had yet to face the test of battle, spent their time offering up prayers to the almighty and confessing their sins to the only man of the cloth remaining among them, Father Valverde. For many, it was a sleepless night filled with the sound of silent desperation.

At the break of dawn each Spanish soldier was given specific instructions regarding his upcoming role in the engagement that would take place shortly after the Inca emperor and his entourage entered the plaza of Cajamarca. Francisco Pizarro inspired the troops with a rousing speech in which he reminded his men that they were soldiers who represented the might of Spain and the power of Christianity, and with the will of God almighty on their side they would either prevail or enter the kingdom of heaven as worthy warriors of the cross. The commander told his men, "Make fortresses of your hearts, for you have no other.[5] A Mass was observed to lift the spirits of the men during which Father Valverde was kept busy absolving each and every soldier for all his past sins.

The large plaza at Cajamarca was enclosed on three sides by buildings, each of which were nearly 200 yards long, that offered convenient hiding places for the Spanish soldiers. It was Huayna Capac, the father of Atahualpa, who had conceived the design of this unique triangular courtyard. Hernándo de Soto and his horse soldiers hid in one stone hallway while Hernándo Pizarro and his cavaliers were concealed in another large hall. Sebastián de Benalcázar was placed in charge of a third company of hidden horsemen. Most of the infantry were divided up and stationed along the ten streets that led to the enormous square. Francisco Pizarro had 24 soldiers who were assigned to follow his direct lead. Bells were hung upon the breastplates of the horses so that during the attack they would produce a loud clanging sound that would further confuse and frighten the natives. The small cannons were placed upon a ceremonial platform known as an usnu. Each soldier was instructed to await the captain-general's signal before commencing with the attack.

A Test of Faith

Lord Atahualpa awoke later than usual on the morning that he was scheduled to meet with Francisco Pizarro at Cajamarca. His nobles urged him to hurry so that he could reach the courtyard, a distance of approximately four miles from the Inca camp, before the sun set but Atahualpa, who was famished from his now completed fast, insisted there was still time to partake of food and drink. The emperor consumed more chicha than he should have with his celebratory meal and consequently was not reasoning with a clear mind.

A noble who had spied on the Spaniards and saw that they were deployed and armed for battle, warned Atahualpa that he must make war against these invaders but the slightly inebriated Inca ruler chose to ignore such advice and honor the awaiting Francisco Pizarro with his presence before executing his own plan of action. However, Atahualpa did send a messenger to Cajamarca to announce that since Spanish soldiers felt the need to enter his camp fully armed then he too felt the need to enter the Spanish compound with warriors who were fully armed.

It was nearly midday before the royal Inca procession finally got under way. Numerous attendants went on ahead to sweep the path clean of all debris. They were followed by three separate and large groups of elegantly attired natives who sang and danced along the freshly swept road. Musicians played a melodious march with their flutes and conch shells. Atahualpa was held aloft on a magnificent litter. The platform and the poles of this royal palanquin were sheathed in gold and silver while two jewel encrusted arches held up curtains decorated with plumes of brilliantly colored macaw feathers designed to conceal the emperor from plain view of the common folk. The leisurely pace was such that numerous stops were ordered so that the ruler could rest and imbibe in even more chicha.

The Spanish soldiers, all of whom had spent several hours crouched in their cramped positions before there was any noticeable sign of movement from the Inca camp, watched from their assigned locations as Atahualpa and his lengthy parade of nobles made their way ever so slowly along the road that led to Cajamarca. Pedro Pizarro, the young page who was to be counted among those that had to endure such a long and frightful wait, recorded, "I saw many Spaniards urinate without noticing it out of pure terror."[6]

The Inca procession had advanced within a half mile of the city when the Spaniards noticed that the natives had suddenly stopped marching and were beginning to pitch camp. Atahualpa then sent a message to Francisco Pizarro stating that since the hour had grown late he would therefore delay his entrance to Cajamarca until the following morning. When Atahualpa stopped the procession and began to set up tents many of the sleep deprived Spaniards feared that the Incas were making preparations for a night attack against them. The captain-general knew that his men, all of whom were near their breaking point, could not possibly endure another long night of dreadful anticipation. Hernándo de Aldana volunteered to go by himself to carry a message to Atahualpa stating that the Spanish commander had gone to great lengths to prepare a magnificent banquet in his honor and hoped to dine with him on this day. Aldana, who apparently had an ear for languages, had picked up some of the Quecha vocabulary and felt comfortable enough to converse without the aid of an interpreter.

After a brief moment of contemplation, Atahualpa replied that he did not wish to disappoint the Spaniards and promised that he would meet with them that very evening. As both a gesture of friendship and an effort to hasten his pace, the inca declared that he would leave the majority of his army behind, while the small force of five or six thousand nobles that accompanied him would enter Cajamarca unarmed. Atahualpa was not quite as naive as many historians have portrayed him to be. The emperor, who still had designs on punishing the Spaniards for crimes committed against his people, made sure a great many of his nobles concealed small axes and slings beneath their garments. Atahualpa was well aware of the size of Pizarro's army and therefore had little reason to suspect that so few would have the audacity to attack a force of so many, even if they appeared unarmed. He also knew from his spies that many soldiers hid behind the walls that enclosed the courtyard, which he took to believe as their cowering out of fear for having beheld the imposing size of his army. Unfortunately for Atahualpa, his two best commanders, Quizquiz and Chalcuchima, were still at Cuzco. Their counsel was sorely missed, for they surely would have pointed out the folly of such a decision.

Atahualpa and his entourage of several thousand nobles continued on toward Cajamarca while the many thousands of armed warriors who remained behind carried on with the chores of setting up camp. As the Incas entered the Cajamarca courtyard, the nobles immediately fell into formation while loudly singing songs of praise to the gods and their ancestors, as well as the divine Atahualpa. They were split into two groups of equal size and positioned to the sides of the emperor and those who held his litter aloft. The royal bodyguards of the emperor wore thin sheets of gold over top their elegant wardrobe. Atahualpa entered the city expecting to be greeted by Francisco Pizarro and his men but found the large plaza filled with only his own people. Believing that the Spaniards were hiding out of fear, he cried out, "Where are the strangers?"[7] It was then that Father Vincente de Valverde, a Dominican friar, stepped out from behind the shadows with the native interpreter Martínillo.

Father Valverde carried a crucifix in one hand and in the other a Christian Bible, or according to other accounts a breviary, as he slowly approached the Inca ruler. Once in the presence of the emperor, the priest went into a long winded dissertation regarding the basic tenets of Christianity. According to Francisco de Xeres, Father Valverde proclaimed to Atahualpa, "I am a priest of God, and I teach Christians the things of God, and in like manner I come to teach you. What I teach is that which God says to us in this book. Therefore, on the part of God and of the Christians, I beseech you to be their friend, for such is God's will, and it will be for your good. Go and speak to the Governor, who waits for you."[8]

The Dominican friar also recited the requerimento to Atahualpa, required reading before the Spaniards had royal and papal approval to launch an assault against any heathen of the New World. Lord Atahualpa became noticeably irritated when it was told to him that he must not only renounce his religion and accept Jesus Christ as his savior but also recognize the Emperor Charles V as his new lord and master. Atahualpa told Father Valverde, "I will be no man's vassal. I am greater than any prince on earth. As for my religion, I will not change it. You say your God was put to death, but mine still lives."[9] A statement which he punctuated by pointing upward and toward the slowly setting sun.

Atahualpa asked to see this book that spoke of such things, and Father Valverde obliged his request by handing over his holy manuscript. The sapa inca, after quickly flipping through the pages and finding that the strange symbols it contained were of no meaning to him, threw the sacred text to the ground in disgust. Martínillo picked up the holy book and after dusting it off he handed it over to Father Valverde. Atahualpa then said to the friar, "Tell your comrades that they shall give me an account of their doing in my land. I will not go from here, till they have made me full satisfaction for all the wrongs they have committed."[10]

Annoyed by the blasphemous remarks and irreverent actions of Atahualpa, Father Valverde turned his back on the Inca ruler and quickly rejoined his comrades. The priest then went up to Francisco Pizarro and said, "Don't you see what is happening? While we are arguing with this arrogant dog the fields are filling with Indians. Set on him! I absolve you."[11]

Father Valverde had provided Francisco Pizarro with a legitimate excuse to execute the murderous plan he already had in mind. The captain-general waved a white towel, the specified signal for the firing of the cannons, which, in turn, was the signal for commencement of the full attack. Pedro de Candia fired two cannons directly into the heart of the assembled Inca crowd. Shots then rang out from all directions after which the infantry and the cavalry burst forth from the numerous entrances that allowed access to the courtyard with startling cries of "Santiago! Santiago y a ellos!" "Saint James! Saint James and at them!"

The shocked and confused Inca nobles tried as best they could to protect Atahualpa from harm but many fell quickly before the blast of the arquebus and the razor sharp edge of the Spanish sword. The grounds of the plaza was quickly stained red with blood. The thrust of the Spanish assault was directed toward the center of the crowd where Atahualpa still sat upon his royal conveyance. Francisco and twenty-four soldiers under his command charged directly at the litter that seated Lord Atahualpa. The arms and hands of the attendants who held aloft the palanquin of the revered Inca ruler were hacked off by the remorseless Spaniards. The litter and the lord of the Incas soon came tumbling down. Pizarro saw that the uncontrollable rage of his soldiers placed the life of Atahualpa in immediate peril, and fearing that such a loss would jeopardize his plans for gaining control of the empire he rushed blindly into the fray. As Francisco reached out to grab the fallen and helpless ruler, a Spanish sword sliced the commanding officer across the hand. The captain-general then cried out above the din of battle, "Let no one wound the Indian upon pain of death,"[12] and with blood-soaked hands he grabbed Atahualpa by the hair and dragged him away from the ongoing slaughter. The fallen royal borla was claimed by a soldier named Estete.

The mass killing continued even after the Inca ruler had been captured and safely locked away in a nearby building. Many natives were trampled to death by their comrades who were desperately seeking to escape the savage fury of the sudden Spanish assault. The attack had occurred with such speed and rage that the nobles never had an opportunity to raise their concealed weapons against the Spaniards. Many of those who managed to escape the courtyard by forcing an opening in one of the walls were chased down and butchered by the Spanish cavalry. The slaughter at Cajamarca continued until all except for Atahualpa had been either killed or had fled to the countryside. The massacre had lasted for but only a half hour, but in that brief space of time several thousand of the Inca nobility were slaughtered and lay strewn across the blood stained courtyard. By the time it was over the sun was beginning to set behind the mountains. The weary but jubilantly victorious Spaniards offered up thanks to God for delivering them from harm and granting them the strength to defeat such a vast horde of heathens.

The encamped warriors who had accompanied Atahualpa part of the way fled immediately after learning that their divine ruler had become a prisoner of the Spaniards. As for the Inca commander Rumiñavi, he apparently feared that Pizarro would harm Atahualpa if he launched any sort of rescue effort. Not knowing what to do, he decided to march his army back to the safe haven of Quito. According to most European accounts, the only Spaniard to suffer a wound was Francisco Pizarro. Some native accounts claim that five Spaniards died as a result of being trampled by their own horses. There even exists a Spanish claim that one of their own died that day.

After the slaughter was complete, Francisco Pizarro invited Atahualpa to dine with him. They sat down to a grand banquet inside one of the halls that overlooked the plaza that was still littered with lifeless bodies. Sobered and humbled by the experience that had so swiftly befallen him, the inca turned to Pizarro and said, "It is the way of war, to conquer or be conquered."[13]

12
The Ransom of an Empire

The Spoils of War

Following a night of wild celebration and much needed rest, the Spaniards awoke in eager anticipation of the spoils that surely awaited them at the nearby abandoned Inca camp. Francisco Pizarro told Atahualpa to command those warriors who had not deserted him to surrender their arms to the Spaniards. Some five thousand prisoners were taken in this manner and a great many of them were put to work clearing the multitude of dead bodies that still littered the courtyard. Most of those who were rounded up were later permitted to return to their homes. Such a seemingly benevolent gesture on the part of the captain-general was actually a calculated decision that played to the advantage of the conquistadors. Lacking the resources to care for such a large group of native prisoners they were freed so that they could spread the news of the Spaniards' incredible victory.

Francisco then dispatched Hernándo de Soto and thirty cavaliers to probe the site of the main Inca camp. Once there the Spaniards rounded up a great many of the concubines and servants of the Inca ruler, as well as several prominent nobles. They were all brought back to Cajamarca where they continued to serve the needs of their now imprisoned ruler as well as those of the Spaniards, the latter of which were often needs of a salacious nature. Inca servants were used to cart the many treasured items of the camp back to Cajamarca. While rummaging through the Inca camp, the soldiers happened upon the bodies of those who had been executed by order of Atahualpa for having cowered before the horse ridden by Captain de Soto.

The victorious soldiers feasted on the food of the Incas, helping themselves to the maize, potatoes, guinea pig and birds, all of which they washed down with the intoxicating chicha beverage. Another slaughter was to soon take place. The Spaniards, in an effort to satisfy their taste for meat, took to butchering the royal herds of llama that traveled in the company of the Inca. Of course the greatest find of all was the vast amounts of gold and silver items that had been left behind. The Spaniards confiscated all they could find, a bountiful haul that, to the delight of all the soldiers, weighed in at eight hundred pounds of gold and nearly 3,500 pounds of silver.

Atahualpa was imprisoned in a large room where he continued to enjoy all the trappings entitled to one possessed of such an elevated status. He was waited on hand and foot by the numerous concubines and servants who stayed at his heavily guarded quarters. He was also permitted to receive a steady stream of nobles and messengers who kept him abreast of all affairs within the empire. It was as if the royal court had simply been moved to Cajamarca.

Francisco Pizarro, who had decided to remain at Cajamarca to await the anticipated arrival of reinforcements from the coast, made it a point to visit Atahualpa at least once a day. The majority of these conversations were filtered through the trusted tongue of Felipillo, the interpreter who had warned the Spaniards of the hostile intentions of the natives at the Isle of Puná. The Spanish commander saw that even during his confinement, Atahualpa remained the absolute ruler of the Inca kingdom. No decision, not even a rescue effort, could be made without his express approval. The Spanish commander was clever enough to realize that he would be able to exert control over the Inca empire as long as he was able to control the Sapa Inca. It was during one of these visits that Pizarro noticed a skull that was trimmed in gold and when he asked Atahualpa about it the emperor replied, "It is the skull of one of my brothers who fought against me and boasted that he would drink maize beer from my head. I had him killed and it is I who drink from his."[1]

A special bond soon developed between captor and captive. Atahualpa began to look forward to the visits of Francisco and on one such occasion he proudly presented the young Quispe Cusi and said to the captain-general, " Take here my sister, my father's daughter, whom I much love."[2] Pizarro accepted the offering of the emperor's half-sister and had her christened Doña Inés Huayllas Uusta. The fifteen year old Inca princess would bless the elderly Spanish commander with a daughter, who was christened Francisca, in December of 1534. The following year she bore a son, whom the father had baptized with the name Gonzalo, the same as that of his father. Hernándo de Soto also spent many hours visiting with Atahualpa and even taught him how to play chess. Atahualpa showed that he was a quick learner by besting his teacher on several occasions.

Atahualpa possessed a keen eye and took note of the Spaniards' uncontrollable lust for any and all items crafted from either the "sweat of the sun" or the "tears of the moon." He believed that he could use their insatiable craving for precious gold and silver to buy back his freedom. The Inca ruler proposed to fill a chamber 22 feet long and 17 feet wide with gold to a height as high as he could reach. The Spaniards thought the Inca ruler was jesting, but when they realized he was serious the captain-general decided to up the ante by stating that the ransom would have to include the filling of a slightly smaller adjoining room twice over with silver. Atahualpa agreed to this request on the condition that the transported treasure would be piled in the same form as which it arrived. In other words, the Spaniards were not to break or melt any of the items in order to reduce their size. Pizarro then brought in a royal official to set down on paper the formal terms of the agreement between Atahualpa and the Spaniards. A red line measuring approximately seven feet above the floor marked the height that the roomful of riches were to reach. The Spaniards pledged not to melt down any of the objects, the bulk of which Atahualpa was counting on to fill up the chambers. Once the agreed upon amounts of gold and silver had been attained then the Spaniards were to grant the emperor his freedom.

The imprisoned sapa inca was given two months to fulfill the terms of his ransom pledge. A great many royal runners were sent out to the four corners of the empire to order the immediate transfer of all items that contained elements of gold and silver, no matter how large or small, to the town of Cajamarca. The priests at the capital city of Cuzco were faced with a difficult decision when the chasqui messengers arrived with orders to send all items made of such sacred substances. Atahualpa was a usurper but, Huascar, the man whom they considered the true ruler had been defeated and was now a prisoner. If they failed to comply with Atahualpa's request and he somehow managed to extricate himself from his present predicament, as he had done before, then there would certainly be hell to pay for not having come to his aid during his hour of need. They decided to send just enough gold to satisfy the demands of Atahualpa while secretly diverting much of the gold and silver to secret hiding places in and around Piscobamba. The secreted gold included eleven gold statues, known as chuquihuancos, cast in the likeness of previous Inca rulers.

Several weeks would pass before the first offerings of gold and silver items began to trickle into the city. Caravans of llamas and native porters came from all four cardinal points carrying on their backs the precious metals that had been demanded by the Spaniards. Pizarro and his troops marveled at the many splendid forms of gold and silver that were divided and deposited in their appropriate ransom chamber.

In the meantime, the imprisoned Huascar learned of Atahualpa's ransom offer and sent word to Francisco Pizarro that he could double any amount that his usurper half-brother pledged to raise. In a message smuggled to the captain-general, the dethroned inca offered to pay the Spaniards an even larger ransom in exchange for his freedom. He boastfully declared: "It will not be up to any line drawn on the wall, but up to the ceiling that I shall fill the room, because I know where the incalculable riches amassed by my father and all his predecessors are hidden, whereas my brother does not know this, and he is therefore reduced to stripping our temples of their ornaments in order to fulfill his promise."[3]

Atahualpa learned of Huascar's secret offer to Francisco Pizarro and, so that the Spaniards understood that there was but one true sapa inca to deal with, he issued secret orders through his messengers that his opportunistic half-brother was to be put to death. Huascar was hacked to pieces in his cell and his lifeless remains were dumped in a nearby river by obedient servants of Lord Atahualpa. The disturbing news of Huascar's brutal assassination made the captain-general realize that Atahualpa still commanded enough authority to exert his will, and demonstrated that he possessed a cold and calculating mind to achieve whatever end he so desired.

The death of Huascar also fueled rumors among the Spanish soldiers that the imprisoned ruler was using his messengers to coordinate an Inca uprising. To convince his captors that he was not plotting against them, Atahualpa urged Pizarro to send some of his men out into his empire to see for themselves that no armies were massing. He informed the captain-general that his subjects could not act upon such a plan without his express permission, and he emphasized that he had never issued such a directive. Francisco decided he would test the truthfulness of Atahualpa's words by sending out two expeditions, one of which was dispatched toward the capital city of Cuzco while a second group embarked for the town of Huamachucho. Both expeditions were expected to obtain any and all intelligence about native movements and determine if the people were complying with the terms of the Spaniards' ransom demands. They were also instructed to return with as much treasure as they possibly could carry.

In Search of Greater Wealth

Frustrated that the wealth of the empire was not flowing into Cajamarca fast enough, Francisco Pizarro sent three of his men to Cuzco, a journey of roughly six hundred miles, to make sure that all of the precious metals, especially the seven hundred gold plates said to adorn the sacred Temple of the

Sun, had been removed and were on their way. Martín Bueno, an officer, Pedro de Moguer and Juan de Zárate, regular soldiers, were transported along the Inca highway in the comfort of luxurious litters provided by the gracious Atahualpa. Once inside the city, the Spaniards were greeted by Quizquiz, the general who was in command of the city. The Inca commander, who had yet to receive confirmation of Atahualpa's rumored predicament, followed the explicit instructions of the sapa inca to show these three Spaniards every possible courtesy and to respect their every wish. He provided Pizarro's emissaries with lodging, food, and drink, after which he gave them a tour of the city and the Coricancha, the golden enclosure where the holy temples stood.

The citizens of Cuzco were unaware of the fact that Lord Huascar was already dead. when Moguer, Bueno, Zárate, and the black slave who accompanied them arrived. Many saw the Spaniards as potential liberators of the usurping army of Atahualpa. The three soldiers, who were carted around on litters, as if they were true sons of the sun, were treated royally by all they came in contact with: Moguer, Bueno, and Zárate, men of minor rank, certainly relished being revered as if they were deified lords. But these three emissaries were hardly worthy of such adulation. They continually mocked the Incas and showed no respect toward them or their customs. Their coarse manner left the Incas with many doubts about the character of these men who came from across the sea.

Quizquiz could not help but notice that these men were mostly interested in those sites which displayed prominent amounts of gold and silver. The three Spaniards stood in awe of the golden Temple of the Sun and marveled at the many Inca mummies who sat upon gold leaf thrones. Though these three, at first, showed great respect toward the sanctity of the Coricancha, their behavior toward the Chosen Women who cared for the temples was clearly less admirable. All three reportedly raped a great many cloistered women, known as mamaconas, during their rather lengthy stay at Cuzco. When the soldiers took to corrupting the respected women of the temple many of the natives changed their reverent view of the Spaniards, concluding that they were loathsome demons who needed to be cast out.

The Inca general was powerless to countermand the sacrilegious order of the three Spaniards that every sheet of gold was to be stripped from the Temple of the Sun. Refusing to participate in the desecration of their sacred temple, the horrified citizens of Cuzco were compelled to watch as the Spaniards pried off all seven hundred thin plates, each of which measured approximately one foot in width and weighed slightly more than four pounds, with crowbars made of copper. After nearly a fortnight of raping and pillaging, the three soldiers were ready to return to Cajamarca. They brought with them a tremendous haul of confiscated silver and two hundred cargos of plundered gold, the weight of which was borne entirely on the backs of 255 llamas and a great many native porters.

After the Spaniards left, Quizquiz told the nobles in his company, "It seems to me they are not gods because they do not know how to speak our language, or how to eat our food properly, as we do. In the houses of the Sun they threw a rock at a golden pitcher that belongs to the Sun's service. Without a doubt they are not gods. Nor has our lord Atahualpa explained to us who they are. I do not know why he did not send somebody with them to explain to us who they were."[4]

The answers to Quizquiz's many concerns arrived ten days after the departure of the three Spaniards. A messenger dispatched by Lord Atahualpa informed the general that he had been kidnapped by Francisco Pizarro, the leader of the three vulgar soldiers who came to Cuzco, and that the gold and silver was part of the ransom demand required for his release. The citizens of Cuzco would learn from this messenger that Huascar had been executed by order of the imprisoned Atahualpa. Quizquiz began preparing the army for battle and ordered much of the remaining gold and silver to be removed at once and hidden in secret locations known to only a select few.

On January 14, 1533, Hernándo Pizarro departed Cajamarca at the head of a force of twenty horsemen, including his half-brothers Juan and Gonzalo, and a dozen foot soldiers. Their destination was the nearby town of Huamachucho, a location where the Inca army was supposedly gathering for a surprise assault against the Spanish army. Finding no evidence of a potential native uprising, Hernándo dispatched a message to his brother that all appeared quiet on this frontier of the empire. Francisco, who had recently learned of a great treasure that was purportedly housed at the temple of Pachacamac, responded with instructions for Hernándo and his men to continue on to the sacred town located near the coast, some four hundred miles away.

For the next thirty days, Hernándo and his men marched along the Inca highway, a route that took them over many mountains and deposited them at seventeen towns along the way. The Spaniards entered the sacred city of Pachacamac unopposed and, against the wishes of the local native priests, they immediately made their way to the holy temple. A sudden and powerful tremor shook the ground at the very moment the conquistadors began to make their way up the hallowed shrine. Convinced that their god was angered and about to destroy his own temple, the priests ceased with their attempts to stop the Spaniards and quickly ran for cover. The conquistadors, however, were not about to let an earthquake stand between them and the fortune they so eagerly sought. The fearless Spaniards forced open the temple door which they hoped would reveal a room full of wealth but were sorely disappointed by what little they saw. There was no vast treasure trove of gold and silver objects to plunder. Other than some evidence of animal sacrifices the only item they found was a wooden idol that represented the god Pachacamac, which to the righteous Spaniards appeared to posses an image of demonic nature. A frustrated Hernándo ordered the statue dragged out into the open and there, before an assembly of horrified onlookers, he ordered it smashed to pieces. The holy temple was thoroughly cleansed and a proper Christian cross was erected for the benefit of the heathens.

Unbeknownst to Hernándo Pizarro, the priests of Pachacamac had advance warning of the Spaniards approach and, knowing of their insatiable lust for silver and gold, they had their temples and dwellings stripped bare of any religious artifact that contained such enticing metallic elements. Pizarro and his troops still failed to appreciate just how quickly news traveled in this remote part of the world. The priests of Pachacamac had already learned of the ransom offer of Atahualpa and messengers had recently brought news of how three wicked Spaniards had stripped gold and silver from the sacred temple at Cuzco and molested many of the Chosen Women who cared for the holy shrines. Fearing the damage that an even larger Spanish force could do, the priest sent the virgin mamaconas into hiding. The precious metals were then secretly stored away from the city or buried deep beneath the ground. A token amount of precious metals was left in the hope that it would be sufficient enough to appease the Spaniards, which, of course, it wasn't. Hernándo managed to recover an estimated 80,000 pesos worth of valuables but that represented only a small fraction of the wealth that previously adorned the city.

While at Pachacamac, Hernándo learned that the Inca general Chalcuchima was camped at the town of Jauja with an army of some 35,000 warriors. According to Miguel de Estete: "The town of Xauxa (Jauja) is very large. It is situated in a beautiful valley, and enjoys a temperate climate. A very large river flows near the town. The land is fertile. The town and district are very populous, and the Spaniards saw one hundred thousand people assemble every day in the principal square. The market places and streets were also crowded. There were men whose duty it was to count all these people, and to know who came in for the service of the troops; and other men had to watch and take note of all who entered the town."

Pizarro and his men scaled the mountains once again to reach the village that was roughly one hundred miles to the east of Pachacamac. Ever since Atahualpa's capture at Cajamarca, Chalcuchima had been uncertain as to what course of action he should take. Upon their arrival at the town of Jauja,

Hernándo Pizarro and his men were greeted by the ghastly sight of row upon row of bloodied lances displaying the impaled and rotting body parts of Huascar's defeated army. An undaunted Hernándo sent a message to the nearby Inca camp requesting that the two commanders meet in private. Chalcuchima agreed to Hernándo's request and at the ensuing conference he was told that Atahualpa greatly desired his presence at Cajamarca. Believing that Pizarro spoke the truth, the Inca general abandoned his troops and elected to travel in the company of the Spaniards. Chalcuchima was permitted to travel in the comfort of a litter that was supported by many attendants. The Inca general was compelled to pay a steep price for the privilege of being escorted by the Spaniards: five thousand pesos of gold and enough silver to shoe the hooves of the horses. Hernándo chose to follow a different route back to Cajamarca, a path that took them 54 days to complete, during which time they stopped to inspect the belongings of 22 towns. At the town of Bombón the Spaniards were fortunate to find and confiscate gold items valued at five thousand pesos.

The Execution of Atahualpa

During the time when Francisco Pizarro was making his way to Tumbes, Diego de Almagro was busy making last minute preparations to join up with his partner. The gold and silver that Pizarro had sent back to Panama helped him to procure another six ships which, besides transporting an additional 150 recruits and 84 horses, hauled an assortment of essential supplies and weapons for continuing with the conquest of the Inca empire. Bartolomé Ruiz was among those who returned to Peru with Almagro.

When Almagro arrived at the Bay of San Mateo he was delighted to see his expedition reinforced with the unexpected arrival of a ship from Nicaragua, captained by Francisco de Godoy, which carried several soldiers of fortune eager to join in the campaign. At this point, Almagro led many of the soldiers on a march by land while the ships went on ahead in a concerted effort to locate Francisco Pizarro and his troops. Almagro was now forced to suffer many of the deprivations experienced on so many occasions by his partner: a lack of food and decent drinking water, and an inhospitable terrain and climate. The commander would lose thirty men during this long and difficult march.

One of Almagro's ships soon reached Tumbes where it was quickly met by a fleet of several hundred balsas. The Spaniards feared they were about to come under attack but were relieved to see that this was simply a welcoming party. Seeing the damage that had been done to the city of Tumbes many soldiers were now eager to abandon this mission and return to Panama. That opinion changed the moment they learned from the few Spaniards who had remained at Tumbes that Francisco Pizarro had succeeded in capturing Atahualpa, the supreme Inca. All were suddenly anxious to resume the march in order that they might join up with their victorious comrades. Shortly thereafter, all of the members of Almagro's party were reunited at Tumbes.

Diego de Almagro and his troops finally reached San Miguel in December of 1532. After learning more about the incredible success of their comrades from those stationed at the Spanish settlement, Almagro and his men continued on along the same route paved by Francisco Pizarro and his soldiers. While on the way to Cajamarca, Almagro learned that his secretary, Rodrigo Pérez, was writing letters which, for reasons known only to him, were intended to stir up trouble between the two partners. He had the secretary tortured until he finally confessed to his malevolent act after which Almagro sentenced him to be hung from the highest mast of the docked ships until pronounced dead.

Almagro and his troops marched to Cajamarca uncontested. With Atahualpa a prisoner the people were afraid that any transgression against the Spaniards would bring undue harm to the sapa inca. Diego made sure his men were on their best behavior so that they would not disrupt the fragile peace that presently existed. Depending on which account you believe, Almagro and his force of 153 soldiers and fifty horses arrived at Cajamarca in either February or April of 1533. We do know that he was reunited with his partner shortly before the expeditions to Cuzco and Pachacamac had returned.

All past differences were forgotten when Francisco Pizarro and Diego de Almagro embraced. They reveled, for the moment, in the long overdue success of their quest, a mission once dubbed as the Company of Lunatics by skeptical settlers back at Panama. The still imprisoned Atahualpa, however, was surely discouraged by the sight of even more Spaniards coming to the aid of his captor. The new Spanish recruits were utterly bedazzled by the sight of all the gold and silver that had been collected so far and amazed to learn that even more was on the way. On a more somber note, Almagro brought with him the mournful news that their faithful partner, Hernándo de Luque, had succumbed to an illness shortly before his departure from Panama.

Hernándo Pizarro rejoined his brother at Cajamarca after an absence of nearly three months. The capture of the renowned Inca commander Chalcuchima greatly outweighed what treasure he and his men had confiscated on their expedition to the holy city of Pachacamac. Hernándo, who possessed a temperament that would not permit him to let bygones be bygones, refused to even speak to Almagro upon his return. Such dissension did not escape the notice of Francisco, who, for the benefit of the greater cause, compelled his brother to meet with Almagro, and from this meeting a promise was extracted from both parties to act civil toward one another. Hernándo and Diego Almagro concealed their intense dislike for one another for the benefit of the mission. It would prove to be but a momentary truce between these two proud conquistadors.

The captured Inca general, was brought before Atahualpa. Even Chalcuchima, a mighty warrior who had conquered many lands for the Inca ruler, bore a small load on his back designed to humble his presence before the magnificent son of the sun. The Inca commander, who was always considered one of Atahualpa's favorites, was greatly disappointed by the cold reception he received. The imprisoned sapa inca showed absolutely no emotion over the sudden and unexpected appearance of one of his generals. It was then that it finally dawned on Chalcuchima that he had been deceived by the cunning Hernándo Pizarro. The Inca general was later imprisoned and subjected to countless rounds of interrogations — inquisitions that were both verbally and physically abusive to the extreme. Hernándo de Soto attempted to extract information from the Inca commander regarding the whereabouts of gold rumored to be hidden near the city. He partially burned the legs of a tied up Chalcuchima but never did acquire the information he desired so greatly, nor did he ever show any remorse for his actions.

Shortly thereafter, Pedro de Moguer, Martín Bueno, and Juan de Zárate, the three Spaniards sent to Cuzco, returned with a large caravan of llamas and native porters that transported a large quantity of silver and gold items to be added to the mounting pile of precious metals that were expected to buy Atahualpa his freedom. The soldiers were amazed by the returning envoys tale of a city filled with many golden delights, and the seven hundred gold plates they brought with them certainly seemed to confirm the validity of such a fantastic report. Of course many of these stories grew grander with each retelling. The golden garden of the Coricancha was a myth that grew from the imaginations of the Spaniards who had seen intricately detailed garden replicas of corn cobs complete with stalks and leaves that were brought out during festivals honoring the gods. This evolved into a story of a golden garden complete with maize, trees, llamas, insects, birds, and grass all of which were made from the "sweat of the sun."

Garcilaso de la Vega, a mestizo who carried the name of his conquistador father, recorded the remembered tales of his Inca ancestors in *The Royal Commentaries of the Indies*, an informative but overly subjective and highly imaginative historical account written nearly seventy years after the Spanish conquest of Peru. His following description of the magnificence of the gardens of the sapa inca became an indelible figment of European imagination:

"Here were planted the finest trees and the most beautiful flowers in the kingdom, while quantities of others were reproduced in gold and silver, at every stage of their growth, from the sprout that hardly shows above the earth, to the full-blown plant in complete maturity. There were also fields of corn with silver stalks and gold ears, on which the leaves, grains, and even the corn silk were shown. In addition to all this, there were all kinds of gold and silver animals in these gardens, such as rabbits, mice, lizards, snakes, butterflies, foxes, and wildcats. Then there were birds set in the trees, as though they were about to sing, and others bent over flowers, breathing in their nectar. There were roe deer and deer, lions and tigers, all the animals in creation, in fact, each placed just where it should be."[5]

To the relief of Francisco Pizarro and his army, both of the expeditions reported that they saw no signs of any planned Inca uprising against the Spaniards. However, Pizarro could see that the sight of so much gold and silver was beginning to wear away at the patience of his troops, all of whom were eager to lay their hands on a share of this grand treasure. Guards had been posted to watch night and day over the steadily growing ransom of Atahualpa but with the arrival of Almagro's reinforcements and news that more precious metal was on the way the captain-general feared that temptation was simply becoming to difficult to control. Even though the amassed treasure had not quite reached the agreed upon line, the captain-general declared that the ransom was officially paid in full and would be melted down at once so it could be divided into shares.

At this point it was decided that Emperor Charles V needed to be informed of all that they had already accomplished. Hernándo Pizarro, the conquistador deemed to be the best qualified to appear before the royal court, was selected to return to Spain in order to provide a full account of the conquest and to present the obligatory quinto, a royal fifth tribute equivalent to one hundred thousand gold pesos. Another factor that played a part in Francisco's choice of Hernándo as his bearer of these glad tidings was recognition of the fact that there still existed a great deal of animosity between his beloved brother and his longtime partner.

A splendid array of gold and silver items that exhibited the most outstanding native craftsmanship were spared from the fires of the furnace. They were sent to the emperor so that he could have the opportunity to admire the many works of splendor that his new vassals were capable of producing. Hernándo would return to Spain in the company of several soldiers who wished to come home to enjoy the rewards that their newfound wealth could afford them. Cristóbal de Mena, a good friend of Diego de Almagro, was one of the men who asked for and received permission to return to Spain. Fearing that Hernándo might not speak honorably of him, Almagro asked Cristóbal de Mena to make sure his good name was not sullied at the royal court. Almagro secretly hoped that would be the last he ever saw of Hernándo Pizarro.

A heated dispute arose over the division of the spoils when Francisco Pizarro announced that since Diego de Almagro and his men had not risked their lives in the capture of Atahualpa they therefore were not entitled to a share of the ransom, only to a stake of future shares of acquired wealth. Almagro felt that he and his men were entitled to a fair share of the treasure on the grounds that they had faced an arduous journey of their own to aid Pizarro and to supply him with additional fire and manpower to complete the conquest of the empire. After much discussion, Pizarro and Almagro reached a compromise which allowed the latter to receive a small but unspecified amount of the ransom. Seeing as to how it was agreed that all would be entitled to a share in the spoils that awaited at Cuzco and other towns, Almagro and his men were therefore eager for an expedited closure on the existing ransom arrangement.

Shortly after Hernándo Pizarro left for Spain the conquistadors took to melting down the huge ransom of Atahualpa into measurable ingots. As many as sixty native goldsmiths toiled day and night over nine blazing furnaces to melt down the great store of silver and gold that had been accumulated at Cajamarca. An estimated 13,000 pounds of gold and 26,000 pounds of silver had streamed into Cajamarca to pay for Atahualpa's freedom, a portion of which had trickled in after the ransom had been declared paid in full. Cups, dishes, jewelry, figurines, the gold plates torn from the Temple of the Sun, and other items made of earth's most precious metals were thrown into the raging fires so they could be cast into bars of equal value. This was truly one of the greatest hauls of treasure ever obtained by a conquering army, especially for one as small as this bold band of Spaniards.

Francisco Pizarro awarded himself a hefty sum of 57,722 pesos of gold and 2,350 marks of silver. He also laid claim to the confiscated gold throne of the Inca. Hernándo Pizarro was paid 31,080 pesos of gold and 2,350 marks of silver. Hernándo de Soto received 17,740 pesos of gold and 724 marks of silver. The horse soldiers were granted 8,880 pesos of gold and 362 marks of silver. Most of the infantry received 4,440 pesos of gold and 180 marks of silver. The captain-general set aside 2,220 pesos of gold for the building of the Church of San Francisco, the first Christian temple to be constructed in Peru by the Spaniards. A mere 20,000 pesos of gold was given to Diego de Almagro to divide amongst himself and his troops. The soldiers at San Miguel received a meager total of 15,000 pesos. A vow of poverty forbade Father

Valverde from sharing in the ransom of Atahualpa — he measured his wealth by the number of heathen souls he was able to convert to Christianity.

Lord Atahualpa demanded his freedom once the ransom had been declared paid in full, but Pizarro kept him a prisoner until he could decide how best to handle such a delicate matter. Even the soldiers were concerned about what might happen once the kidnapped ruler was released: once free, would he rally his people to avenge the massacre of the Inca nobles? The debate over the fate of the sapa inca continued while he remained confined to his cell. Some thought he should be sent back to Spain, while there were a few who believed he should be put to death at once. Others felt that as a prisoner, the Inca ruler could serve them equally well as both a human shield against native stirrings of discontent and a puppet ruler who would allow them to wield power over the entire empire. There were a number of honorable soldiers who believed that the captain-general should stick to the terms of the original agreement, which clearly called for the release of the emperor. Hernándo de Soto was the most prominent member of the faction who called upon Francisco to give Atahualpa his due freedom. Pizarro had much to consider but, thanks to the intrigue of his trusted interpreter, a course of action was soon decided upon.

The brash Felipillo had developed an attraction for one of Atahualpa's favorite concubines, a beautiful young woman by the name of Sancta. The sly and salacious glances that the interpreter cast toward Sancta had not gone unnoticed by the emperor. Over time, Felipillo's lustful desires got in the way of his better judgment and he forced himself upon the royal concubine. Atahualpa caught him in the act and said, "Evil yinga dog, and with my wife. It truly appears I am a prisoner. If I were not, you know I would exact such a punishment that no knowledge would remain of you and your lineage and all those of your nation."[6]

Felipillo knew that he had committed an unforgivable offense that under Inca law warranted his being put to death. To save himself from such a terrible fate, the interpreter did everything he could to make sure the emperor would never be in a position to pass judgment upon him. Noticing how susceptible the Spaniards were to even the slightest rumor, Felipillo played on the Spaniards fear that the Incas were preparing an attack by telling Francisco Pizarro that native commanders were busily gathering warriors in the south lands. The captain-general had placed great trust in the words of this interpreter ever since he had warned him of the treacherous plans of the natives at the Isle of Puná. That same trusted interpreter now claimed there were already two hundred thousand warriors, thirty thousand of whom were said to be Palta cannibals who were eager to dine on the flesh of the Spaniards, massing for a full scale attack upon Cajamarca.

Concerned by the ominous tone of this report presented by Felipillo, Francisco Pizarro had Chalcuchima interrogated, but the Inca general refused to lend credence to such gossip. He then questioned Atahualpa who also said that these were rumors without any basis of fact. Even though his two previous reconnaissance missions and Almagro's expedition had seen no evidence of any emerging native uprising, Pizarro decided he could not afford to take any chances. The troops were placed on full alert and sentries were posted. Hernándo de Soto and a small detachment of men were sent to Huamachucho, the town already visited by Hernándo Pizarro, to determine if the natives were massing there as claimed by Felipillo. Pizarro now had it in his mind to do away with the threat that Atahualpa posed, which meant the emperor would have to die.

One night, while still a prisoner at Cajamarca, Atahualpa peered up at the heavens and saw a comet streaking across the night sky, an ominous sign similar to that which had been witnessed by his father shortly before he passed away. The Inca ruler was convinced that a similar fate now awaited him.

The trial of Atahualpa took place almost immediately after the departure of Hernándo de Soto, one of the imprisoned Inca ruler's staunchest Spanish defenders. Pizarro and Almagro were the judges at the secret hearing that tried a conspicuously absent defendant. The Inca ruler was charged with a dozen trumped up crimes, the most notable of which claimed he committed incest and polygamy; was an idolater as well as a usurper; and that he had secretly ordered the execution of Huascar, his imprisoned half-brother. The treacherous Felipillo served as interpreter for the native witnesses compelled to testify. There were twelve Spanish officers who objected to the unjust proceedings but they were overruled by their superior officers. Atahualpa was found guilty on all counts and sentenced to die for his many crimes.

Most of the soldiers who wished to see the Inca ruler put to death were those who had arrived under the command of Diego de Almagro. It seemed to them that as long as Atahualpa remained alive they would never be able to share equally in the treasures of this land. Father Valverde agreed with the verdict and gave his blessing to the grisly sentence of death by fire rendered against the heathen ruler. When told of the verdict, Atahualpa said to Pizarro, "What have I done, or my children, that I should meet such a fate? And from your hands, too, you, who have met with friendship and kindness from my people, with whom I have shared my treasures, who have received nothing but benefits from my hands!"[7] Realizing that his fate was sealed, Atahualpa asked Francisco Pizarro to take care of his beloved sons and daughter still residing at Quito. Pizarro made a promise to the condemned ruler that he failed to keep.

The death sentence of Atahualpa (courtesy Library of Congress).

Shortly after sundown on a summer evening that some historians have reported as being the date of August 29, 1533, but which more likely than not occurred several weeks earlier, Atahualpa was escorted by Friar Valverde from his chamber cell to the same courtyard where he had been taken prisoner some nine months earlier. His hands and feet were bound by heavy chains that rattled as he shuffled past a horde of Spanish and native onlookers. The humbled Inca ruler was tied to a stake surrounded by bundles of twigs that were to be ignited in order to carry out the fiery sentence imposed by the Spaniards. Death by burning would deny the son of the sun his god given right of immortality. The rites of passage between the realm of earth and the heavens above specified that his mortal body had to be mummified. The Dominican friar promised Atahualpa that he could be executed in a less gruesome manner, one in which his flesh would not be consumed by flames, if he agreed to convert to the faith of the Spaniards. To avoid eternal damnation, the condemned emperor accepted Valverde's offer to become a Christian. Agreeing to save his soul by converting to the faith of his oppressors was the only way Atahualpa could save his body so that it could be preserved for the day that his soul would return to earth.

Immediately after being administered the rites of baptism and christened as Juan de Atahualpa, the sapa inca was slowly and painfully garroted by a Canari warrior who twisted the rope until his life was extinguished. After being pronounced dead, the inca was left sitting on his stool, his slumped carcass held in place by ropes secured to the stake. A collective sigh of sorrow rang out from those who watched the Inca ruler die. A great many wives and concubines, including Sancta, committed suicide shortly thereafter so that they could continue to serve the needs of the emperor in the hereafter. In death as in life, Atahualpa was deceived by his captors. A portion of his body was burned along with his clothes and instead of handing his remains over to the followers of the Inca so that he could be preserved and interred in the prescribed sacred manner, he was, come the following morning, buried beneath the grounds at Cajamarca. Several days later, however, his body disappeared from its grave — removed by loyal subjects who hid and cared for his remains that were now mummified in the proper manner.

Hernándo de Soto returned from his mission to learn of the state of native unrest of which he found no evidence — two days after the execution of Atahualpa. The captain confronted Francisco Pizarro and demanded to know why he had not sent the prisoner back to Spain to be judged by the emperor or, at the very least, had him exiled to Panama to end the threat he supposedly posed. Francisco blamed the decision to execute the emperor on his officers, but those same officers laid the blame squarely at the feet of the captain-general.

News of Atahualpa's demise spread quickly throughout the land. Now that the emperor was dead there was no longer a need to continue paying the ransom, and just as quickly the gold and silver that was earmarked for Cajamarca ceased to arrive. Much of the gold and silver of the Incas was then hidden in order to keep it from the clutches of the greedy Spaniards.

13
Laying Claim to Cuzco

The March to Cuzco

Three of Huascar's brothers were being held prisoner at Cajamarca when the Spaniards first arrived, two of whom were ordered to be executed by a vengeful Lord Atahualpa. A third brother, Tupac Huallpa, who is sometimes mistakenly referred to as Toparca, was crowned as the new sapa inca by Francisco Pizarro immediately following the execution of the imprisoned emperor. Tupac Huallpa's coronation at Cajamarca was performed before the approving eyes of a great many local chiefs who had been summoned to the elaborate ceremony put on for the benefit of all concerned parties. Most in attendance saw Tupac Huallpa as the legitimate heir to the throne while the captain general merely saw him as a convenient means to wield control over the entire Inca empire.

Francisco Pizarro and his troops were now eager to lay claim to the tremendous store of wealth said to await them at the capital city of Cuzco. The most impatient of these soldiers were certainly those who served directly under Diego de Almagro. Their late arrival at Cajamarca had deprived them of an equal share of Atahualpa's ransom, but now that the Inca ruler was dead and buried they could share equally in the wealth that existed at Cuzco and all the other towns subject to the rule of the Incas. The victorious Spaniards set out for the Inca city of Cuzco in August of 1533. They were accompanied by the puppet ruler Tupac Huallpa, his sister-wife Azarpay, and the Inca general Chalcuchima, all of whom were transported in the cushioned comfort of royal litters.

The execution of Atahualpa had won for the Spaniards the immediate support of the large portion of the empire that had been ruled by Huascar. Because of this, the Spaniards were well received at most of the towns residing along the path leading to Cuzco. They did, however, encounter armed resistance at the town of Jauja from an Inca force led by Mayta Yupanqui, another of Atahualpa's loyal commanders. However, thanks mostly to the natives' terrible fear of the horse and the superiority of Spanish weaponry, the conquistadors were, after much effort, able to break the ranks of the native warriors. The Spaniards gave chase to the fleeing Incas and killed a great many even after the battle had clearly been won. After routing the Quito army that opposed them, Pizarro decided to spend a fortnight at Jauja to provide his men with a much needed and well deserved rest. He also wanted to give the slower moving baggage train led by Alonso de Riquelme an opportunity to catch up with them. During their stay at Jauja, a town much larger than Cajamarca, the Spaniards were treated well and the captain-general reciprocated by making sure his men remained on their best behavior.

An irate Francisco Pizarro was convinced that Chalcuchima was responsible for this sudden uprising. The Inca general denied any responsibility, but the captain-general was unconvinced of his innocence and ordered the prisoner to be shackled and placed under constant and heavy guard. The most devastating loss at Jauja was the sudden and inexplicable passing of Tupac Huallpa, whose death occurred shortly after the arrival of Alonso de Riquelme, the treasurer who brought much needed provisions to continue with the completion of the conquest as well as the immense treasure obtained at Cajamarca. Blame for the inca's untimely demise, which was thought to be a case of intentional poisoning, was placed squarely at the feet of Chalcuchima. News of the murder of Huaritico, an Inca prince that Pizarro had sent on ahead to Cuzco to announce their arrival, by troops loyal to Atahualpa merely added to the mounting woes of the imprisoned Inca general.

Francisco and his men continued on to the valley of Jaquijahuana. Here, just fifteen miles shy of their intended destination, they halted so that Chalcuchima could be formally tried for the death of Inca Tupac Huallpa and for inciting the natives to take up arms against the Spaniards. Chalcuchima's fate was a foregone conclusion: he was found guilty and sentenced to be burned alive for his many alleged crimes. The native commander was immediately tied to a hastily planted stake and offered the opportunity to save his soul by accepting Christ as his savior. He staunchly refused to be baptized and prayed aloud to Viracocha, the god of creation, as his body was slowly and painfully consumed by flames.

While Chalcuchima was being judged at Jaquijahuana, Hernándo de Soto was off on yet another reconnaissance mission, this time with sixty mounted soldiers to make sure the path ahead was clear of any obstacles. They soon discovered that the natives had attempted to bar the way by placing large boulders and fallen trees in the road. Shortly after crossing the Apurímac River, Hernándo and his men reached the mountain called Vilcaconga where they were waylaid by a reorganized force of several thousand warriors under the command of Mayta Yupanqui. To escape certain death, the conquistadors had to ride as fast as they could through the ranks of the enemy. Once Hernándo reached the high ground he ordered his men to turn and counterattack the native warriors who were still in dogged pursuit. Not a single soldier or horse emerged unscathed from the fierce encounter that followed. At least five Spanish soldiers were killed during this fierce confrontation and all of the horses suffered from exhaustion brought on by the heat of battle and the treacherous terrain. Though the Peruvians suffered far more losses, the Spaniards, however, could not afford the loss of any more men. With night fast approaching, Hernándo decided to have his soldiers retreat to safer ground in the hope that a good night's rest would restore the strength of his men and horses for the next engagement. A messenger was dispatched to make the main force aware of their dilemma and to urge them to come to their aid. Luckily, Diego de Almagro arrived in the nick of time with the remaining cavalry and this combined force proved strong enough to drive the natives back into the mountains.

The native resistance encountered by the Spaniards at Vilcaconga were the remnants of the army that had fled Cajamarca following the capture of Atahualpa. The army of Quito was attempting to join forces with the warriors stationed at Cuzco in an attempt to prevent the conquistadors from claiming the city they had only recently conquered. In order to feed themselves, the Quito warriors sacked and pillaged any village they came upon, and then, in an effort to deprive the advancing Spaniards of food and shelter, they torched all of the buildings, including the royal storehouses. The Inca army also destroyed numerous suspension bridges and several aqueducts during their retreat from Jauja. Such destructive acts resulted in the afflicted natives of this region extending a warm welcome to the Spaniards, whom they saw as their redeeming saviors.

Shortly after the execution of Chalcuchima a common looking native strode into the Spanish camp and proclaimed that he was Manco, son of Huayna Capac, half-brother of Huascar, and thus the rightful heir to the vacant Inca throne. The prince was around twenty years old at that time and had spent the last several weeks of his young life doing his best to evade capture from the hands of Atahualpa's vindictive warriors. Manco requested the help of the Spaniards in securing his claim to the throne. Francisco Pizarro granted him his wish, while brazenly claiming that he had come to this land to overthrow and punish the usurper Atahualpa. The crafty captain-general knew that by installing Manco as the new sapa inca the Spaniards would be perceived by many as the liberators of Cuzco.

The Puppet Inca

The Spanish soldiers encountered a minor ambush on their last leg to Cuzco but it proved to be of little consequence. As they neared the city of Cuzco the Spaniards saw the numerous rotting corpses of those who had the misfortune of being related to Huascar or who were concubines of the emperor still hanging from the poles where they were placed by the victorious army of Atahualpa. Tens of thousand of Quizquiz's warriors came out to bar the way of the advance Spanish force that was under the command of Hernándo de Soto. The resolute Spanish captain led the cry of "Santiago" and the determined Spaniards who followed him attacked the host of natives who meant to do them harm. They were soon joined by the main force under the command of Francisco Pizarro and Diego de Almagro. The battle raged until nightfall, at which point, Quizquiz and his warriors withdrew to higher ground. Following the retreat of Quizquiz's army, many Inca lords of Cuzco came out to greet and welcome the Spaniards as their liberators.

With Manco Inca by their side, Francisco Pizarro and his army paraded triumphantly into the city on the 15th of November 1533. The natives filled the streets to catch a glimpse of these mighty warriors from across the sea who had helped rid Cuzco of the invading warriors from Quito. In a grand coronation ceremony witnessed by nearly every citizen of Cuzco, Francisco Pizarro placed the royal borla upon the head of Manco to officially crown him as the new sapa inca. Manco had for himself a meager sized home, a small entourage of servants, and the illusion of supreme power. Everything else, the palaces, the lands, the herds of llamas, and the precious metals belonged to the Spaniards. The captain-general claimed the magnificent Casana palace, built by Apu Cinchi Roca to honor his brother Huayna Capac, for himself, which purportedly contained a courtyard that could comfortably house 3,000 people. Meanwhile, Father Valverde went to work claiming the souls of the natives by systematically converting them to the one true faith of Christianity.

Francisco Pizarro imposed a ban on all individual looting but the temptations of so much valuable gold, silver, and precious stones, all of which seemed to be present everywhere, were simply too great to keep under control. The rape of Cuzco continued unabated throughout the day and the night, the soldiers' barbaric behavior fueled by the intoxicating effects of the chicha which they consumed with reckless abandon. Graves were robbed, temples were plundered, houses were looted, and sacred mummies were relieved of all their earthly valuables. Bands of conquistadors went from house to house and temple to temple pillaging anything of value. The conquista-

Pizarro's entry into Cuzco (courtesy Library of Congress).

dors wasted little time stripping the city of its many valuable possessions. The enclosed temple of the Coricancha, which housed subsidiary shrines dedicated to the celestial bodies that governed the universe, were sacked of all their remaining precious metals and jewels, after which the soldiers turned their attention to the palaces of the nobles. After having desecrated the sacred Coricancha, the zealous Spaniards transformed it into a Christian Church — the Church of Santo Domingo, which was built upon the solid stone foundations of the sacred Inca temple.

The royal palace of Huayna Capac had not been disturbed during the ransom of Atahualpa and therefore it yielded a tremendous amount of treasure for this covetous cast of conquistadors. Tombs were pried open to plunder any and all valuable offerings. The finding of such abundant amounts of wealth simply fueled Spanish desire for more treasure. Convinced that there were even more valuables buried away, the Spaniards had many poor souls tortured in order to learn the whereabouts of additional hidden stores of precious metals and other items of value. These painful extractions ultimately yielded many more incredible finds. At a nearby cave they located a fairly large cache of hidden delights: animal figurines cut in gold and vases made of the same valuable substance. They also found twelve life size statues, some made of pure silver, the rest of fine gold.

The citizens of Cuzco took care to hide the sacred mummies of their ruling Inca ancestors prior to the Spaniards taking control of the city. In fact, the mummies of the deceased Inca rulers were so secretly hidden that they remained beyond the grasp of the ever searching Spaniards until the year 1559. The ceaseless search for the mallquis, the mummified bodies of the Inca nobility, turned the conquistadors into unrepentant grave robbers. No burial site was left unturned and any worthy possessions, such as gold or silver ornaments, that were laid to rest with a corpse were stripped away in order to line their own pockets. Such ghoulish behavior yielded the Spaniards a significant amount of gold and silver which, consequently, encouraged even more similar atrocities. Such illicit dissections led to the destruction of a great many mummified remains which, to the Incas, meant that the souls of the dead had also been robbed of their opportunity to return again to earth.

The gold and silver collected at Cuzco amounted to nearly half the ransom haul obtained at Cajamarca, which itself consisted of a great quantity of the precious metal sent from Cuzco to pay for the release of Atahualpa. Added to this pot were the precious items that the Spaniards had looted from villages on their march from Cajamarca to Cuzco, a haul that had an estimated value of 580,200 pesos. Included in this horde of valuables were silver planks, measuring twenty feet long, one foot wide, and 2 to 3 inches thick. The amassed treasure was stockpiled in the town square where it was closely guarded. A few of the more magnificently crafted items were set aside after which native goldsmiths were once again employed to melt down the treasure into more manageable ingots. The obligatory royal quinto was set aside and what remained was then divided among the officers and the soldiers.

The concentration of so much wealth in the hands of so few Spaniards was the source of much gambling and was also at the root of an astounding inflationary spiral in prices. Francisco Lopez de Jérez, a notary, recorded that a jug of wine cost 60 pesos of gold, a pair of boots ranged from 30 to 40 pesos, a cape went for 125 pesos, and the purchase of a sword would set a man back 50 pesos. Those wise enough to return to Spain once they had the opportunity were among the few who enjoyed the benefits of their newfound wealth. Many a fortune was won and lost from gambling. In one celebrated instance, a soldier by the name of Mansio Serra de Leguizamón lost a gold disc, a sacred image of the sun known as Punchao, which gave rise to the Spanish expression, "he gambles away the sun before it comes up." How Leguizamón ever came to own such a grand piece that once hung in the Temple of the Sun to begin with is still somewhat of a mystery.

Shortly after taking over Cuzco, Francisco Pizarro sent Hernándo de Soto out at the head of a company of fifty horsemen and several foot soldiers to search for the retreating army of Quizquiz. The captain-general wanted to make sure they were not massing for another assault. Captain de Soto engaged the natives in several battles but was ordered to return to Cuzco after warriors were spotted near and around the city. The search for Quizquiz would resume after the passage of a few weeks.

Francisco Pizarro sent his partner, Diego de Almagro, along with Hernándo de Soto and a significant portion of the cavalry unit to seek out and subdue the retreating Inca army under the command of Quizquiz, the Quito commander who had helped conquer Cuzco for Atahualpa. The Spaniards were supported on this mission by Inca Manco and a company of five thousand Cuzco warriors who were eager to confront the troops that had defeated the army of Huascar and occupied their city. Fearing that something might happen to the titular ruler that would upset the delicate balance of power, Francisco Pizarro had Manco recalled to Cuzco. The Inca warriors, however, remained under the command of Almagro. The Spanish force had little difficulty finding the army of Quizquiz and succeeded in driving the Quito warriors back to the town of Jauja where Almagro and his army nearly annihilated what remained of the Inca troops.

Quizquiz and his greatly reduced and demoralized band of warriors took flight towards the city of Quito. Along the way they continued to harass Spanish efforts with their guerrilla style tactics. Many of Quizquiz's captains beseeched their commander to seek a peaceful resolution with the Spanish army that now controlled Cuzco. Quizquiz refused to listen to such talk and then went on to proclaim that the army would continue to fight the Spaniards from other locations, particularly the highlands. Shortly after finding their way to a village near Quito, several warriors, all of whom were weary of the long campaign that seemed to them to be a hopeless cause, entered Quizquiz's quarters wielding axes and clubs and proceeded to bludgeon their leader until there was no longer any life left in his body.

The Arrival of Pedro de Alvarado

In March of 1534, while he was still at Cuzco, Francisco Pizarro learned that Pedro de Alvarado, the legendary conquistador who had played a pivotal role in helping Hernán Cortés conquer Mexico and who was now the respected governor of Guatemala, had come to South America to claim a share of the region's legendary wealth. Alvarado had heard of the tremendous treasure trove of riches that Pizarro and Almagro had recently uncovered and set sail from Guatemala with an army of approximately 500 well armed soldiers and 327 horses to stake his claim to the northern province of the Inca empire.

He also brought four thousand conscripted Guatemalan Indians to serve as porters during his march to conquer the unclaimed city of Quito. Concern over this unexpected news prompted Pizarro to dispatch Diego de Almagro with a small force to meet with Alvarado. The captain-general authorized his partner to use any and all means at his disposal to dissuade the governor of Guatemala from completing his intended quest.

After thirty long days at sea the Alvarado expedition reached the Cape of San Francisco, situated along the coast of Ecuador. Continually contrary currents made for such slow progress that when the Spaniards finally arrived at the Bay of Caráquez most agreed that the time had come to go ashore. It was a recently apprehended native who captured the fancy of Alvarado and his men by boasting of the vast store of riches that awaited them at the city of Quito. Alvarado planned to march inland toward the direction of Quito while most of the ships followed along the coast. Some of the vessels were sent back to Nicaragua and Panama to recruit more men and to obtain more provisions for the conquest.

Pedro de Alvarado procured the services of a knowledgeable native guide who was to lead him and his army along the most direct route to the city of Quito. Unfortunately, the path chosen took them through an extremely difficult mountain range pass. The Spaniards found small quantities of gold at the villages they happened upon, all of which they helped themselves to. What they found was just enough to demonstrate that stories of a great treasure housed at Quito were probably true. They hadn't traveled very far before the native guide suddenly abandoned them at a village called Las Golondrinas. Unsure of which route to follow, a greatly angered Alvarado captured many natives at neighboring villages in the hope of finding a suitable replacement guide. It was later claimed by several observers that the Guatemalan porters feasted upon the flesh of many of the natives captured by the Spaniards.

Continuing onward, the Spaniards found the crossing of this stretch of the snow capped Andes a more laborious ordeal than they could have ever imagined. The extreme heights caused many Spaniards to become disoriented and nauseous. Some fell to the ground and began to vomit food, fluids, and blood. Many of the afflicted believed they were near death and sought out a priest to confess their sins. Only after their bodies had adjusted to the rarefied air of such high altitudes, often a matter of only a few hours, were they able to continue on with their quest.

The ice and snow, the latter of which was so deep in certain places that it reached the girth of the horses, made the climb up the Andes an even more difficult task. Howling and biting winds cut like a knife through what little clothing that the Spaniards wore. Hundreds of scantily clad native porters, who

Portrait of Pedro de Alvarado (courtesy Library of Congress).

were not accustomed to such extreme cold, and several Spaniards froze to death. It wasn't long before the food ran out and the Spaniards had to resort to eating the raw flesh of the horses that had succumbed to the rigors of this ordeal. A number of wives had chosen to accompany their husbands on this expedition and many of them perished alongside their loved ones. Their climb was also complicated by a thick cloud of ash caused by the sudden eruption of a distant volcano. The grayish powder that fell like snow from the sky not only blinded the view of the soldiers but also greatly irritated both their eyes and their lungs.

Many of the Spaniards abandoned their weapons and treasure in a desperate effort to lighten their load. The Guatemalans perished at a far faster rate than the Spaniards. Those who stopped to rest soon froze to death and those who collapsed from exhaustion were left where they had fallen. One's own survival was suddenly the only order of business. Many members of this expedition suffered snow-blindness, and many more lost toes, fingers, and even entire limbs to the ravages of frostbite. Nearly two thousand native porters would become fodder for the constantly circling vultures by the time the expedition came upon a more hospitable region. The majority of the horses and eighty-five Spanish soldiers would not survive the perilous passage over the steep slopes of the Andes.

While Pedro de Alvarado and his troops were spending several weeks trudging along the difficult snowy pass, Sebastián Benalcázar, who had been appointed commander of the San Miguel settlement shortly after the execution of Atahualpa, and 140 Spanish soldiers along with a large contingent of natives left their post at San Miguel and managed to reach Quito before either armies of Diego de Almagro or the governor of Guatemala. Benalcázar had been led to believe by the natives of his region that Quito held riches far greater than what had been obtained at Cajamarca and even exceeded the wealth that once existed at Cuzco. The natives, who were quick to notice that the Spaniards were always on guard and therefore susceptible to any suggestion of a potential native uprising, also whispered that the Incas of Quito were preparing to launch an attack to reclaim their kingdom. Benalcázar decided to head to Quito without waiting for approval from Francisco Pizarro. He did, however, send his commander a note explaining why he felt compelled to march on Quito.

The city of Quito was under the control of Rumiñavi, the Inca commander who fled Cajamarca after the capture of Atahualpa, when the advancing force of Spaniards arrived. Rumiñavi had crowned himself ruler of the city after having executed Quilliscacha, a brother of Atahualpa, and used his flayed flesh to make a ceremonial drum for himself. When it was learned that the Spaniards were closing in on Quito from several directions, Rumiñavi had much of the city's gold and silver carted off and thrown into the deepest part of a nearby lake to keep it from falling into the hands of the enemy. Additional amounts of the "sweat of the sun" and the "tears of the moon" were buried in caves and deep ravines and those who fulfilled this deed were killed in order that such hiding places would forever remain a secret.

Meanwhile, the army commanded by Sebastián Benalcázar was bolstered by the unexpected arrival of three thousand Canari warriors. The Canaris, who had suffered greatly at the hands of Atahualpa, offered to forge an alliance with the Spaniards. Benalcázar gladly welcomed them to the Spanish camp. It was a native alliance that would serve the Spaniards well. Shortly thereafter, Benalcázar and his troops encountered sudden resistance from Inca warriors who had managed to overcome their terrifying fear of the horse. They killed two horses and inflicted wounds upon many of the Spaniards, none of which, thankfully for them, proved to be fatal. Elated by this victory over one of their worst fears, the natives chopped off the head and limbs of one fallen horse and sent them back to their chiefs as proof of both their valor and the horses' mortality. Many warriors forfeited their lives in order to prove that the noble horse could be killed.

Fearing that more traps lay ahead along the road to Quito, Benalcázar decided to take a back way over the hills in order to reach the city. A native guide took them by a route that carefully avoided the royal road. Meanwhile, Rumiñavi learned from his spies of the approach of Benalcázar's army and immediately sent his warriors out to engage the enemy. After crossing a nearby river, the Spaniards were surprised to see a legion of heavily armed and well attired warriors led by Rumiñavi, who looked on from the comfort of his royal litter. The Quito army had dug a number of camouflaged pits that were lined with sharp stakes to trap and impale the Spaniards and their horses, but Benalcázar and his men skillfully managed to avoid them. The warriors from Quito were greatly frightened by the presence of the charging horse and fled almost as soon as the battle had begun. The cavalry gave chase and killed a great many of the fleeing warriors. Many natives were taken prisoner, including a wife of Huayna Capac. Miraculously, the Spaniards prevailed without the loss of a single soldier. Both the Spaniards and the Incas believed that this swift victory was the result of divine intervention.

The volcanic eruption of nearby Mt. Cotopaxi — the same fiery expulsion experienced by Pedro de Alvarado and his troops — coincided with the arrival of Sebastián Benalcázar and his troops. Since this was seen as an ominous sign, a great many natives sued for peace. After having defeated many warriors on his march to Quito, Benalcázar decided to give diplomacy a chance. He sent a native messenger to Rumiñavi to ask him to cease with his attacks and to embrace the Spaniards as friends. Rumiñavi listened to the message recited by the emissary and, after careful consideration, he replied, "Look at the ruses with which they want to deceive us and with what words they want to convince us, so they can take away from us the treasure they think is in Quito in order to later kill us and take our wives and daughters to keep as concubines! Who saw in Cajamarca how the other cruel bearded ones cajoled Atahualpa, with what cunning they took most of the treasure from the Temple of Coricancha, what ways they sought to kill him then, falsely accusing him with such effrontery. God forbid we should trust these people who neither told the truth nor will tell it; let us rather die by their hands and their horses so that they do not oppress and force us to willingly follow their excesses and fulfill their pretensions."[1] The emissary was then executed for having dared to utter such a deceitful message.

Unable to stop the advance of Benalcázar and his army, Rumiñavi decided to deny the Spaniards of the fortune they hoped to earn by setting fire to the city and carting off to the mountains with a significant amount of the remaining wealth. Before abandoning Quito, he ordered the nobles, the wives and concubines of Huayna Capac and Atahualpa, and the women of the temple to leave before the vile Spaniards had their way with them. Some left, taking with them as much treasure as they could carry. However, many told the ruler that they could not abandon their city. Rumiñavi had all who refused to obey his command put to death and ordered their bodies cast unceremoniously into a deep ravine. Such an act prompted many more to evacuate the city at once. The buildings of Quito were set on fire shortly before the Spaniards arrived.

Sebastián Benalcázar took control of the city which, in claiming it for his commanding officer, he christened San Francisco del Quito. The Spaniards were bitterly disappointed by the sight of charred buildings, some of which were still smoldering when they entered, and what little treasure the city had to offer. The native guide had told Benalcázar that there was so much gold and silver at Quito that it would take all of the Spaniards and their porters a great many trips to cart it all away. The nobles of Quito were rounded up and tortured in an effort to learn of the whereabouts of Atahualpa's missing treasure but none knew the locations of the secret hiding places. After learning of Rumiñavi's doings the Spaniards began a fervent search for the self-proclaimed ruler of Quito and the numerous precious items which once adorned the city. Their efforts were merely rewarded with the discovery of Rumiñavi and his small entourage. Once found, the Inca commander was returned to Quito where, in an effort to learn where all the gold and silver had been hidden, he was subjected to an intense interrogation. When he failed to tell them what they wanted to hear, the frustrated Spaniards had him put to death. Benalcázar and his men did learn of one hiding place that yielded a fair amount of gold and silver items. Their search, however, was cut short by the unexpected news that Diego de Almagro and his army had reached the city of Quito.

The Marshal, a title that Diego de Almagro was often known by, had expected to join up with Benalcázar at San Miguel, and therefore was surprised to find that the young officer had taken control of Quito on his own authority. Almagro suspected that Sebastián had designs on claiming the city and the surrounding lands for himself. Benalcázar assured him there was no intent on his part to deceive either Pizarro or Almagro and backed up this claim by immediately turning over command of the city to the Marshal. While awaiting the anticipated arrival of Pedro de Alvarado, the deceitful interpreter Felipillo, who had been assigned to the command of Almagro following the execution of Atahualpa, deserted the Marshal and crossed over to the camp of the invading force from Guatemala to offer his services as both guide and interpreter.

Pedro de Alvarado and the members of his expedition suffered greatly following the desertion of their native guide. Still unsure of which path to follow, Alvarado sent several of his officers along with a number of soldiers off in different directions to locate the surest route to Quito. It was during these scouting expeditions that the natives managed to capture a soldier by the name of Luz. The Spaniards later found the lifeless body of their comrade separated from his head. The soldiers understood the meaning of this message and wisely chose to avoid that particular route.

A strange fever spread rapidly amongst Alvarado's weary soldiers. Many became delirious and a few fell into a coma from which there was no awaking. One soldier became so confused that he thought the horse was his enemy. With sword in hand, the fever stricken Spaniard killed his own steed and several other horses before being subdued and placed in irons by his comrades.

Meanwhile, squads of Alvarado's soldiers were still seeking to find the royal road that would lead them to Quito. Frustration and disillusionment took hold of many men as basic needs began to greatly outweigh their precious desires. Their priority was now finding food and that meant locating villages which they could force to provide them with all that they required. Then one day the surviving troops were delighted to learn that the long journey was nearly at an end. Several of Almagro's scouts were captured by Alvarado's men and brought before the adelantado. Pedro de Alvarado gave them a warm welcome and handed them a message to take back to their commander which stated that his intentions in this land were entirely honorable. The governor of Guatemala also stated that he had been granted approval by the Crown to conquer and settle the northern lands that had not been awarded to either Pizarro or Almagro. Alvarado requested to meet in person with Almagro at Riobamba to discuss their present situation.

Diego de Almagro wisely pursued a peaceful resolution to Spanish claims over this contested territory. Following a lengthy round of negotiations, the Marshal was able to arrive at an arrangement deemed suitable to both commanders. Almagro was able to buy off the man who had been Hernán Cortés's second-in-command during the conquest of Mexico with a payment of 100,000 pesos. For this seemingly handsome price Almagro was to receive Alvarado's pledge to return to Guatemala, his fleet of twelve ships, his remaining army, and all of the armaments and supplies he brought on this expedition. Alvarado's officers and soldiers felt they had been sold out by their commander but the Marshal soothed their anguish with a promise that all would share in the splendid treasures of this land. In truth, the amount paid to Alvarado was little more than recompense for what he had personally invested in this disastrous venture. This agreement also called for the return of the deserter Felipillo, who was granted a full pardon for his faithless act but who was never again trusted by Almagro or any other Spaniard.

Before returning home, Pedro de Alvarado had an opportunity to meet with Francisco Pizarro at the holy city of Pachacamac, where the two triumphant conquistadors embraced and toasted to their own successes. Hernándo de Soto was dispatched to Cuzco to procure the necessary funds to pay off Alvarado so that he could return to Guatemala.

14
The Revolt of the Incas

A Question of Control

Hernándo Pizarro and his accompanying crew reached the port at Seville in January of 1534. He brought with him the celebrated royal quinto, a treasure trove the size of which was so great that it dazzled all who had the privilege to behold it. Hernándo personally selected the most elegant items to bring to Calatayud, where the emperor was presently holding court. Pizarro graced the royal court with his striking presence and refined manner. He spoke eloquently of the great deeds of his brother and how these heroic achievements had enriched and enlarged the emerging empire of Spain.

Hernándo's mission to the court of the emperor was a rousing success. Emperor Charles V, who because of his desperate need for additional funds to finance his far flung and ambitious activities throughout the Holy Roman Empire, was willing to grant all that the Pizarros desired and then some. Francisco Pizarro was bestowed with the noble rank of a marquis while Hernándo Pizarro was honored with an appointment as a knight of the Order of Santiago. Also present at the royal court were men sent by Diego de Almagro to make sure his interests were not once again forsaken, a necessary move on the part of the Marshal when taking into account the deep-seated hatred that existed between him and the emissary who represented his interests at court. For his dedicated service to Spain, Almagro was granted the right to explore, conquer, and settle a designated region to be called New Toledo, which comprised the lands that make up much of the present day nation of Chile. As for the extraordinary crafted figurines and pieces of jewelry that had been spared from the furnaces at Cajamarca, the emperor, after having briefly marveled at their exquisite beauty, had them all melted down into more tangible coin to meet his steadily mounting financial obligations.

The exploits of the Pizarro brothers and Diego de Almagro in South

America excited the interests of a great many Spanish citizens. The fortunes of those who chose to retire to Spain was sufficient proof of the incredible amount of wealth waiting to be had by those who were willing to risk undertaking such a bold adventure. Because of this, Hernándo Pizarro was able to return to Panama with a much larger crew then he had left with.

While Hernándo was away receiving accolades from the emperor, Francisco was busy formulating plans for restructuring the conquered empire of the Incas so that it would better suit his needs as well as those of Spain. The city of Cuzco was simply too far inland to carry on commercially viable trade with the other established Spanish settlements of the New World. In January of 1535, before setting off for the coast to locate a more suitable site for the founding of a new capital for his empire, Francisco named Hernándo de Soto governor of Cuzco. During his stay at the Inca capital, Hernándo took as his mistress Tocto Chimpu, a daughter of the late Lord Huascar. She was considered by all who had the pleasure of seeing her as being a woman of stunning beauty. She gave de Soto a daughter who was christened Leonor, named for the mother of the famed conquistador.

Prior to his departure, the captain-general called for a moratorium on all individual looting. He also instructed Hernándo and his brothers, Juan and Gonzalo, to recognize and respect the rights and property of the Incas. Francisco Pizarro feared, and rightly so, that the greed of his own men might give the natives a reason to rebel. Unfortunately, he failed to take into consideration the covetous and cruel nature of his own brothers. Following these instructions, Francisco and his brigade of soldiers marched westward until they arrived at the verdant valley of Rimac, situated near the mouth of a river that was roughly two leagues from the Pacific Ocean, where the captain-general halted to found El Ciudad de los Reyes, the City of the Kings, a city that was later renamed Lima, the capital and largest city of Peru.

The appointment of Hernándo de Soto as governor of Cuzco did not sit well with Juan and Gonzalo Pizarro, both of whom did everything in their power to undermine his authority. The slighted siblings were helped by the fact that Hernándo de Soto was a better soldier than an administrator. News of the escalating dissension between the officers at Cuzco forced the captain-general, who was preoccupied with designs on his new city, to take immediate action. To avoid taking sides with the feuding factions, the captain-general appointed Diego de Almagro, who was still at Quito, as Hernándo de Soto's replacement. Juan and Gonzalo, who were named interim commanders, were even more disappointed by their brother's choice of Almagros as governor of Cuzco and elected to ignore his appointment. A discouraged Hernándo de Soto continued to serve in a lesser role as city alderman. Juan, who believed

Captain de Soto was scheming with Almagro and others to obstruct his role in governing the affairs of Cuzco, challenged the alderman to a duel. The two mounted knights would certainly have fought to the death if others had not intervened at that moment.

Diego de Almagro received advance news of his royal land grant during his march back to Cuzco, a city which he believed fell within the boundaries of his province of New Toledo. The Pizarros disagreed with the Marshal's conclusion but seeing as to how he now commanded a far larger force, due to his recent acquisition of the army that had served under Pedro de Alvarado, Juan and Gonzalo Pizarro decided it would be best to hand over command of the city to Almagro. Since Hernándo Pizarro had still not reached Lima with the official decrees, Francisco thought his partner was somewhat presumptuous in claiming the Inca capital for himself. He sent a message back to Juan and Gonzalo ordering them to resume command of the city until it could be determined if Cuzco rested within the boundaries of New Toledo or New Castile. Unfortunately, Juan and Gonzalo were no longer in a position to do as their brother wished.

The Marshal befriended Inca Manco during his governorship of Cuzco and even permitted him to to take up residence in one of the Inca royal palaces. However, the rape of Cuzco continued almost unabated, especially by those who once served under the command of Pedro de Alvarado. These soldiers sought a just reward for their many hardships and unexpected abandonment by staking their claim to any item deemed to have value. The women of the Inca nobility became the prized possessions of the conquistadors. The officers, according to order of rank, laid claim to the women, taking the most beautiful of the noble women as their concubines. The remainder were doled out according to order of rank.

Cuzco had become a city divided between those who supported Diego de Almagro and those who were allied to the Pizarro camp. News of this growing dissent reached Lima, and Francisco now felt compelled to ride back to Cuzco to settle this festering dispute. Once there, he patiently listened to the complaints of his comrades but it soon became evident to all that the captain-general wished to retain control of the city. The persuasive Francisco convinced Almagro to momentarily put aside his claim to Cuzco until the Crown was able to rule on the current boundary dispute. An accord was reached in which each partner agreed under oath to respect the rights of the other, that all communications with the Crown would be done with the full knowledge of the other party, and that they were to share equally in the profits of their lands. Once this pact was agreed to, Diego de Almagro marched into Chile with his his army to seek out more rich civilizations to conquer while Francisco returned to the coast to continue with the building of his new city.

Juan Pizarro was named governor of Cuzco following the departure of Diego de Almagro, while Gonzalo served as his trusted lieutenant The conquistadors at Cuzco continued to confiscate and melt down every gold and silver item they were able to lay their hands upon. Not matter how much precious metals they were able to find, it was never enough to satisfy their needs. Juan and Gonzalo Pizarro constantly pressured Inca Manco to find more gold for them and these repetitious requests prompted the Inca ruler to remark, "Even if the snows of the Andes turned to gold still they would not be satisfied."[1] Respect for the Spaniards' own appointed sapa inca lessened in proportion with the diminishing supply of gold and silver items he was able to offer them.

A noteworthy example of the extreme cruelty and cupidity exhibited by the conquistadors toward the helpless citizens of Cuzco can be found in the unseemly actions of Gonzalo Pizarro, the youngest half-brother of the captain-general. Gonzalo overheard stories of the vast personal treasure of Viracocha Inca, the eighth ruler of the Inca empire, that was supposedly stored at a secret hiding place which contained his mummified body. He tortured and killed a great many natives — some of whom where burned alive in his presence to learn of its exact whereabouts. After locating the objects he had longed for at the town of Jaquijahuana, the same site where the Inca general Chalcuchima had been executed, Gonzalo confiscated all of the treasure and then ordered that the sacred mummy was to be burned. Those charged with the care of the earthly body of Viracocha Inca painstakingly collected all the ashes of the Inca ruler and placed them in an urn, which they then hid along with the idol that was carved in his likeness.

Inca Manco was to suffer numerous humiliations at the hands of his Spanish overlords. Gonzalo Pizarro, in particular, showed his lack of respect for the Inca emperor by forcing himself upon one of the ruler's favorite wives. In an effort to to halt the lecherous advances of Gonzalo, Manco tried to deceive him by passing off a woman named Ynguil (flower), a concubine who bore a striking resemblance to his sister, the woman whom the Spanish officer longed for. The ruse was exposed when after Gonzalo embraced and kissed her in front of all, Ynguil screamed aloud that she did not wish to be with such a foul and vulgar person. Gonzalo then merely took that which Manco did not wish for him to take.

The personal insults, both in private and in public, escalated to the point where a frustrated Manco felt he must take action before he met with the same terrible fate that had befallen Atahualpa. Many Inca nobles had experienced similar agonies, and having grown weary of watching their women being raped, their temples desecrated, their possessions confiscated, and the constant disrespect shown toward members of the Inca nobility, they began meeting in secret with Manco to formulate a plan for winning back their city, their empire, and their self-respect. The plan called for Manco to quietly slip out of the city so that he could rally the people to rise up against their Spanish oppressors and drive the invaders back to the sea and to the lands from whence they came. They needed to act fast before more Spanish soldiers arrived, an increase that if too great would surely dash all hope of ever winning back their nation.

Under cover of darkness, Manco was able to easily sneak out of Cuzco in the company of several wives, a few nobles, and several attendants without being noticed by the Spaniards. His movements, however, were not furtive enough to escape the notice of the Canari spies who had managed to infiltrate the secret meetings of the Incas. The Canari Indians had first come under Inca rule when they were conquered by Tupac Yupanqui. Unfortunately for the Canari, they had sided with Huascar during the long Inca civil war and because of this alliance Atahualpa had cruelly executed all of the Canari natives who surrendered to him. The fact that it was Canari warriors who inflicted a noticeable wound upon the royal ear of Atahualpa also contributed to the victorious inca's disdain for this highland tribe. The opportunity for exacting revenge came with the sudden arrival of the Spaniards and the persecuted Canari warriors were quick to ally themselves to the cause of the conquistadors. They immediately informed Juan Pizarro of Inca Manco's escape.

The Spanish commander and several cavaliers immediately gave chase and succeeded in capturing the fugitive ruler before he had a chance to get very far. After being found hiding in a nearby thicket of reeds, Manco was returned to the city in chains. The captured and bound Inca ruler was tied to the tail of Gonzalo Pizarro's horse and paraded through the streets of Cuzco, a sight that stirred up much resentment among the people. Following this public humiliation, Manco was imprisoned and placed under constant guard. During his incarceration, the Inca ruler was subjected to even harsher indignities: he was forced to watch as the wives who visited him were raped repeatedly by his Spanish guards. Some of those who watched over him pulled out the measure of their manhood and micturated on the humbled emperor. The guards even singed Manco's eyelashes with the flames of their candles. A number of Inca nobles managed to escape during Manco's imprisonment and they riled up the neighboring villages with tales of how the incarcerated Inca ruler was being horribly mistreated by the Spaniards.

It was during these turbulent times at Cuzco that Hernándo Pizarro found his way to Lima whereupon he presented his brother with the royal papers that confirmed the generous grants and titles that had been bestowed by a grateful Emperor Charles V. In an effort to restore order to the Inca capital, Francisco sent Hernándo to Cuzco to take over command of the city.

Hernándo Pizarro arrived at Cuzco in January of 1536. Emperor Charles V had decreed that the ruling Inca should be shown all the respect normally accorded a reigning monarch and Hernándo sought to comply with this royal edict by courting the imprisoned Manco with an overt show of kindness. The Spanish officer, who had forged a genuine friendship with Atahualpa and was therefore greatly saddened by the news of his execution, was able to establish a comfortable rapport with the imprisoned Manco and it wasn't long before the titular Inca ruler was granted his freedom. Manco further ingratiated himself with the benevolent Spanish captain by revealing a number of the secret places where the Incas had hidden a token amount of their valuable items.

Shortly after Gonzalo Pizarro left Cuzco on a mission to avenge a recent native uprising that had resulted in the death of several Spanish soldiers, Manco managed to convince Hernándo Pizarro to grant him permission to leave the city. He promised to bring the Spanish commander a golden statue shaped in the likeness of Huayna Capac, his father, if he allowed him to go on a pilgrimage to a site located at the Yucay Valley which honored the former Inca ruler. Hernándo's officers and a number of native allies warned him that this was simply a ploy by the sapa inca to attempt another escape but the captain, who had been blinded by the newly forged bonds of friendship and vivid visions of a life size statue made of pure gold, permitted Manco to leave Cuzco in the company of just two armed Spanish guards.

The Siege of Cuzco

When Manco failed to return after a week, Hernándo began to fear that he just might have been played for a fool. He then dispatched sixty horse soldiers under the command of his brother Juan to the Yucay Valley to locate, capture, and return the fugitive Inca ruler. Not too far from the city the Spanish search force came upon the two soldiers who had accompanied the Inca ruler and they confirmed what everyone already suspected: the pilgrimage was simply a ruse that would enable Manco to rejoin his people in order to organize and lead an assault against the Spaniards at Cuzco.

Juan and his cavaliers continued with their pursuit and finally found what they were looking for, and much more, at the Yucay Valley. Here they saw that Manco had amassed a large native army that was fully prepared to do battle with the Spaniards. The determined captain and his troops crossed a separating stream while having to carefully shield themselves from a torrential downpour of projectiles hurled by an opposing Inca force. The moment that Juan and his soldiers had made their way to the other bank the natives attacked in full force. The cavaliers immediately closed ranks and charged forward at a steady stride. This highly effective maneuver led to the death of many an Inca warrior and eventually forced the natives to withdraw.

The victorious but weary Spaniards made camp near the base of a mountain. The next morning Juan decided to renew his pursuit of Manco but soon found the way barred by thousands of warriors who bombarded them with rocks and various other projectiles. Such tactics succeeded at keeping Juan and his troops at bay for several days. While contemplating his next move, Juan Pizarro received an urgent message which ordered him to return to Cuzco at once. They rushed back to find the city surrounded by tens of thousands of armed and enraged natives. Juan and his men were prepared to cut a swath through the ranks of the enemy but were somewhat surprised to see the warriors step aside and allow them to pass through unmolested.

Following his escape from Spanish authority, Manco rallied his people and hurriedly organized an army of nearly 50,000 warriors to lay siege to the city of Cuzco. However, Manco decided not to order an attack upon the Inca capital until his volunteer army, composed mostly of peasant farmers, was at full force. The arrival of those supporting troops took several weeks after which the ranks of the Inca army swelled to well over 100,000 men, a seemingly insuperable number of warriors. The various tribes who assembled at the Valley of Cuzco wore their varied and vibrant tribal colors with great pride as they united under the banner of the Incas. At night the warriors who besieged Cuzco lit thousands of campfires, an eerie reminder to those inside that they were still surrounded.

In the meantime, the Spaniards, who numbered but a mere 190 soldiers, and their approximately 1,000 Canari allies, were kept busy fortifying themselves behind a city that lacked adequate defensive structures. Messages, like the one sent to Juan, were also sent to Francisco Pizarro at Lima to urge more soldiers to come to their aid during this desperate hour.

The day after Juan's return to Cuzco the massive army assembled by Manco launched a furious and full scale attack. Heated stones were wrapped in cotton and catapulted by slings into the city, a number of which landed on the thatched roofs and, as intended, quickly ignited a brilliant burst of fire. The flames spread swiftly from one building to another and before long the entire city was engulfed in fire and smoke. The Spaniards, who now found it difficult to either breathe or see, sought sanctuary in the palace of Viracocha and the accompanying open courtyard. The fact that the ichu grass covered roof of the building that shielded the Spaniards from harm never caught fire was later attributed to an act of divine intervention but the reality of this supposed miracle was simply that the soldiers and their native allies had taken the precaution to douse the flammable roof with water. Both sides could only watch as the great city of Cuzco burned out of control. It would take several days before the fires finally burned themselves out. The palace of Viracocha, the Temple of the Sun and the Temple of the Virgins were among the few buildings that managed to escape the devastating effects of this conflagration intact.

Skirmishes were a regular and daily occurrence. The Incas quickly regained control of much of Cuzco, leaving the beleaguered Spaniards and their staunch allies cornered in a small sector of the city. Fearing that the end was near, many soldiers sought absolution from the three priests who were present. A frustrated Hernándo Pizarro led several cavalry assaults that succeeded in slaughtering a large number of Inca warriors but failed to bring about an end to the siege. In one of these surprise attacks he was able to inflict a great deal of damage before the natives regrouped, after which the cavaliers found themselves suddenly immobilized by swarms of native warriors bent on avenging the loss of their comrades. The discouraged Spaniards retreated but not soon enough to save the life of Francisco Mejía. Both he and his horse were captured and dragged to a nearby visible location where the Spaniards inside Cuzco were to witness the swift beheading of both man and beast.

The Spaniards discovered that the Incas were quick to adapt to Spanish tactics. Many of the natives took to brandishing Spanish weapons taken from those they had killed and some, including Manco, even learned to ride the horses they had captured. The natives discovered that they could bring down both horse and rider with a well thrown lasso. The Inca warriors, as the Spaniards would painfully learn for themselves, had a rather effective arsenal of weapons at their disposal. The sling, or huaraca, was an effective long range instrument that could fling small stones with a fair degree of accuracy to distances of thirty yards. The javelin could also be hurled a great distance with an equal degree of deadly accuracy. A spiked mace made of copper was used for hand to hand combat — a blow from it could easily smash to pieces an opponent's bones. The bola, which consisted of three rocks attached to strings made from the tendons of the llama, was a weapon that easily and effectively entangled the legs of a horse, resulting in the downfall of both the rider and beast. The Inca army was divided into squadrons of well equipped archers, slingers, and macanas — a double edged sword — ax and club wielders, as well as spear or lance hurlers.

Those Spaniards who were captured in battle were immediately beheaded and their severed and still bloody heads were thrown into the streets of the city in an effort to strike terror into the hearts of their enemy. The Spanish soldiers at Cuzco reciprocated with equally gruesome acts intended to instill fear amongst the Incas. Captured warriors had their hands or arms chopped off, while some lost their nose. Several women suffered the painful removal of one or both breasts. The mutilated victims were then set free so that others might see what happened to those who dared to oppose the Spaniards.

Francisco Pizarro dispatched troops to Cuzco to aid his beleaguered brothers but these soldiers were ambushed and cut down in the mountain passes by a military force sent by Manco to drive off the Spaniards who were settling along the coast. The few Spanish soldiers who survived this deadly encounter struggled back to Lima to warn the captain-general that the Incas were coming. The sighting of such a large native army advancing toward the city sent many of the newly arrived settlers into a confused state of panic. The city was saved from being overrun by a hastily organized ambush. A hidden force of Spanish cavalry led by Francisco Pizarro charged at the advancing Inca warriors and eventually, after much effort, they succeeded in forcing the natives to retreat to a hill located on the other side of the Rimac river. The natives, however, maintained control of the passes, thereby preventing any attempt by the Spaniards of the coast to rescue their besieged comrades at Cuzco. Francisco sent messages to the governors of Mexico, Guatemala, Nicaragua, and Panama requesting their immediate help before all that he had recently won was lost forever.

The Incas launched their assault of the Spanish occupied city of Cuzco from the hillside fortress of Sacsahuaman. Since the Inca capital was conceived as a city without walls, Sacsahuaman was designed and built after the Chanca invasion of 1438 as a safe haven for the people in the event of another such invasion. The enormous stone stronghold was used by 1,500 of Manco's warriors to continually pelt the conquistadors and their Canari allies with a various assortment of deadly projectiles. Seeking to put an end to this lethal threat, Juan Pizarro led a cavalry assault against against the fortress which was answered with a steady barrage of javelins and rocks hurled by the Inca defenders. The determined Spaniards and their Canari allies scaled the towering walls with ladders and, after much effort, managed to break through the first line of defense but were immediately pinned down by natives stationed along an even higher second wall. During the battle Juan removed his helmet, presumably because it was irritating a previous facial wound. He was almost instantly struck down by a stone hurled from high above. Though immobilized by the crushing blow to his jaw the wounded officer continued to urge his men on until they managed to breach the second wall. The seriously wounded Juan was then brought back to the city where he clung to life for another two weeks before finally succumbing to the painful effects of his injuries.

The attack against the Inca stronghold continued under the command of Hernándo Pizarro. Inca Manco sent five thousand additional warriors to protect the fortress but eventually the Spaniards and the Canari warriors breached the third and final wall which, after a fortnight of intense and steady fighting, finally gave them control of Sacsahuaman. An Inca noble, by the name of Cahuide, who had fought with exceptional courage and conviction, leapt to his death when he saw that the Spaniards were about to emerge as the victors.

Despite the loss of the Sacsahuaman fortress, Manco continued to assail Cuzco, a siege that, in one form or another, lasted for nearly a year. Unfortunately his efforts were hindered when, after the passage of five months, Manco had to send many of his warriors home so that they could tend to their fields, lest the rest of the native population should starve. This was, after all, an agrarian based society. The inca took a large body of warriors to the town of Tambo until the time came to resume the siege. Another body of troops remained near Cuzco to keep a watch on the Spaniards and to make sure no supplies or reinforcements found their way to the city.

Hernándo took advantage of the native withdrawal by sending out armed parties to gather much needed food. They managed to round up nearly two thousand llamas that helped to satisfy their craving for meat. Starvation was the great enemy of the Spaniards at Cuzco and several would perish from the terrible pangs of an unsatisfied hunger. This, of course, had been part of Manco's plan, but he was betrayed by traitors to the cause who secretly smuggled food to the barricaded Spaniards.

The Spanish commander sought to put an end to this long struggle by surprising and capturing Inca Manco at his new stronghold. Hernándo led a force of eighty horse and several foot soldiers on this daring mission. Unfortunately for the Spaniards, Manco had anticipated such a move and therefore his troops were well prepared for Hernándo's assault. They permitted the Spaniards to advance without any interference, but the moment they were in range the natives let loose a deadly barrage of projectiles from their well concealed positions. The startled Spaniards quickly regrouped and then resumed their attack. Hernándo, after being repulsed twice and finding his troops on the verge of being massacred, was forced to order a retreat back to Cuzco.

The arrival of Spanish reinforcements from the coast helped bring an end to Manco's rebellion. Unable to reclaim the city of Cuzco, the Inca ruler and his remaining army retreated to Ollantaytambo where there stood a large fortress that protects the entrance to the Urubamba canyon. Also at Ollantaytambo, if one looks long and hard enough, the stone face of the god Viracocha can be seen protruding from the side of the mountain. The Spaniards pursued and attacked them at Ollantaytambo but the Incas prevailed. Despite their victory, Manco realized the Spaniards would eventually return in greater numbers. He decided that he needed to find a place that was unknown and inaccessible to the conquistadors, so he and his twenty thousand faithful followers fled into the secluded jungles of the neighboring highlands. They relocated to an Inca palace at Vitcos, situated in the Vilcabamba Valley and nestled serenely between the Urubamba and Apurímac rivers. The Spaniards eventually found them at Vitcos and after a bloody confrontation Manco led his few remaining followers farther northward into the heavily wooded hills until he found an ideal location to build a new Inca city he called Vilcabamba. From this location, Manco continued to effectively harass the efforts of the Spaniards with his well organized guerrilla tactics.

15
The Return of Almagro

A Land of Unfulfilled Promises

Many of the conquistadors chose to go their separate ways following the accord reached between Diego de Almagro and Francisco Pizarro. Almagro left Cuzco on July 3, 1535, with 570 soldiers and twelve thousand native warriors and porters to explore and settle the province that had been granted to him by Emperor Charles V. Most of the soldiers who had come over from Guatemala with Pedro de Alvarado now followed the Marshal on his expedition to conquer and plunder the rich villages and cities that were sure to be found in the region designated as New Toledo. Villac-Umu, the high priest of the sun, and Paullu, the half-brother of Inca Manco, also traveled in the company of Almagro. Pizarro returned to the coast shortly thereafter to continue with the building of his new city while Hernándo de Soto, who after suffering the humiliation of being denied an opportunity to participate in Almagro's quest and Pizarro's continued reluctance to offer him any significant position within his regime, decided the time had come to return to Spain to enjoy his newfound wealth and ponder what would be his next great adventure. A caravan of several hundred llamas and a large number of native porters carried the 100,000 pesos of gold that he had amassed in the New World. Hernándo abandoned Tocto Chimpu, his mistress, and Leonor, their daughter, when he returned to Spain.

When Diego Almagro entered the province of Paria, the natives warned him that Chile was nothing like the lands of Peru. There were no rich empires, nor were there any temples sheathed in gold. Instead, it was a land of many extremes that was inhabited by a great many savage tribes. Almagro and his men believed the natives were merely trying to steer them away with well-rehearsed lies. Cristóbal de Molina would later remark that Almagro was "so obsessed by greed and by ambition to rule great kingdoms, and so full of the tales that lying Indians told him about the riches of Chile, that he thought nothing of the country he was actually in."

Felipillo, the native interpreter who always seemed to be at the center of intrigue, also accompanied the Marshal on his expedition to conquer the presentday region of Chile. They hadn't gone very far before Felipillo once again deserted his commanding officer. He was hunted down and after being judged guilty of desertion and conspiring to incite the neighboring tribes to attack the Spanish expedition the notorious interpreter was sentenced to a particularly cruel manner of death by an unforgiving Almagro. The Spanish commander had each limb of the betrayer of Atahualpa securely tied to a separate horse. At the same time, the four horsemen rode off at full speed, the force of which ripped the arms and legs of Felipillo from his torso, which then spurted blood in all directions. The limbless interpreter, while writhing in agony upon the ground, pleaded with the Marshal to put him out of his misery. Felipillo was left to lie on the ground until he finally bled to death.

Villac-Umu, the high priest who had set out with the Marshal, also abandoned the mission and on his trek back to Cuzco he preached to the people of the many atrocities committed by the Spaniards and urged them to take up arms in defense of their way of life. The high priest arrived at Cuzco in time to accompany Inca Manco on a journey that was supposed to locate for Hernándo Pizarro a statue literally worth its weight in gold but which instead united the emperor with the armed citizens of Peru who had been aroused into action by the efforts of the high priest and other Inca nobles who had escaped Cuzco. Inca Paulla, on the other hand, chose to remain with Diego de Almagro.

The route that Diego de Almagro took to reconnoiter the region he had been granted led the expeditionary force through the steep slopes of the Andes, a most formidable barrier to the inviting valley of Copiapó. The difficulty of the precipitous climb through the mountains was made even harsher by the bone chilling cold and the slippery accumulation of snow and ice that blanketed the rugged mountain peaks. Any man who stopped, even for a moment, ran the very real risk of immediately freezing to death. In one such incident, a soldier leading his horse decided to take a break, and in that brief instance both man and horse froze like a statue for all to see. Many men, especially the scantily clad native porters, froze to death during this difficult stage of the journey.

The tremendous supply of food brought on this expedition was soon exhausted and the discouraged soldiers were forced to scoop away snow in a desperate search for roots to feed upon. Eventually, the famished adventurers reached a point where they were forced to eat from the bodies of the horses that had frozen to death. Thirty horses perished during this exhaustive expedition. The Spaniards raided villages for food and enslaved many of the inhabitants to serve as replacements for the numerous native porters who had died on the journey. These subjugated natives were chained or tied with ropes while compelled to carry the heavy provisions of the expedition. A frustrated Almagro showed his cruel side on several occasions during this ill-fated campaign. In one instance, some thirty native chiefs were, by the Marshal's orders, burned at the stake, in a desperate effort to learn where they could find kingdoms as rich as that of the Incas. After much suffering the surviving members of the expedition ventured southward until coming upon the Aconcagua river where they were unmercifully attacked by the fierce Mapuche natives. It was at this point that the frustrated Almagro decided to try his luck to the north. This chosen path brought the troops to the Atacama desert, a barren land that deprived all of both food and water.

At the more hospitable valley of Coquimbo, Diego de Almagro was reinforced by the unexpected, but certainly welcome, arrival of Rodrigo de Órgoñez and a small company of cavalry soldiers. Órgoñez, a veteran of the Spanish campaigns in Italy and an exemplary officer who would faithfully serve the Marshal to whatever end, had left Cuzco after recruiting more men and provisions and set out at great speed to catch up with his commander. They rode during a period when the natives were preparing to rise up against the Spaniards. Two of Órgoñez's men were crushed to death by boulders when they walked into a ravine where the natives had laid a trap. Two more soldiers were killed when the natives chased Órgoñez away from their lands. Rodrigo and his men suffered greatly while in the mountains, just as Almagro and his men had, where two conquistadors froze to death alongside a great many native porters.

Juan de Rada, Almagro's majordomo, also arrived with the royal decrees brought back from Spain by Hernándo Pizarro which stipulated the territory that fell under the Marshal's purview. Many of the men had grown weary of this fruitless campaign and expressed a fervent desire to return to Cuzco, which, according to this notice, seemed to confirm as being situated well within Almagro's rightful territory. When a scouting party that had been sent on ahead prior to the arrival of Órgoñez and Rada returned after an absence of nearly two months with the sobering news that the land for the next one hundred leagues had little to offer, Almagro conceded to the requests of his men and ordered an immediate return to Cuzco. It was the end of a nearly two year long quest that resulted in the death of many men and left the survivors with nothing of value to show for the terrible ordeal they had been forced to endure.

Diego de Almagro and what remained of his tattered and weary force were surprised to learn of the native uprising at Cuzco. Once they came near the city, Almagro sent an emissary to the Inca camp to seek a conference with Manco. The inca, who had been on friendly terms with the Marshal, agreed to such a meeting. However, some of Manco's spies spotted a meeting between Diego de Almagro and Hernándo Pizarro in which the former expressed to the latter that the newly revised land grant of the Spanish Crown placed the city of Cuzco within his jurisdiction and he was fully prepared to claim what was rightfully his. Hernándo refused Almagro's request for an orderly transfer of power, and now the beleaguered and outnumbered troops at Cuzco had to count the returning Spaniards among their host of enemies. Those who had spied on this conference did not know of the enmity between the two officers and therefore suspected that some new form of treachery was being planned by their Spanish oppressors. Manco immediately sent fifteen thousand warriors to punish Almagro and his troops for having betrayed his trust. The Spaniards were caught off guard by this sudden assault but quickly regained their composure and, thanks to their superior weapons and tactics, they were able to fend off a vastly larger native force.

The New Lord of Cuzco

Having prevailed over the Inca force sent against them, Almagro and his troops now set their sights on taking control of Cuzco. The Marshal sent a message to Hernándo Pizarro demanding that he immediately relinquish control of the city to him or suffer the consequences of his resolve. Hernándo, who from the beginning harbored an intense hatred of Almagro, adamantly refused to comply with the Marshal's ultimatum. A truce was established by intermediaries but it was not long before this accord was broken. Diego suspected that Hernándo was not adhering to the terms of their truce when he noticed that the Spaniards at Cuzco were hurriedly fortifying their position. Once Almagro learned that Alonso de Alvarado, the nephew of Pedro de Alvarado, was marching from Lima with a large body of troops to reinforce the army stationed at Cuzco he decided to take control of the city while he still had the opportunity.

It was during the night of April 8, 1537, that Almagro and his troops, under cover of darkness, quietly entered Cuzco uncontested and laid claim to the city. A startled Hernándo and Gonzalo Pizarro, along with about twenty other soldiers, refused to yield to the inevitable and from their quarters they kept Almagro's men at bay with their excellent swordplay. Rodrigo de Órgoñez, the Marshal's young right hand officer, ended the futile confrontation by setting fire to the thatched roof. Those inside escaped into the waiting arms of Almagro's men just moments before the roof collapsed. Órgoñez brought the captured Pizarro brothers before his commander and then urged him to execute both of them at once, reasoning that if the role had been reversed they certainly would not show the Marshal or his officers any manner of mercy.

The city that Diego de Almagro reclaimed had been greatly ravaged by the long siege. Many of the buildings that still stood were just shells; the standing remains of what the fire had failed to consume. One of the first official acts of the Marshal was to crown Paullu, the half-brother of Manco, as the new emperor, a move that Almagro hoped would forge a favorable alliance with the neighboring native settlements. The Marshal's troops, fueled by the frustration of their long and fruitless expedition, wasted no time laying claim to all of the silver and gold they could get their hands on. The pillaging and raping that took place was even worse than that which had occurred while the Pizarros were in charge.

Meanwhile at Lima, Francisco Pizarro had managed to round up an army of 450 soldiers, a force divided almost evenly between the ranks of cavalry and infantry, to aid in the rescue of his besieged brothers at Cuzco but was forced to abandon these plans once he learned that his partner had managed to gain control of the city. Instead, he sent emissaries to the Inca capital in an effort to negotiate a peaceful settlement to the current crisis at Cuzco. The man at the head of this embassy was none other than Gaspar de Espinosa, the licentiate who had helped found the colony of Panama and the silent partner who had provided the essential funding for Pizarro, Almagro, and Luque to launch their ambitious expeditions to search for the rich kingdoms rumored to lie to the south. Pizarro had asked his old benefactor to come to Peru to help mediate the escalating tension that existed between him and his partner Almagro. Espinosa, who was by then a man of more than seventy years of age, saw this undertaking as an opportunity to check on the progress of his investment and a chance to participate in one last adventure, willingly accepted Pizarro's offer to come to Lima. The veteran conquistador reached the city of Cuzco where he witnessed the charred remains of the razed city, but unfortunately on August 25, 1537, he passed away of unknown causes before having an opportunity to settle the long-standing boundary dispute that centered around the Inca capital.

After gaining control of the city, Almagro decided that he would send an expedition under the command of Rodrigo de Órgoñez to locate Inca Manco and punish him for having dared to assail his troops following their return from the disastrous expedition into the barren regions of Chile.

Órgoñez and his troops caught up with the fugitive Inca ruler and his still sizable army at Vitcos and immediately engaged them in battle. The element of surprise favored the conquistadors greatly and the engagement quickly turned into a Spanish rout. However, Órgoñez and his soldiers were so busy looting the village of Vitcos of its many valuable possessions that they missed their golden opportunity to capture Manco, who took advantage of the Spaniards' momentary lapse of judgment and retreated to higher ground, an elevated region that was too difficult for the horses to climb. The capture of twenty thousand natives and fifty thousand "Peruvian sheep" seemed to satisfy Órgoñez and his men that they had succeeded in ending the Inca rebellion once and for all. The captured warriors were later released and permitted to return to their homes.

In the meantime, the relief force sent by Francisco Pizarro, which was under the command of Alonso de Alvarado, was slowly but steadily closing in on the city of Cuzco. The commander had originally left Lima with 350 soldiers but was soon reinforced by an additional 150 soldiers sent by the captain-general. Diego de Almagro sent emissaries to Jauja to inform Alvarado of his victory at Cuzco and demanded that he recognize and yield to his authority. The officer responded by arresting and imprisoning the emissaries, after which he sent a message to Almagro reminding him in no uncertain terms that Francisco Pizarro was his commander. As the Marshal prepared to march against Alvarado, Órgoñez once again urged him to lop off the heads of the imprisoned Pizarro brothers. The commander, however, could not bring himself to act on this advice. Almagro led his army against the troops of Alvarado at the Battle of Abancay in July, where, after Órgoñez won a pivotal engagement, the veteran commander emerged as the victor. Alvarado surrendered his sword to Almagro and the victorious commander returned to Cuzco with vastly increased provisions and a much larger army. The Spanish civil war for control of Peru was under way and Almagro now appeared to be the stronger of the former partners.

16
The War of the Spaniards

Almagro Marches on Lima

Francisco Pizarro had not remained idle during the period of upheaval that was disrupting the entire Valley of Cuzco. The conquerer of Peru had sent out a desperate plea for help to Spanish settlements at Mexico, Santo Domingo, Panama, and even to Pedro de Alvarado at Guatemala to aid in bringing about an end to the Inca revolt. Pizarro's request was heeded by many sympathetic Spanish leaders, each of whom responded by sending either soldiers, supplies, weapons, or a combination thereof. An elderly Gaspar de Espinosa, the silent partner whose financial backing made it possible for Pizarro and Almagro to sail to Peru, personally brought over 250 soldiers from Panama; Hernán Cortés, the conqueror of Mexico, sent a boatload of supplies and weapons; and from Nicaragua and Guatemala there came additional volunteers and assorted military provisions.

Fearing that he was on the verge of losing his newly established realm to Inca Manco, Francisco mustered an army of 450 soldiers, half of which were cavalry, and began his march toward Cuzco. He hadn't traveled very far before learning that not only had Diego de Almagro returned to once again stake his claim to the city that was at the center of the dispute but that his former partner had also defeated the seasoned troops of Alonso de Alvarado he had dispatched to aid his brothers against the Incas. Such a loss was of grave concern to Pizarro: the addition of Alvarado's defeated men and the surrendering soldiers at Cuzco combined with those who had returned from the Chile expedition provided Almagro with an army that vastly exceeded the size of his own. Not wishing to risk the lives of any more of his men, including his imprisoned brothers at Cuzco, Francisco decided to return to Lima to make preparations for an assault with a much larger army.

The captain-general tried to open up a dialogue with his old partner by sending emissaries to Cuzco but those negotiations quickly broke down with the untimely death of the mediator Gaspar de Espinosa and Almagro's reluctance to concede any ground during those short-lived discussions. Francisco sent a gentle rebuke to Diego and then requested a meeting where he hoped the two could attempt to reconcile their differences. Órgoñez managed to convince Almagro that there was more than sufficient reason to decline such an offer. Rodrigo also convinced his commander that it would be in their best interest to take the battle to Pizarro at Lima rather then wait for him to come to Cuzco.

Before striking out for Lima, Órgoñez once again pleaded with the Marshal to execute the two imprisoned Pizarro brothers. Diego de Alvarado, the brother of Pedro, and an officer who now faithfully served the Marshal, counseled against such an extreme measure. Alvarado had struck up a friendship with Hernándo Pizarro while playing cards with the prisoner. He also had fallen heavily into debt to Hernándo and, being the gentleman that he was, promptly offered to pay what he owed. The prisoner, however, refused to accept the money, a gracious gesture that left a favorable impression upon the deeply indebted officer. Alvarado told Almagro that such an act would not sit well with either Francisco Pizarro or, more importantly, Emperor Charles V, who had taken a strong liking to Hernándo. Almagro chose to favor the counsel of Diego de Alvarado over that of Rodrigo de Órgoñez. The Marshal also decided that he would bring Hernándo with him on his march to the coast to confront Francisco Pizarro, hoping to use him as a bargaining chip during their negotiations. Gonzalo Pizarro and Alonso de Alvarado were to remain imprisoned under heavy guard at Cuzco. A frustrated Órgoñez warned his commander that there would come a day when all would regret such a decision. He reminded the Marshal that "A Pizarro was never known to forget an injury; and that which they had already received from Almagro was too deep for them to forgive."[1]

Diego de Almagro and his army marched uncontested toward the city of Lima. Feeling confident that he alone would soon reign supreme over this land, the Marshal decided, upon reaching the Valley of Chincha, a spot situated about 150 miles to the south of his intended destination, to found a settlement comparable to the one recently established by Francisco Pizarro. It was here that he learned of the disturbing news that Gonzalo Pizarro, Alonso de Alvarado and several other prisoners had cleverly gained their freedom by bribing their jailers. Órgoñez again pleaded with his commander to do away with Hernándo while he still had the opportunity, but the Marshal could not bring himself to order the execution of his prisoner. A slightly disappointed Almagro and his somewhat skeptical troops proceeded to make their way to Lima.

A Pact with the Devil

A hastily arranged meeting between Francisco Pizarro and Diego de Almagro took place on November 13, 1537, at Mala to discuss their precarious predicament. The meeting quickly dissolved into a war of words between the two stubborn commanders and after not getting his way, Francisco stormed back to his camp. Fray Francisco de Bobadilla, from Lima, was left to mediate the many differences that still divided the Spanish camps.

Determined to gain the release of his brother, Francisco sent a message to his former partner which stated that in exchange for Hernándo he would agree to Almagro's continued control of Cuzco while an official survey was conducted to determine once and for all exactly which territory the city belonged to. To assuage any fears Almagro might have concerning a possible reprisal, the captain-general pledged that Hernándo would leave the country within six weeks of his release. The arrangement also stipulated that both armies were to cease all hostilities and return at once to their respective camps. Órgoñez, as well as many other officers and soldiers, complained that the arrangement was far too favorable toward the Pizarro camp. Órgoñez once again begged his commander to end the life of Hernándo but once again it was Diego de Alvarado who pleaded for the life of the prisoner. Francisco, who was intent upon obtaining the freedom of his brother, made some minor concessions that sounded more than fair to the trusting ears of Almagro. An accord was finally reached by which the two conquerors of Peru agreed to abide. Unable to change the mind of his commander, Órgoñez said, "What has my fidelity to my commander cost me?"[2] He then answered himself by running joined fingers across his throat.

Diego de Almagro personally released Hernándo Pizarro from his present manner of confinement and then turned him over to several of his officers who were to escort him to the town of Mala. Once there, they where all warmly received by a grateful Francisco who treated the emissaries to a grand feast before permitting them to return to their commander. Once Almagro's officers had left the Pizarro camp, the captain-general assembled his army and recounted all of the transgressions perpetrated by his former partner and told them that the time had come to exact a fitting revenge. Francisco turned the campaign over to the just released Hernándo and the recently escaped Gonzalo. The captain-general, who never had any intention of honoring the terms of the agreement, then sent a message to Almagro that officially announced the annulment of their recently signed treaty. He demanded that the Marshal return to the previously recognized borders of New Toledo, which did not include Cuzco, a city that he was ordered to relinquish at once or die

16. The War of the Spaniards   189

Pizarro and Almagro swearing peace (courtesy Library of Congress).

trying to defend his claim to it. Almagro, who already was suffering from numerous infirmities related to his profession and his advancing years, was in a state of shock over this sudden and dramatic turn of events. Was there no honor among conquistadors?

The Defeat of Almagro

The despondent Diego de Almagro had to be carried upon a litter during the long march back to Cuzco. His delicate condition became so precarious at one point that the troops had to stop at the town of Bilcas for nearly three weeks before the Marshal was strong enough to continue the journey. Too weak to make any decisions, Almagro relinquished command of the army to Rodrigo de Órgoñez, his trusted officer who, even after all of his commander's bad decisions, pledged to defend the city of Cuzco to the very end. Neither of the former partners would physically participate in the coming battle that would decide once and for all who would reign supreme over the empire of Peru. Francisco Pizarro, who deemed himself too old for another military campaign, gave command of his avenging army to Hernándo and Gonzalo, both of whom were eager to make their brother proud. While the captain-general retired to Lima his brothers gave chase with an army of nearly seven hundred well-armed soldiers.

While Almagro's army awaited the inevitable showdown with their fellow countrymen, the natives arrived in great numbers to witness the spectacle that was about to unfold. The residents of the neighboring towns, as well as those who had taken refuge in the mountains, heard that the Spaniards were about to do battle with one another, and, eager to see the conquistadors spill their own blood, they flocked to the hills by the thousands to witness this epic event. The Spaniards did not disappoint them.

After finding their way back to Cuzco, Rodrigo de Órgoñez, who was a well trained and highly disciplined field commander, marched out of the city to meet the advancing army of the Pizarros. Órgoñez had approximately five hundred soldiers, divided almost evenly between cavalry and infantry. He positioned his infantry in the middle and they were flanked by the horse soldiers. The troops were also supported by six small cannons known as falconets.

The Pizarro brothers and their troops emerged from a mountain pass where they were immediately rewarded with the sight of Órgoñez and his soldiers who were well positioned to contest their advance. Seeing as how it was already late in the evening, Hernándo had his men make camp in order that they might be well rested and sufficiently prepared for the confrontation that was to take place the following morning. Both camps were within full view of one another. The natives, who had been busy all day jockeying for the best spots to view the upcoming struggle, camped out in the mountains. There was no communication between the Spanish camps; what needed to occur was well understood by all.

The call to arms was sounded at both camps during the early morning hours of April 26, 1538. The commanders on each side rallied their troops with speeches that reminded the men of the greater cause they were about to fight for. Hernándo and Gonzalo spoke of their unjust imprisonment and how Diego de Almagro had wrongfully claimed Cuzco for himself. They also reminded them of Almagro's previous assault against Spanish soldiers under the command of Alonso de Alvarado. Órgoñez reminded his soldiers of the treachery of the Pizarros and their plot to deny the Marshal the city that belonged to him.

Gonzalo Pizarro was given charge of the infantry which, at his command, advanced at a steady pace toward the river that separated the opposing armies. Once in range, Rodrigo de Órgoñez and his troops unleashed a heavy barrage of firepower that felled a great many of Gonzalo's men. Pizarro's army managed to regroup and return fire, at which point Órgoñez's army suffered heavy casualties. Hernándo then led the charge of his cavalry and Rodrigo accepted the challenge by leading his loyal cavaliers into battle. The horses, all of which were clad in armor, galloped at full speed until their riders were close enough to clash swords with one another.

Órgoñez hoped to throw the enemy into a state of confusion by slaying their leader. He charged directly toward a cavalier he believed to be Hernándo Pizarro. The lieutenant of Almagro brought down that soldier as well as two others, and believing that he had killed the commander of the opposition he cried out "Victory!" At that very moment he was struck by a shot from an enemy's arquebus which grazed along his forehead. Though protected by his helmet, some fragments had penetrated his visor and left the officer slightly dazed and confused. His horse was struck down and Órgoñez momentarily found himself pinned to the ground. He frantically freed himself only to find that he was now surrounded by Spanish soldiers of the other side. Realizing that he faced an insurmountable disadvantage, the half blind Órgoñez asked if there was a knight present to whom he could surrender his sword. A less than chivalrous soldier by the name of Fuentes pretended to hold such a title and accepted the sword of Órgoñez. Fuentes then pulled a dagger and plunged it into the heart of the surrendering officer. The same soldier then chopped off the head of the dying commander and placed it on a pike which he held up high for the enemy to see. The fateful prediction that Órgoñez had made at Mala had now come to pass.

The troops of Rodrigo de Órgoñez quickly fell into disorder following the demise of their commander and hurriedly retreated toward Cuzco. Surrender was not an option. The Battle of Salinas had raged for nearly two hours and in its wake there laid 150 dead Spanish soldiers. After all of the Spaniards had fled the battlefield, the natives swooped down from the mountainsides and rewarded themselves with the attire and weapons of the fallen soldiers. The stripped bodies were left where they fell so that the vultures might enjoy a feast of their own. In the war for control of Peru, more Spaniards died at the hands of their comrades than were killed by native warriors.

Killing Him with Kindness

Having watched the devastating defeat of his army from a safe distance, a weak and terribly despondent Diego de Almagro attempted to ride off on his mule in search of a safe haven. His pace, however, was not swift enough to elude his persistent pursuers. The Marshal was captured at the ruins of Sacsahuaman, placed in heavy chains, and dragged to Cuzco where he was imprisoned at the Coricancha temple. A joyous Francisco Pizarro embarked for the city of Cuzco shortly after learning that his troops had emerged as the victors. He stayed at the town of Jauja, where he was met by the son of his former partner who had been granted permission to leave Cuzco. The young Diego de Almagro, who had accompanied his father on the expedition to Chile, remained at Jauja until the trial of the elder Almagro was concluded, whereupon he was escorted to the captain-general's house at Lima.

At Cuzco, a gravely ill and deeply melancholy Diego de Almagro was nursed back to health by a reassuring Hernándo Pizarro, who made it a point to regularly visit the imprisoned Marshal. Hernándo expressed concern for Diego's delicate condition and made sure that he received sufficient food, drink, and medical attention to aid in his recovery. Almagro was convinced that Hernándo remembered how he had spared his life on more than one occasion and was now returning the favor. The slowly recovering prisoner failed to realize that Hernándo was simply restoring him back to health so he would be of sound mind and body to appreciate the vengeful manner of punishment that he was about to face. Once Almagro's confidence and health were restored, the cold hearted Hernándo convened a secret tribunal where the prisoner, without benefit of any sort of defense, was judged guilty of treason and condemned to die at once. All who had a complaint against the defendant were encouraged to give testimony, well rehearsed remarks which were duly recorded in the official record of the staged proceedings. The guilty verdict was rendered on July 8, 1538.

When Diego de Almagro learned of his suddenly determined fate he immediately asked to speak with Hernándo Pizarro. The captain visited the prisoner and took great delight in seeing a tearful Almagro beg for his life. The Marshal reminded him that the Crown would not look kindly upon such an act. Hernándo, who was no longer inclined to show any pity or mercy toward the prisoner, responded that his fate was now sealed and then brought closure to their meeting by telling Almagro that he should spend what little time he had left on earth making peace with his maker.

The condemned Almagro heeded the advice of Hernándo Pizarro and spent his last few hours of life dictating a will which, among other bequeathments, named his young mestizo son Diego as his successor. The Panamanian woman who bore Almagro a son had been christened Ana Martínez. A great many Spaniards from both camps pleaded with Hernándo to show mercy towards Diego de Almagro. At the very least, they asked that the Marshal should be spared the indignity of suffering a traitor's death, an execution by beheading. Hernándo's mind could not be swayed. The only concession he would make was to allow the condemned Almagro to be garroted in his cell rather than to suffer a public beheading. Moments after the Marshal had confessed his sins and received the last rites from a friar, the executioner slowly but steadily tightened a cord wrapped around the neck of the prisoner until he was pronounced dead. Not content with this manner of death, a vengeful Hernándo reneged on his solemn pledge by having the lifeless body of Almagro dragged to the courtyard where, before a large crowd of startled onlookers, he was beheaded. The bloody severed head of the one-eyed Almagro was placed on a pike and held aloft for all to see. It was an ignominious end for one of the original partners of the Company of the Levant.

17

The End of an Era

The Assassination of Francisco Pizarro

To those around him, Francisco Pizarro appeared somewhat distraught when he learned that his brother had taken it upon himself to judge and execute his former partner. It must be remembered, however, that the Pizarros were known to be great actors and in this tragic tale many suspected that Hernándo was merely following the orders of his brother, who had longed to rid himself of Diego de Almagro but was constrained by the court of public opinion. Francisco returned to Cuzco, once again flaunting himself as the liberator, conqueror, and protector of the great Inca city. He showed no sympathy toward the soldiers who had faithfully followed the banner of the Marshal. They were stripped of their titles and their estates were confiscated and awarded to members of the loyalist faction. Shunned by their Spanish comrades, these soldiers without a cause to serve were reduced to paupers who had little hope of ever rising above their imposed poverty-stricken status.

Shortly after the execution of Diego de Almagro, Hernándo Pizarro collected a great store of gold bullion that was earmarked for shipment to Castile. It was thought that such a magnificent offering of this most sought after of all metals would be enough to eclipse the complaints of those who had sailed on ahead to Spain to inform the court of the unpleasant circumstances surrounding the death of the Marshal. Before leaving for Spain, Hernándo warned Francisco to keep an eye on the men of Chile, prophetically reminding him that these were desperate men who would surely resort to violence if an opportunity presented itself. After a farewell embrace, the brothers laid eyes upon one another for the very last time. Hernándo made his way back to Spain in July of 1539 and immediately traveled to the city of Valladolid, where the royal court was currently in session.

Despite all the riches he had brought with him, Hernándo found his reception at the royal court to be far less cordial than his previous appearance. Diego de Alvarado, who had been entrusted to look after the inheritance of the younger Almagro until he was of legal age, had preceeded him at court, and even though the officer had twice saved the life of this Pizarro, he could not forgive him for having so callously taken the life of Diego de Almagro. Alvarado informed the officials at court of the heinous act of revenge that had been perpetrated by a remorseless Hernándo. In his own defense, Pizarro relied on his charm in an effort to allay the numerous concerns of those who sat in judgment of him. Alvarado became so incensed over the delay in reaching a verdict that he challenged Pizarro to a duel. Hernándo declined, but in a strange twist, a seemingly healthy Diego died five days later of an unexplainable ailment, the mystery of which caused many to suspect that he had been poisoned. Though never formally charged with any crime, Hernándo Pizarro was, however, placed under house arrest at the Medina del Campo compound for the next twenty years. In 1551, while still incarcerated, an elderly Hernándo married his eighteen year old niece, Doña Francisca, the progeny of the union between his half-brother Francisco and the Inca princess Quispe Sisa, who was christened Doña Inés.

The royal court then turned its attention toward the conduct of Francisco Pizarro, fearing that the conqueror of Peru now imagined himself as being beyond the reach of Spanish jurisdiction. Vaca de Castro, a member of the Royal Audience of Valladolid, was sent to assess and pass judgment on the present situation in Peru, the latest addition to a rapidly expanding Spanish empire.

Once he turned eighteen years old, Diego de Almagro, who came to Peru after Cuzco was claimed by the Spaniards to join his father in the conquest and settlement of New Toledo, inherited all of his father's extensive land holdings, claims which were supported by the royal decree of Emperor Charles V. However, Francisco Pizarro declared that he would not recognize any claims put forth by the half-breed progeny of his former partner and a native woman of Panama. The captain-general convinced himself that the New Toledo province granted to the elder Almagro was part of an award to the enterprise of the Company of the Levant, and now that the partnership had, due to the death of his two partners, been dissolved he was therefore entitled to all of its remaining assets. Even though Pizarro refused to recognize the claims of the young Almagro, he did permit him to maintain a permanent residence at Lima, a location where he could keep a close eye on him. It was here that a number of men who once served the Marshal, and who now transferred their allegiance to his young son, met in secret to conspire on a way to exact revenge against an unforgiving and uncompromising Francisco Pizarro.

The complaints of the younger Almagro and the impoverished soldiers who had served his former partner were, at that time, the least of the captain-general's concerns. The more pressing matter at the moment was the Inca resistance movement that seemed to be taunting him. From his mountain stronghold, Inca Manco continued to harass the Spanish settlements with a series of well orchestrated guerrilla style attacks, particularly against Spanish caravans, while managing to avoid all of the captain-general's determined efforts to capture him. To put an end to these intolerable raids, Gonzalo Pizarro was dispatched with a large force to find and capture the persistent Manco. Gonzalo's army defeated the Inca rebels in several pitched battles but Manco always seemed to elude his grasp. Once, while pursuing the fugitive Inca ruler, Gonzalo and his men were halted by a river that ran before them and as they pondered the best way to get across a figure emerged from the other side and exclaimed, "I am Manco Inca! I am Manco Inca!"[1] The fugitive ruler went on to say that he and his warriors had killed two thousand soldiers during the great uprising and that he intended to kill them as well, in order to regain possession of the lands and treasures that belonged to his forefathers. To strike fear into the hearts of the rebellious faction, the Spaniards burned alive the captured high priest of the Incas, Villac-Umu. Undeterred, Manco and his warriors resumed their raids against Spanish interests once Gonzalo returned from his less than successful mission.

Frustrated by the numerous unsuccessful attempts to capture Manco Inca, the captain-general sought to reach a peaceful settlement to their many differences. When the distrustful Inca ruler refused his invitation to a meet with the Bishop of Cuzco, Francisco Pizarro decided to send an offering of gifts, tribute which included a splendid looking pony that he hoped would demonstrate that his intentions were truly sincere. An African slave who was one of Pizarro's servants was selected to carry this array of tribute to the Inca. Along the way the unsuspecting emissary and his two native guides were waylaid by warriors in the service of Manco who, after taking the lives of those who served Pizarro as well as that of the pony, ran off with the valuable tribute items they carried for the Inca ruler.

A greatly angered Francisco Pizarro was quick to take revenge for the murder of his unarmed emissary. Cura Occlo, a beautiful young woman who was a favorite wife of Manco and, unfortunately, a prisoner of the captain-general, was stripped naked and tied to a tree. Unfortunately, the coya, who had repelled Spanish attempts to violate her body by covering herself with feces, could not protect herself from the wrath of Francisco Pizarro. After being beaten to a bloody pulp with rods in the hands of overzealous Canari Indians, Cura Occlo's tormentors ended her pain and suffering by piercing her swollen and scarred body with a great many arrows. The Inca queen bore her torture and death with quiet dignity, never once uttering a scream or a cry. Many of the Spanish soldiers who witnessed this malevolent means of retaliation employed by their commander simply hung their heads in shame. Her ravaged body was placed in a canoe and allowed to float down the Yucay River so that the rebellious Inca could see what had become of Cura Occlo, his beloved sister wife. Manco was heartbroken when he learned of what had happened.

Meanwhile, the stirrings of discontent at Lima were on the verge of coming to a head. The impoverished former followers of Diego de Almagro were delighted to hear that the Crown had sent a judge from Spain. Two Almagro loyalists were selected to meet the royal judge at the port where he was expected to arrive in order to inform him of their numerous grievances. Unfortunately, the arrival of Vaca de Castro was delayed, the duration of which was long enough to cause many to suspect that his vessel had perished at sea.

Unable to wait any longer for help that might never arrive, several of the frustrated members of the Almagro faction decided to take matters into their own hands. Juan de Rada, once an officer of high rank within the army of the Marshal, was looked upon as the leader of a group consisting of approximately twenty other disgruntled soldiers who secretly schemed to assassinate Francisco Pizarro. They set a date of Sunday, June 26, 1541, as the day they would execute their daring plot. The plan was to strike the captain-general dead as soon as he emerged from church following Sunday Mass.

One of the conspirators, however, had a sudden change of heart and felt compelled to confess the upcoming assassination plot to a priest, who, in turn, reported it to a member of Francisco Pizarro's inner circle. The captain-general dismissed the report as the words of a clergyman who merely wished to get in his good graces. Francisco also felt that even if the rumor were true, the malcontents simply did not posses enough courage to act upon their boastful claims. He did, however, tell the story to his chief judge, Velázquez, who also scoffed at the report. However, the story must have caused him some concern, for Pizarro chose not to attend church that Sunday morning.

When Francisco Pizarro and his regular entourage failed to appear from church as usual, the conspirators feared that their plot had somehow been revealed and that at any moment soldiers would come to arrest them. As they debated over which course of action to take one of the conspirators threatened that if they did not follow through with the planned assassination he would personally reveal to the Pizarro camp the names of all involved in the plot. Juan de Rada and his cohorts paraded down the street chanting with a growing sense of confidence, "Long live the king! Death to the Tyrant!"[2]

Though many citizens came out to see what all the ruckus was about no one made an effort to stop them.

Juan de Rada and his party of determined assassins entered Francisco Pizarro's courtyard and struck down an unarmed servant who bravely attempted to block their way into the governor's palace. One of the guards entered the room where the captain-general was entertaining about twenty guests and shouted "Help, help! the men of Chile are all coming to murder the Marquis!"[3]

Several of Francisco Pizarro's guests, who just moments earlier had been enjoying the food and company of their gracious host, left by way of an open window the instant they learned of the danger that was rapidly approaching. Martín de Alcantára, a half brother of the captain-general, was among the loyal few who remained to defend the Marquis. An officer by the name of Francisco de Chaves was ordered to lock the door while another soldier was sent to get help. The brazen Chaves, however, decided to open the door slightly so he could teach the rabble outside a lesson with his sword. This was all the opening that Juan de Rada and his men needed. Chaves was bested by the blade of his opponent and as his pierced body fell to the floor the assassins flung open the door and rushed in for the kill.

Francisco Pizarro was hurriedly strapping on his gear as the conspirators broke through the door to his chambers. When he saw that Martín de Alcantára was in trouble the Marquis tossed aside the cumbersome breastplate he was attempting to put on and rushed into the fray. Unfortunately, Martín was slain before he was able to reach him. The elderly Pizarro showed he still possessed the strength and skill to defend himself by striking down two of the assassins.

Juan De Rada and his men eventually cornered the captain-general but despite their superior numbers they could not penetrate past the blade of their skillful opponent. The frustrated De Rada shouted "Why are we so long about it? Down with the tyrant!"[4] He pushed one of his men toward Pizarro who responded by running the man through with his sword. However, before the marquis could extricate his sword another soldier slashed him across the throat with his blade. As the weary and wounded captain-general slowly fell to the floor the assassins hacked away until there was little life left within his body. Knowing that death was near, Francisco dipped his finger into the pool of his own blood and made the sign of the cross on the floor. The captain-general expired his last breath after planting a kiss on his hastily made cross of blood.

The victorious Juan de Rada and his men went out into the streets and shouted, "The tyrant is dead! The laws are restored! Long live our master the

The Killing of Pizarro (courtesy Library of Congress).

emperor and his governor Almagro!"⁵ The conqueror of Peru, and the last of the partners of the Company of the Levant, was buried in the cathedral without the benefit of any ceremony.

After the young Diego de Almagro was proclaimed ruler of Peru, the men of Chile took to looting the city of Lima. The homes and wealth of those who served Francisco Pizarro were confiscated and distributed among the Almagro loyalists. Those who were part of Pizarro's inner circle were rounded up and tortured in an effort to find out where the captain-general kept his secret stash of wealth — the vast treasure that was never reported to the Spanish crown. Several of Pizarro's comrades were put to death. With the Almagro faction now in control of Lima and the empire, Father Vincente de Valverde fled Peru shortly after the assassination of Francisco Pizarro. His ship stopped at the island of Puná where he was killed and eaten by native cannibals who had not forgotten or forgiven the Spaniards for their many past transgressions.

The Murder of Manco Inca

Manco learned of Francisco Pizarro's assassination while he was still carrying on guerrilla campaigns against the Spaniards from his hidden stronghold of Vilcabamba. Vaca de Castro, the Spanish judge who had been sent by the Crown to settle the many differences between the Pizarro and Almagro camps, finally arrived in Peru and, when he learned of the recent death of the conqueror of Peru, he immediately raised a royal army to restore order and to protect the interests of Emperor Charles V. His army would quickly settle the issue by defeating the Almagro force at the Battle of Chupas. Diego Méndez, a captain who played an important role in the assassination of Francisco Pizarro, was captured at the battle of Chupas. Somehow, both he and six other imprisoned comrades managed to escape from their confinement and sought refuge in the mountains where they happened upon the secret hideout of the Incas at Vilcabamba. The Spanish refugees offered their services to Inca Manco in exchange for his protection.

Manco's nobles advised the Inca not to trust the seven Spaniards who had come to their mountain retreat and called for their immediate death. Manco, however, wanted to learn from them. Méndez and his cohorts taught the Inca warriors how to ride horses, use Spanish weapons — especially the arquebuses — and drilled them in the intricacies of Spanish tactics of warfare.

However, when these fugitives learned that Spain had sent a viceroy to replace Vaca de Castro and restore order to the land they saw an opportunity to redeem themselves for their seditious crimes by offering proof that they had found and killed the Inca ruler who had wreaked such havoc on Spanish efforts to colonize Peru. The soldiers invited the Inca ruler who who had so graciously sheltered and fed them for many months to join them in a popular native game called quoits. While drinking a toast from tumblers made of gold, Diego Méndez pulled out a concealed knife and repeatedly stabbed Manco until the unsuspecting Inca fell to the ground. Tito Cusi, the nine year old son of Manco, witnessed the brutal attack. When he tried to rush to the aid of his fallen father one of the Spaniards picked up a spear and hurled it directly at him. The frightened but unharmed prince hid in the bushes while the Spanish assassins made their escape. Leaving Manco for dead, Diego and his comrades attempted to escape on their horses. News of what happened spread swiftly among the members of the tribe and soon every warrior of Vilcabamba was looking for the treacherous Spaniards.

In their haste to escape to the city of Cuzco the small group of murderous Spaniards ran smack into a squadron of Manco's warriors who were searching for them. Several soldiers were speared to death and those who escaped such a fate soon met a fiery demise when Indians set fire to the building where they sought protection. The severed heads of the seven Spaniards were prominently displayed for all to see. Manco lived for another five days before finally succumbing to his wounds. When told of how the attempt on his life had been avenged, a weary Manco responded, "Do not be surprised that they have killed me in this corner; they killed my brother Atahualpa while he was in possession of all his power and empire."[6] Before dying he named Sayri Tupac as his successor. With these final words the sun slowly set upon the empire that once belonged to the Incas.

Chapter Notes

Chapter 1

1. J.H. Parry, *The Discovery of South America*, page 117.
2. William H. Prescott, *History of the Conquest of Peru*, page 830 (n. 3 cites Herrera as his source).
3. Robert Silverberg, *The Golden Dream: Seekers of El Dorado*, page 21.

Chapter 2

1. J. H. Parry, *The Discovery of South America*, page 176.

Chapter 3

1. William H. Prescott, *History of the Conquest of Peru*, page 860 (n. 25 cites Herrera as his source).

Chapter 4

1. Cecil Howard, *Pizarro and the Conquest of Peru*, page 21.
2. Pedro de Cieza de León, *The Discovery and Conquest of Peru*, page 125.

Chapter 5

1. Hammond Innes, *The Conquistadors*, page 268 (cites Cieza de León as source).
2. *Ibid.*
3. David M. Jones and Brian L. Molyneaux, *The Mythology of the Americas*, page 307 (cites Vega as source).
4. Donna Rosenberg, *World Mythology*, page 475.
5. Pedro Sarmiento de Gamboa, *History of the Incas*, page 48.
6. Jones and Molyneaux, page 308 (cites Vega as source).
7. Bertrand Flornoy, *The World of the Inca* (n. 4 cites Garcilaso de la Vega as source).
8. Sarmiento de Gamboa, page 76.

Chapter 6

1. Father Cobo, *History of the Inca Empire*, page 134.
2. Juan de Betanzos, *Narrative of the Incas*, page 29.
3. *Ibid.*, page 76.
4. Alfred Netraux, *The History of the Incas*, page 58.
5. Time Life Books, *Incas: Lords of Gold and Glory*, page 48.

Chapter 7

1. William H. Prescott, *History of the Conquest of Peru*, page 877 (n. 3 cites Herrera as his source).
2. Pedro de Cieza de León, *The Discovery and Conquest of Peru*, page 131.
3. Stuart Stirling, *The Last Conquistador*, page 61.

4. Cecil Howard, *Pizarro and the Conquest of Peru*, page 16.

Chapter 8

1. Stuart Stirling, *Pizarro: Conqueror of the Inca*, page 28.
2. David Duncan, *Hernando de Soto: A Savage Quest in the Americas*, page 118.

Chapter 9

1. Hammond Innes, *The Conquistadors*, page 277 (cites Cieza de León as source).
2. Father Bernabe Cobo, *History of the Inca Empire*, page 160.
3. Innes, page 280 (cites Garcilaso as source).
4. Innes, page 280.
5. Cobo, *Inca Religion and Customs*.
6. Innes, page 279 (cites Cieza de León as source).
7. Juan de Betanzos, *Narrative of the Incas*, page 195.
8. Ibid., page 235.

Chapter 10

1. Stuart Stirling, *The Last Conquistador*, page 36 (cites Francisco de Xerez and were the words of Diego de Trujillo).
2. Hammond Innes, *The Conquistadors*, page 235.
3. Juan de Betanzos, *Narrative of the Incas*, page 248.
4. Ibid., page 250.
5. William H. Prescott, *History of the Conquest of Peru*, page 921 (n. 3 cites Oviedo as his source).
6. Innes, page 240.

Chapter 11

1. John Hemming, *Discovery of Lost Worlds: the Lost Cities of the Incas*, page 250.
2. Hammond Innes, *The Conquistadors*, page 284 (cites Cieza de León as source).
3. Ibid., page 287.

4. William H. Prescott, *History of the Conquest of Peru*, page 930.
5. Time Life, *Incas: Lords of Gold and Glory*, page 24 (no source cited).
6. John Hemming, *The Conquest of the Incas*, page 38.
7. Prescott, page 939.
8. Carmen Bernard, *The Incas: People of the Sun* (cites Xeres as source).
9. Time-Life Books, *Ancient America*, page 150 (no source cited).
10. Prescott, page 940.
11. Time-Life Books, *Ancient America*, page 150 (no source cited).
12. Time Life Books, *Incas: Lords of Gold and Glory*, page 26 (no source cited).
13. Time-Life Books, *Ancient America*, page 150 (no source cited).

Chapter 12

1. Alfred Metraux, *The History of the Incas*, page 60.
2. Rafael Varon Gabai, *Francisco Pizarro and his Brothers*, page 182.
3. Hammond Innes, *The Conquistadors*, page 293.
4. Juan de Betanzos, *Narrative of the Incas*, page 270.
5. Robert Silverberg, *The Golden Dream: Seekers of El Dorado*, pages 33, 34 (cites Garcilaso de la Vega).
6. de Betanzos, page 272.
7. William H. Prescott, *History of the Conquest of Peru*, page 974.

Chapter 13

1. Pedro de Cieza de León, *The Discovery and Conquest of Peru*, page 283.

Chapter 14

1. Michael Wood, *The Conquistadors*, page 18.

Chapter 16

1. William H. Prescott, *History of the Conquest of Peru*, page 1045.

2. Cecil Howard, *Pizarro and the Conquest of Peru*, page 113 (no source cited).

Chapter 17

1. Michael Wood, *The Conquistadors*.
2. Cecil Howard, *Pizarro and the Conquest of Peru*, page 122.

3. Ibid., page 124.
4. Ibid., page 124.
5. Ibid., page 125.
6. Father Cobo, *History of the Inca Empire*, page 176.

Bibliography

Acosta, Jose de. *Natural and Moral History of the Indies*. Durham, NC: Duke University Press, 2002.

Bernard, Carmen. *The Incas: People of the Sun*. New York: Abrams, 1994.

Betanzos, Juan de. *Narrative of the Incas*. Translated by Roland Hamilton and Dana Buchanan. Austin: University of Texas Press, 1996.

Bierhorst, John. *Mythology of South America*. New York: Morrow, 1988.

Canseco, Maria Rostworowski de Diez. *History of the Inca Realm*. Translated by Harry B. Iceland. Cambridge: Cambridge University Press, 1999.

Cobo, Father Bernabe. *Inca Religion and Customs*. Translated by Roland Hamilton. Austin: University of Texas Press, 1990.

———. *History of the Inca Empire*. Translated by Roland Hamilton. Austin: University of Texas Press, 1979.

Cotterell, Maurice. *The Lost Tomb of Viracocha*. London: Headline, 2001.

Descola, Jean. *The Conquistadors*. New York: Viking Press, 1957.

Dickey, Thomas, John Man, and John Wiencek. *The Kings of El Dorado*. Chicago: Stonehenge Press, 1982.

Duncan, David Ewing. *Hernando de Soto: A Savage Quest in the Americas*. New York: Crown, 1995.

Editors of National Geographic. *Lost Empires, Living Tribes*. Washington, D.C.: National Geographic Society, 1982.

Editors of Reader's Digest. *Mysteries of the Ancient Americas*. Pleasantville, NY: Reader's Digest, 1986.

Editors of Time-Life. *The Search for El Dorado*. Alexandria, VA: Time-Life Books, 1992.

Flornoy, Bertrand. *The World of the Inca*. Garden City, NY: Doubleday, 1958.

Gabai, Rafael Varon. *Francisco Pizarro and His Brothers: The Illusion of Power in Sixteenth Century Peru*. Norman, OK: University of Oklahoma Press, 1997.

Gamboa, Pedro Sarmiento de. *History of the Incas*. Mineola, NY: Dover, 1999.

Gardner, Joseph L., ed. *Mysteries of the Ancient Americas: The New World Before Columbus*. Pleasantville, NY: Reader's Digest, 1986.

Hardoy, Jorge E. *Pre-Columbian Cities*. New York: Walker, 1973.

Hemming, John. *Discovery of Lost Worlds: The Lost Cities of the Incas*. New York: Heritage, 1979.

———. *The Conquest of the Incas*. New York: Harvest Books, 1970.

Howard, Cecil. *Pizarro and the Conquest of Peru*. New York: American Heritage, 1968.

Innes, Hammond. *The Conquistadors*. New York: Knopf, 1969.

Johnston, Darcie Conner, and James M. Lynch. *Incas: Lords of Gold and Glory*. Alexandria, VA: Time-Life Books, 1992.

Jones, David M., and Brian L. Molyneaux. *The Mythology of the Americas*. New York: Lorenz Books 2001.

Kamen, Henry. *Empire: How Spain Became

a World Power 1492–1763. New York: Harper Collins, 2003.

Kennedy, Mike Dixon. *Native American Myth and Legend*. London: Blandford Books, 1996.

Kropp, Miriam. *Cuzco: Window on Peru*. New York: Crowell, 1956.

Leon, Pedro de Cieza de. *The Discovery & Conquest of Peru: Chronicles of the New World Encounter*. Durham, NC: Duke University Press, 1988.

Leonard, Jonathan Norton. *Ancient America*. New York: Time-Life Books, 1967.

Littleton, Scott, gen. ed. *Mythology: The Illustrated Anthology of World Myth and Storytelling*. London: Baird, 2002.

Mason, J. Alden. *The Ancient Civilizations of Peru*. New York: Penguin Books, 1968.

McFagen, Brian. *Kingdoms of Gold, Kingdoms of Jade*. London: Thames and Hudson, 1991.

Metraux, Alfred. *The History of the Incas*. New York: Schocken Books, 1969.

Morison, Samuel Eliot. *The European Discovery of America: The Southern Voyages A.D. 1492–1616*. New York: Oxford University Press, 1974.

Moseley, Michael E. *The Incas & Their Ancestors*. London: Thames and Hudson, 1992.

Osborne, Harold. *Mythology of the Americas: South American Mythology*. London: Hamlyn, 1970.

Parry, J.H. *The Discovery of South America*. New York: Taplinger, 1979.

Prescott, William H. *The World of the Incas*. New York: Tudor, 1970.

_____. *The Conquest of Peru*. New York: Random House, 1953.

Restall, Matthew. *Seven Myths of the Spanish Conquest*. New York: Oxford University Press, 2003.

Rosenberg, Donna. *World Mythology*. Lincolnwood, IL: NTC, 1994.

Silverberg, Robert. *The Golden Dream: Seekers of El Dorado*. Athens, OH: Ohio University Press, 1996.

Spence, Lewis. *Mexico and Peru: Myths and Legends*. London: Crowell, 1920.

Stierlin, Henri. *The Pre-Columbian Civilizations: The World of the Maya, Aztecs, and Incas*. New York: Sunflower Books, 1979.

Stirling, Stuart. *Pizarro: Conqueror of the Inca*. Gloucestershire, England: Sutton, 2005.

_____. *The Last Conquistador: Mansio Serra de Leguizamon and the Conquest of the Incas*. England: Sutton, 1999.

Stuart, George E., and Gene S. Stuart. *Discovering Man's Past in the Americas*. Washington, D.C: National Geographic Society, 1969.

Thomas, Hugh. *Rivers of Gold: The Rise of the Spanish Empire, from Columbus to Magellan*. New York: Random House, 2003.

Urton, Gary. *Inca Myths*. Austin: University of Texas Press, 1999.

Verrill, A Hyatt. *Great Conquerors of South and Central America*. New York: New Home Library, 1943.

Wasbard, Simone. *The World's Last Mysteries*. Pleasantville, NY: Reader's Digest, 1976.

Wood, Michael. *The Conquistadors*. Los Angeles: University of California Press, Berkeley, 2000.

Wood, Peter. *The Spanish Main*. Alexandria, VA: Time-Life Books, 1979.

Index

Abancay, Battle of 185
Acamama 60, 61
Acla 23
Alcantara, Martin de 97, 98, 122, 198
Alcavicca 60, 61, 70
Aldana, Hernando de 136
Almagro, Diego de 21, 25, 27, 32, 34, 35, 36, 37, 38, 40, 41, 42, 43, 44, 46, 47, 94, 95, 97, 98, 99, 100, 101, 102, 104, 106, 112, 147, 148, 149, 150, 151, 153, 156, 158, 159, 162, 163, 164, 167, 168, 169, 170, 171, 172, 180, 181, 182, 183, 184, 186, 187, 188, 189, 190, 191, 192, 193, 194, 197, 200
Almagro, Diego de (son) 193, 195, 196, 197, 200
Altiplano 55, 79
Alvarado, Alonso de 183, 185, 186, 191
Alvarado, Diego de 187, 195
Alvarado, Pedro de 134, 162, 163, 166, 167, 168, 171, 180, 183, 186, 187
Amaza 78
Amazon 56, 81
Amparaes 89
Ancasmarca 71
Andagoya, Pascual de 21, 24, 26, 27, 28, 29, 34
Andahuaylas 118
Andalusia 27
Andes 2, 29, 31, 52, 56, 62, 80, 81, 88, 91, 93, 109, 128, 129, 163, 164, 172, 181
Antisuyu 78, 88, 90
Apu Achache 108
Apu Cinchi Roca 109, 159
Apu Conde Mayta 70, 71, 72
Apurimac 91, 157, 179
Arguello, Hernando de 23, 24
Atacames 41, 42
Atahualpa 107, 110, 114, 115, 116, 117, 118, 119, 120, 121, 122, 123, 124, 125, 126, 127, 128, 129, 130, 131, 132, 133, 134, 135, 136, 137, 138, 139, 140, 141, 142, 143, 144, 145, 146, 147, 148, 149, 150, 151, 152, 153, 154, 155, 156, 157, 158, 160, 161, 162, 164, 165, 166, 167, 172, 173, 174, 181, 201
Auquituma 111
Ayamarcas 69, 73
Ayar Auca 58, 59, 60
Ayar Cachi 58, 59, 60
Ayar Manco see Manco Capac
Ayar Uchu 58, 59, 60
Ayauire 79
Aymara 76, 78, 79
Azarpay 156
Aztec 2, 3, 35, 53, 86, 93, 96, 107, 123, 134

Balboa, Vasco Nunez de 13, 14, 16, 17, 18, 19, 20, 21, 22, 23, 24, 25, 26, 27, 34, 95, 104
Bastidas, Rodrigo de 8, 13, 14
Benalcazar, Sebastian de 21, 102, 104, 105, 106, 135, 164, 165, 166, 167
Biru 26, 29
Bobadilla, Francisco 7
Bobadilla, Maria de 22
Bocanegra, Andres de 52, 53
Bombon 118, 147
Botello, Luis 23
Briceno, Alonso 45
Bueno, Martin 144, 149

Cabo Blanco 52
Cacha 57
Cahuide 178
Cajamarca 78, 82, 107, 109, 118, 120, 121, 123, 124, 125, 126, 127, 128, 129, 130, 131, 132, 133, 134, 135, 136, 137, 139, 140, 141, 142, 143, 144, 145, 146, 147, 148, 151, 152, 153, 155, 156, 157, 158, 161, 165, 166, 169
Cajas 125, 126
Calatayud 169
Calca 75, 76
Canari 88, 117, 120, 155, 165, 173, 175, 177, 196
Candia, Pedro de 45, 50, 51, 95, 97, 138
Capac Nan (royal road) 91

Capac Toco, Inca 58
Capac Yupanqui 73, 81
Cape Pasado 48
Caquea-Xaquixahuana 75, 76
Caranga 89, 110
Caret 17
Caribbean 5, 12
Caribs 32
Carrion, Anton de 45
Cartegena 9, 12
Castilla del oro 25
Castillo, Bernal Diaz de 21, 25
Castro, Vaca de 195, 197, 200
Cayambes 110, 111
Ceretita 17
Chachapoya 88, 109
Chalcuchima 118, 119, 137, 146, 147, 148, 149, 153, 156, 157, 158, 172
Chan-Chan 53, 81, 82, 83
Chanca 75, 76, 80, 82, 85, 177
Charles V, Emperor 94, 95, 96, 138, 150, 169, 174, 180, 187, 195, 200
Chaves, Francisco de 198
Chavin 86
Chilcca 81
Chile 169, 171, 180, 181, 184, 192, 194, 198, 200
Chillka 59
Chimbo Cisa 121
Chimborazo 48
Chimo, Valley of 81
Chimor 54
Chimpu Orma 73
Chimu 50, 52, 53, 82, 83; *see also* Chanca
Chincha 81, 187
Chinchaysuyu 78, 90, 108, 109
Chita Mama Roncay 73
Choco 78
Cholula 134
Chucuito 88, 109
Chunco 88
Chupas, Battle of 200
Cieza de Leon, Pedro de 83, 84, 108, 116
Cinga 109
Cinto 107
Ciquinchara 123, 124, 127, 128
Coaque 101, 102
Coati 80
Cobo, Bernabe 115
Cochabamba 89, 109
Colla Capac 79
Collaguas 70
Collao 78, 88, 109
Collasuyu 73, 78, 88, 90, 109
Collique 52
Colmenares, Rodrigo de 17, 18
Colombia 13
Colon 16
Colon, Diego 17
Columbus, Christopher 7, 8, 17, 20, 102

Comogre 18
Company of the Levant 28, 148, 193, 195, 200
Copacati 80
Copiapo 181
Coquimbo 182
Cordoba, Gonzalo 7
Cori Ilpaycahua 71
Coricancha 61, 83, 84, 90, 119, 144, 149, 160, 166, 192
Cortes, Hernan 2, 13, 27, 95, 96, 107, 123, 124, 134, 162, 168, 186
Cosa, Juan de la 8, 9, 10, 13
Cotopaxi 48, 166
Coya Miro 121
Cuba 12, 25, 96
Cuellar, Francisco de 45
Cuichu 84
Cuntisuyu 78, 90
Cura Occlo 196, 197
Cusi Inca Yupanqui see Pachacuti
Cusi Rimay 87
Cuxi Yupanqui 116, 117, 118, 120
Cuyumarc 71
Cuzco 2, 57, 58, 60, 61, 62, 64, 69, 70, 71, 74, 75, 76, 77, 78, 80, 81, 82, 83, 84, 86, 87, 88, 90, 91, 107, 108, 109, 114, 115, 116, 117, 118, 119, 120, 121, 125, 128, 137, 142, 143, 144, 145, 146, 148, 149, 151, 156, 157, 158, 159, 160, 161, 162, 165, 168, 170, 171, 172, 173, 174, 175, 176, 177, 180, 181, 182, 183, 184, 185, 186, 187, 188, 190, 191, 192, 194, 201

Dabaibe 2, 17, 18, 27, 104
Darien 8, 14, 16, 17, 18, 19, 21, 22, 23, 24, 25, 27, 28, 102, 104
Davila, Gil Gonzalez 104
Dona Francisca 195
Dona Ines 195

Ecuador 2, 100, 109, 163
Egyptians 66
El Mar del Sur, 20, 22, 23, 24, 27
El Nino 82
Enciso, Martin Fernandez de 12, 13, 14, 16, 17, 21, 22, 95
Espinosa, Gaspar de 22, 23, 25, 27, 28, 36, 37, 104, 184, 186, 187
Esquivel, Juan de 13
Estete, Miguel de 139, 146
Extremadura 7

Felipillo (interpreter) 54, 95, 103, 132, 141, 152, 153, 168, 181
Ferdinand, king 7, 8, 16, 19, 21, 22

Gallo, Isle of 39, 40, 41, 42, 44, 45, 46, 97
Garabito, Andres, de 23
Godoy, Francisco de 147

Gonzalez, Francisca (Francisco's mother) 7
Gorgona, Isle of 46, 47, 54
Gualpaya 108
Guama Tupa 73
Guamanga 78
Guaro, Valley of 69, 81
Guatemala 162, 163, 164, 167, 168, 177, 180, 186
Guayaquil, Gulf of 48, 102, 111
Guayna Achache 111

Halcon, Pedro de 45, 53
Haysquisrro 59
Hispaniola 7, 8, 11, 12, 13, 14, 16, 17
Huacas (sacred sites) 60, 84
Hualla 61
Huamachucho 143, 145, 153
Huanacauri 59, 60, 61
Huanaypata 60
Huancabamba 126
Huarco 81
Huaritico 157
Huascar 107, 114, 115, 116, 117, 118, 119, 120, 121, 132, 142, 143, 144, 145, 147, 153, 155, 158, 159, 162, 170
Huatanay 60, 86
Huayllaca 72
Huayna Capac 49, 87, 107, 108, 109, 110, 111, 112, 113, 114, 115, 116, 117, 120, 135, 158, 159, 160, 166, 174
Hurtado, Bartolome de 13, 14, 18

Ica 81
Illapa (god of thunder) 56, 65, 84
Inca Roca 71, 72, 73, 75, 79
Incas 2, 3, 27, 31, 41, 48, 50, 59, 60, 61, 62, 63, 64, 66, 67, 68, 69, 70, 71, 73, 75, 76, 81, 82, 83, 85, 86, 87, 88, 90, 91, 93, 109, 110, 111, 117, 122, 123, 128, 140, 141, 149, 150, 156, 173, 201
Inti (sun god) 58, 59, 61, 64, 66, 79, 80, 84, 89, 91, 114, 134
Inti Cancha (Temple of the Sun) 83, 84, 86, 89, 90
Intl Capac Yupanqui 71
Inti Urco 74, 75, 76, 77
Isabella, queen 7
Italy 7

Jamaica 13, 96
Jaquijaguana 74, 157, 172
Jauja 118, 121, 146, 157, 158, 162, 192
Jerez, Garcia de 45
Jerez de los Cabaleros 104

Kolka (god of stars) 56

Lake Titicaca 55, 56, 78, 79, 80, 89, 93, 109
Lambayeque Valley 52
Las Golondrinas 163

Leguizamon, Mansio Serra de 161
Leon, Hernan Ponce de 105
Leon, Juan Ponce de 13
Lima 170, 171, 174, 175, 177, 183, 184, 185, 186, 187, 188, 190, 192, 197, 200
Limatambo 118
Llanos 81
Lloque Yupanqui 69, 70
Lucanas 78
Lunaguana 81
Lupaca 79
Luque, Hernando de 27, 28, 36, 37, 44, 46, 47, 94, 95, 97, 98, 99, 148, 184

Machu Picchu 86
Mala 81, 188, 192
Mama Anahuarque 78
Mama Cachua 69
Mama Chicya 73
Mama Choque 73
Mama Cuca 69
Mama Cura 58, 59
Mama Cusi Rimay 114
Mama Huaco 58, 59, 61
Mama Kocha (water goddess) 56
Mama Michay 72
Mama Occlo 58, 59, 62, 87
Mama Quilla (moon goddess) 56, 67, 80
Mama Raua 58, 59
Mama Roncay 73
Mama Tancaray 70
Manco Capac 57, 58, 59, 60, 61, 62, 69
Manco Inca 158, 159, 162, 171, 172, 173, 174, 175, 176, 177, 178, 179, 180, 181, 183, 184, 185, 186, 196, 197, 200, 201
Manco Sapaca 69
Manta 57
Mapuche 182
Mara 59
Martinez, Ana 193
Martinillo (interpreter) 54, 95, 137, 138
Maska 59
Maya 3
Mayta Capac 69, 70, 71
Mayta Yupanqui 157, 158
Medina del Campo 194
Mejia, Francisco 176
Mena, Cristobal de 150, 151
Mendez, Diego 200, 201
Mexico 2, 35, 36, 53, 86, 95, 104, 107, 123, 124, 162, 168, 177, 186
Mihicnca Mayta 113
Minchancaman 81, 82
Moche 82
Moguer, Pedro de 144, 149
Mohica 86
Moina Caytomarca 73
Mojo 109
Molina, Alonso de, 45, 49, 50, 51, 53, 107
Molina, Cristobal de 180

Montejo, Francisco 25
Montenegro, Francisco de 30, 31, 33
Mundi Map 8
Munoz, Hernan 23
Muru Uanca 75

Narvaez, Panfilo 13
Nasco 81
Navarre 7, 97
Navarro, Francisco 97, 102, 122
Nazca 86
New Andalusia 8
New Castile 27, 96, 171
New Toledo 169, 171, 180, 188, 195
Nicaragua 2, 36, 37, 40, 102, 104, 105, 122, 147, 163, 177, 186
Nicuesa, Diego 8, 10, 16, 17, 22
Ninan Cuyochi 114
Nombre de Dios 16, 98, 100

Ojeda, Alonso de 5, 8, 9, 10, 11, 13, 14, 16, 22
Ollantaytambo 179
Oma 69, 85
Order of Santiago 97, 169
Orgonez, Rodrigo 182, 183, 184, 185, 187, 188, 190, 191, 192
Ovando, Nicolas de 7, 8, 13

Pacha Kutic 71
Pachacama 81
Pachacamac 113, 114, 145, 146, 148, 168
Pachacuti Inca Yupanqui 73, 74, 75, 76, 77, 78, 79, 80, 81, 83, 84, 85, 86, 87, 111
Pachamama (mother earth) 56
Pahuac Hualpa Mayta 73
Paita 52, 123
Pallusta 59
Panama 2, 13, 14, 20, 21, 25, 26, 27, 28, 30, 34, 35, 36, 42, 43, 44, 45, 46, 47, 51, 53, 54, 94, 96, 98, 100, 101, 104, 105, 123, 147, 148, 155, 163, 170, 177, 184, 186
Panciaco 18, 19, 20
Paracas 86
Paria 89, 180
Pata Yupanqui 75
Paua 73
Paullu 180, 181, 184
Paz, Martin de, 45, 48
Pearl Islands 20, 23, 28, 29, 30, 31
Pedrarias 21, 22, 23, 24, 25, 26, 27, 28, 36, 37, 40, 104, 105
Peralta, Cristobal; de 45, 48
Perez, Rodrigo 148
Peru 2, 26, 27, 37, 44, 45, 81, 94, 96, 100, 104, 105, 107, 113, 122, 123, 131, 147, 149, 151, 180, 181, 185, 186, 188, 192, 195, 200, 201
Pincos 118
Pisco 81
Piura River, 124

Pizarro, Francisco 2, 3, 5, 7, 8, 10, 11, 12, 13, 14, 16, 17, 19, 20, 21, 23, 24, 27, 28, 29, 30, 31, 32, 33, 34, 35, 36, 37, 38, 39, 40, 41, 42, 43, 44, 45, 46, 47, 48, 49, 50, 51, 52, 53, 54, 94, 95, 96, 97, 98, 99, 100, 101, 102, 103, 106, 107, 112, 122, 123, 124, 125, 126, 127, 128, 129, 130, 131, 132, 133, 134, 135, 136, 137, 138, 139, 140, 141, 142, 143, 144, 145, 146, 147, 148, 150, 151, 152, 153, 155, 156, 157, 158, 159, 161, 162, 165, 167, 168, 169, 170, 171, 172, 174, 175, 177, 180, 181, 184, 185, 186, 187, 188, 189, 190, 194, 196, 197, 198, 199, 200
Pizarro, Gonzalo (brother) 97, 106, 145, 170, 171, 172, 173, 174, 183, 187, 188, 190, 191, 196
Pizarro, Gonzalo (father) 7
Pizarro, Hernando 97, 98, 99, 103, 106, 127, 132, 133, 135, 145, 146, 147, 148, 149, 150, 151, 153, 169, 170, 171, 173, 174, 176, 178, 182, 183, 187, 188, 190, 191, 192, 193, 194
Pizarro, Juan 97, 98, 106, 145, 170, 171, 172, 173, 174, 175, 177, 178
Pizarro, Pedro 98, 102, 136
Pleiades 84
Pocona 109
Poechos 54, 124
Posesion (port) 105
Pucara 79
Pueblo Quemado, 34
Puerto de la Hambre (Port of Famine), 31, 32
Puerto de Pinas 29
Puerto Viejo 102
Puna, isle of 48, 49, 102, 103, 106, 107, 111, 112, 141, 152, 200
Punchau 84
Punta de Aguja 52
Punta Pinas 26
Pururaucas 76

Quechua 61, 68, 76, 79, 80, 89, 136
Quilisachi Urco Guarang 75
Quilliscachis 69, 165
Quipu 68, 92
Quirirmanta 60
Quispe Cusi 141
Quito 88, 107, 109, 110, 112, 114, 115, 116, 117, 119, 125, 139, 153, 157, 158, 159, 162, 163, 164, 165, 166, 167, 168, 170
Quizquiz 118, 119, 137, 144, 145, 159, 161, 162

Rada, Juan de 182, 197, 198
Raura Occlo 115
Ribera, Nicolas de 36, 42, 45, 104, 105
Rimac 170
Rio Corrales 48
Rio de San Juan 35, 37, 112
Rio Negro 18
Rio San Mateo 39
Riobamba 168

Rios, Pedro de los 40, 44, 46, 47, 94, 95
Riquelme, Alonso 102, 157
Ruiz, Bartolome, 37, 38, 40, 41, 42, 45, 46, 47, 48, 53, 97, 104, 147
Ruminavi 134, 139, 165, 166, 167
Rutuchico (ceremony) 69

Saavedra, Catalina de 43
Sacsahuaman 85, 86, 177, 178
St. Matthew (bay) 40
Salcedo, Garcia de 96, 97, 102
Salinas, Battle of 192
Salu 85
San Miguel (bay) 20
San Miguel (settlement) 123, 124, 126, 148, 151, 164, 167
San Sebastian 5, 10, 11, 12, 13, 14
Sancta 152, 155
Sanoc, 69
Santo Domingo 5, 8, 13, 14, 186
Sayri Tupac 201
Sechura Desert 52, 124, 127
Seville 8, 95, 104, 169
Sinchi Roca 59, 69, 70
Soras 78
Sorra Luce, Domingo de 45
Soto, Hernando de 21, 104, 105, 106, 125, 126, 127, 132, 133, 135, 140, 141, 149, 152, 153, 155, 157, 158, 159, 162, 168, 170, 171, 180
Susurpuquiu 74, 83
Sutic Guaman 69

Tacachuincay 70
Tafur, Juan 44, 45, 46
Taguapica 56, 59
Tahuantinsuyu 3, 58, 77, 90
Talavera, Bernardino de 5, 11, 12, 13
Tambo of Urcos 57
Tambochacay 60
Tampu 59
Tambu-tocco 58, 59, 60
Tangarala 121, 123
Tapia, Vazquez de 25
Tarco Huaman 71
Tenochtitlan 2, 134
Tiahuanaco 55, 80, 89, 109
Ticcicocha 88
Tito Cusi 201
Titu Cusi Hualpa (Yahuar-Huacac) 72, 73
Tocay Capac 72
Toco, Maras 58
Toco, Sutic 58
Tocto Chimpu 170, 180
Tocto Coca 110

Toledo 95
Toltecs 86
Torre, Juan de la 45
Trujillo 7, 26, 97
Trujillo, Diego de 101, 122
Tullumayo 86
Tumbala 103
Tumbes 40, 41, 45, 48, 49, 50, 51, 52, 53, 95, 96, 97, 100, 101, 102, 103, 106, 111, 112, 122, 123, 147, 148
Tumibamba 110, 111, 112, 114, 116, 117
Tupac Huallpa 156, 157
Tupac Yupanqui 73, 81, 82, 84, 86, 87, 88, 89, 90, 108, 173
Turbaco 9, 10

Uraba, Gulf of 3, 10, 14
Urraca 25
Urubamba 78, 179
Uscovilca, 75, 76
Uxula Urco Guaranga 75

Valderrabano, Andres de 23
Valladolid 194
Valley of Moyna 73
Valverde, Vincente (priest) 98, 122, 134, 135, 137, 138, 152, 153, 154, 155, 159, 200
Vargas, Isabel de 97
Vega, Garcilaso de la 149
Veragua 8, 10
Vespucci, Amerigo 8
Vicaquirao 72, 75
Vilcabamba 78, 179, 200, 201
Vilcaconga 158
Vilcas 78, 118
Villac-umu 180, 181, 196
Viracocha (god) 48, 50, 55, 56, 57, 58, 62, 65, 75, 76, 80, 83, 84, 121, 157, 176, 179
Viracocha Inca (Hatun Tupac Inca) 73, 74, 75, 76, 77, 172
Virgins of the Sun 64, 67
Vitcos 78, 179, 185

Xeres, Francisco 132, 137

Yahuarpampa 76
Yanamayo 81
Yawar Cocha (lake of blood) 111
Ynguil 172
Yucay 174, 197

Zaran 125
Zarate, Juan 144, 149
Zuazo, Alonso 16

www.ingramcontent.com/pod-product-compliance
Lightning Source LLC
Chambersburg PA
CBHW032056300426
44116CB00007B/762